The Nature Company Guides

WORLD TRAVEL

A GUIDE TO INTERNATIONAL ECOJOURNEYS

The Nature Company Guides

WORLD TRAVEL

A GUIDE TO INTERNATIONAL ECOJOURNEYS

CHRISTOPHER P. BAKER, BEN DAVIDSON,
JEREMY HART, DWIGHT HOLING, BRIAN JACKMAN,
JUDY JACOBS, SHIRLEY LAPLANCHE, BOBBIE LEIGH,
DAVID MCGONIGAL, SUSANNE METHVIN, GREG MORTIMER,
PAOLO PERNA, EVERETT POTTER, DAN STRICKLAND,
WANG SUNG, STEVEN THRENDYLE, THERESA WALDROP,
EUGENE J. WALTER JR, MICHAEL WOODS

With illustrations by Rob Mancini

CONSULTANT EDITOR
DWIGHT HOLING

THE
NATURE
COMPANY

TIME
LIFE
BOOKS

The Nature Company Guides are published by Time-Life Books

Conceived and produced by Weldon Owen Pty Limited
43 Victoria Street, McMahons Point, NSW, 2060, Australia
A member of the Weldon Owen Group of Companies
Sydney • San Francisco
Copyright 1996 © US Weldon Owen Inc.
Copyright 1996 © Weldon Owen Pty Limited

The Nature Company owes its vision to the world's great naturalists:
Charles Darwin, Henry David Thoreau, John Muir, David Brower,
Rachel Carson, Jacques Cousteau, and many others.
Through their inspiration, we are dedicated to providing products and
experiences which encourage the joyous observation, understanding, and
appreciation of nature. We do not advocate, and will not allow to be sold in
our stores, any products that result from the killing of wild animals for trophy
purposes. Seashells, butterflies, furs, and mounted animal specimens fall into
this category. Our goal is to provide you with products, insights, and
experiences which kindle your own sense of wonder and help you to feel
good about the world in which you live.
For a copy of The Nature Company mail-order catalog, or to learn the
location of the store nearest you, please call 1-800-227-1114.

THE NATURE COMPANY
Priscilla Wrubel, Ed Strobin, Steve Manning,
Georganne Papac, Tracy Fortini

TIME-LIFE BOOKS
Time-Life Books is a division of Time Life Inc.
Time-Life is a trademark of Time Warner Inc. U.S.A.

VICE PRESIDENT AND PUBLISHER: Terry Newell
EDITORIAL DIRECTOR: Donia A. Steele
DIRECTOR OF NEW PRODUCT DEVELOPMENT: Regina Hall
DIRECTOR OF SALES: Neil Levin
DIRECTOR OF FINANCIAL OPERATIONS: J. Brian Birky

THE NATURE COMPANY GUIDES
PUBLISHER: Sheena Coupe
MANAGING EDITOR: Lynn Humphries
PROJECT EDITORS: Jenni Bruce, Scott Forbes
COPY EDITOR: Gillian Hewitt
EDITORIAL ASSISTANTS: Louise Bloxham, Edan Corkill, Vesna Radojcic
ART DIRECTOR: Hilda Mendham
DESIGNER: Clare Forte
ASSISTANT DESIGNER: Clive Collins
JACKET DESIGN: John Bull
PICTURE RESEARCH: Gillian Manning
ILLUSTRATIONS: Rob Mancini
MAPS: Mike Lamble; Mark Watson, Pictogram
PRODUCTION MANAGER: Caroline Webber
VICE PRESIDENT INTERNATIONAL SALES: Stuart Laurence
COEDITIONS DIRECTOR: Derek Barton

Library of Congress Cataloging–in–Publication Data
World travel : a guide to international ecojourneys/Christopher P. Baker ...
[et al.]; with illustrations by Rob Mancini; consultant editor, Dwight Holing.
    p. cm. — (The Nature Company guides)
    Includes index.
    ISBN 0–7835–4804–4
    1. Ecotourism. I. Baker, Christopher P., 1955– ,
II. Holing, Dwight. III. Series: Nature Company guide.
IV. Title. V. Series: Nature Company guide.
G155.A1W68 1996   96–636
910' .2'02—dc20   CIP

Manufactured by Kyodo Printing Co. (S'pore) Pte Ltd
Printed in Singapore

A Weldon Owen Production

> *Land, then, is not merely soil; it is a fountain of energy flowing through a circuit of soils, plants, and animals ...*
>
> ALDO LEOPOLD (1887–1948),
> American writer and naturalist

CONTENTS

FOREWORD

—◆—

Wanderlust. What a vigorous word. It describes a deep and powerful stirring that seems to have been a part of the human psyche from our earliest history. The wanderings of ancient humans took them on foot across the volcanic plains of Africa and through the jungles of Asia, then over land bridges from the Siberian tundra to North and South America. Epochs later, that same urge to explore took Europeans to Africa and beyond in ships. Today, it urges us toward the farthest reaches of our solar system.

My own wanderlust was awakened when I was very young. Maybe it was the wonderful stories of Albert Schweitzer and other missionaries in Africa, Asia, and the Pacific. Or maybe it was the spell cast by my Uncle Carl's collection of *National Geographic* magazines. Whatever the cause, there I was—surrounded by seas of corn stretching to the flat Midwestern horizon—dreaming of the tropics.

Twenty years later, with the Peace Corps, I was able to live my tropical dream for two years in the rain forests of West Africa. Since then, I've always had some African dust clinging to my shoes, and no matter where on this planet my wanderlust takes me, I have to get back there every few years.

So be forewarned: this book may well be the start of something. Our authors have chosen some of the most unusual spots in the world. Places to dream about. Places to go. Take out your globe, give the Earth a spin, and see where your finger lands. Then open this book to discover that area's natural glories. All that's left is to get your visa and pack your bag …

Perhaps I'll see you in Africa?

PRISCILLA WRUBEL
Founder, The Nature Company

INTRODUCTION

Tourists doubling as conservationists: that is the possibility raised by ecotourism. But how does this appealing concept translate into reality? How can we ensure that tourist dollars are really aiding conservation initiatives and benefiting the local communities that must safeguard natural resources?

Groups such as World Wildlife Fund recognize that tourism often damages the habitats it seeks to celebrate. In the Annapurna region of Nepal, for example, WWF found that visiting trekkers were using ten times as much fuelwood as local villagers—a demand that strained both the environment and the communities themselves, which needed wood for heating, cooking, and building. So we helped develop a program that offers villagers alternatives to fuelwood, requires trekkers to purchase cooking kerosene from village-operated concessions, and provides for locally managed timber plantations.

On Tanzania's Mafia Island, WWF has worked with villagers to create a marine park that will protect the island's coral reefs and generate local income. In Belize, WWF provides ongoing support to the Cockscomb Basin Wildlife Sanctuary and Forest Reserve—a tourist center with the highest density of jaguars in the world.

Through projects such as these, models for ecotourism are being developed worldwide. We know, too, that travelers must be well informed if they are to make responsible choices about where to go and what to do. *World Travel* samples the breathtaking natural habitats that we can visit and explains what we can do to leave the planet better off for our presence. It is up to all of us to travel in a way that preserves our precious natural legacy.

Kathryn S. Fuller

KATHRYN S. FULLER
President, World Wildlife Fund

Something will have gone out of us as a people if we ever let the remaining wilderness be destroyed ... if we pollute the last clean air and dirty the last clean streams and push our paved roads through the last of the silence.

WALLACE STEGNER (1909–93),
American writer

CHAPTER ONE

THE ECOTRAVELER

WHAT IS ECOTOURISM?

Ecotourism can be a highly effective tool for conserving the world's remaining wilderness areas, but it depends on careful management and travelers behaving responsibly.

Herodotus, one of the world's first tourists, traveled around Greece 2,500 years ago just to satisfy his curiosity. Since that time, readily available air travel and the desire to visit the beautiful and unusual have resulted in tourists leaving no corner of the globe untouched. Today, 500 million people a year travel internationally for pleasure, and natural areas are among their favorite destinations.

The growing popularity of nature travel can be either a burden or a boon to wild places. Environmentally irresponsible travel can destroy the fragile beauty that attracts visitors in the first place. But when undertaken appropriately, nature travel can lead to further protection of wild lands and their wildlife.

HOW IT WORKS

Visiting natural areas has developed into a new form of travel known as ecotourism. Coined in the 1980s by the Mexican ecology economist Hector Ceballos-Lascuria, the term refers to ecologically sensitive travel that combines the pleasures of discovering and understanding flora and fauna with opportunities to contribute to their protection. Integral to ecotourism is a sensitivity to traditional cultures.

Many view ecotourism, or ecotravel, as an important

NATURE TRAVELERS *roam the globe seeking out pristine wilderness areas, such as Costa Rica's cloud forests (above), and endangered species, such as the blue and yellow macaw (above left), shown here in a painting by Edward Lear (1812–88).*

conservation tool. The theory is simple. Natural areas that have been preserved and protected draw tourists to a region. The money the visitors spend on transportation, food, lodging, guides, and park fees supports the local economy by creating jobs and a sustainable economic infrastructure. This, in turn, encourages government and local community members to try to put a halt to unsustainable activities, such as logging and poaching. They learn that if the natural areas go, so do the tourists and their dollars, pounds, marks, or yen.

Ecotourism's growing economic significance has gained it widespread acceptance in both the private and public sectors. Each year, tourism produces US$55 billion worth of goods and services, accounting for 25 percent of international trade in services and 12 percent of the world gross product. Although less than one-tenth of this comes from nature-oriented travel, ecotourism has become the fastest-developing sector of the industry, growing at nearly 30 percent a year.

Around the world, developed and developing countries are setting large areas of their territories aside as reserves in order to attract ecotourists and their spending power. Kenya, for example, uses its parklands to generate US$450 million a year. That means that each lion is worth US$27,000 a year and a herd of elephants about US$610,000. This has given rise to an East African saying, "Wildlife pays, so wildlife stays".

Costa Rica has set aside about 30 percent of its land as conservation areas: tourism now ranks as the country's leading source of income, ahead of bananas and coffee. Ecotourism in the Galápagos Islands brings Ecuador more than $180 million a year.

TREKKING LIGHTLY

Large numbers of people visiting a sensitive area can cause extensive environmental problems. Nepal receives more than 200,000 visitors each year. The demand for firewood for lodges built to accommodate the flood of trekkers has lowered the tree line around Annapurna by several hundred feet. Yaks that are used to carry trekking gear have degraded the environment by increasing erosion. Litter is an additional problem.

Ecotourism depends on careful management. Facilities must be properly sited and buffer zones between wild lands and cultivated or populated areas established. Tour operators and guides need to be trained, and, in many cases, the number of visitors limited. Local people need to be involved at all times. The more they benefit from nature tourism, the more they will help preserve natural areas and wildlife.

WILDLIFE PAYS *It is estimated that each herd of elephants in Kenya is worth US$610,000 to the local ecotourism industry.*

On the user side, ecotourists must be committed to traveling in a way that avoids harming wild places. They must act responsibly and be willing to help protect sites and their inhabitants.

ECOTRAVEL FOR ALL

Anyone can be an ecotraveler —old, young, physically fit, physically challenged. You can be an ecotourist whenever you go hiking or camping, by leaving wild places exactly as you find them. You can volunteer to help an environmental group restore a natural area. You can travel with an organized study tour to increase your knowledge of a specific part of the world. And when you are traveling, you can support the economies of the places you visit by purchasing local goods and using local services to help encourage the area's protection.

Ecotourism benefits natural areas and nature travelers alike. When your visit is a tool for conservation, the sight of pristine scenery and wildlife and the experience of being in wild places take on greater importance and enjoyment, and your bond with the natural world becomes stronger.

EARLY NATURE TRAVELERS

People have often traveled for discovery and conquest, for trade, or to find somewhere safe to live, but only recently have they traveled solely for the pleasure of seeing wild places.

Traveling in Europe in the eighteenth century was a perilous business, with highwaymen aplenty, verminous inns, and warfare spasmodically erupting. Well-born young men would often be dispatched, tutor and servants in tow, to visit foreign courts, view the antiquities, learn languages, and generally broaden the mind. When travelers crossed the Alps, they usually considered this country to be "dismal" and "misshapen" and were eager to be gone. And there was reason enough for this attitude, given the dangers—wild weather, bears, wolves, bandits. Only a few brave tourists dared to venture along alpine paths to see waterfalls and snowy peaks.

It was not until writers of the English Romantic movement began extolling the glories of wild places in the early 1800s—a time when people were beginning to want to escape the rapidly growing cities—that a shift in sensibility occurred among travelers.

Poets William Wordsworth and Samuel Taylor Coleridge were captivated by the late eighteenth-century accounts of explorers such as Mungo Park, who traveled in Africa, and artist William Bartram, who roamed the forests of southeastern North America with his father John, a botanist. In his *Travels*, William Bartram wrote with delight of the extraordinary places, plants, and animals he encountered. The "mighty fountain" in Coleridge's "Kubla Khan" was

BRITISH EXPLORER *Sir Henry Morton Stanley (1841–1904) wore this pith helmet (left) on his travels through Africa.*

inspired by Bartram's detailed description of an "inchanting and amazing crystal fountain".

By the middle of the century, Thomas Cook was promoting tours to the Scottish Highlands, and in 1863 he offered the first guided trip to Mont Blanc. By then, largely through the popularity of the works of poets such as Byron and Shelley, the Swiss Alps had become the most glamorous destination imaginable.

The Romantics were followed by a generation of adventurers, such as David Livingstone, whose journeys into deepest Africa became the stuff of legends. Among them were a number of intrepid women, including Ida Pfeiffer, who left her home in Germany in 1846 to explore the Amazon.

TOUR OPERATOR *Thomas Cook was among the first to offer trips to wilderness areas such as the Swiss Alps (below).*

HOLIDAY TOURS Organised by THOS. COOK & SON.

The wisest, happiest, of our kind are they That ever walk content with Nature's way.

"By the Side of Rydal Mere", WILLIAM WORDSWORTH (1770–1850), English poet

FIELD STUDIES *Clearly, the illustrator of this "hippopotamus" (left) had little experience of the real thing. In contrast, the work of John James Audubon (below) was based on careful study of specimens he had collected.*

IN THE NEW WORLD

Nature travel also became popular in the United States as explorers and naturalists sent back word of their fabulous experiences. Meriwether Lewis and William Clark's expedition from St Louis to the Pacific and back, which began in 1804, provided the first records of hundreds of plants and animals and descriptions of vast wildernesses. This inspired others to follow. John James Audubon spent much of the early 1800s in the southern and eastern states observing birds. His 1838 masterpiece, *The Birds of America*, containing hand-colored plates of over 1,000 birds, still inspires nature lovers to seek out wild places.

Nature travel has changed considerably since Audubon's day. Back then, naturalists generally shot their subjects in order to identify and paint them. Today, the National Audubon Society is a leading proponent of ecotourism and has established a code of ethics for nature travelers.

IN MUIR'S FOOTSTEPS

The most influential person of all during the early years of nature travel was John Muir. In 1867, at the age of 29, he walked from Indiana to Florida to see the Appalachian forests. He then traveled to California and was so moved by the Sierra Nevada that he spent the next decade in the range.

Further travels took Muir to Alaska, Australasia, Russia, India, and the Philippines.

Muir's experiences led him to become an ardent conservationist (he founded the Sierra Club) and crusader for national parks—places, he argued, that are as vital to the welfare of people as they are to the natural resources they protect.

Muir's writings encouraged many people in the United States to visit wild places. By 1920, nearly a million tourists were visiting the country's national parks and monuments each year. By 1950, the figure had reached 30 million; by the 1990s, it stood at 270 million.

Since the end of the Second World War, travel to natural areas has boomed worldwide. By the 1970s, Nairobi had 65 safari companies handling all the tourists who came with cameras instead of guns, wanting to see animals rather than hunt them. In Ecuador's Galápagos National Park, visitors have increased from around 10,000 to over 45,000 a year in the last decade.

SACRED MOUNTAINS AND CHERRY BLOSSOM

Throughout history, there have been cultures that see all nature as sacred, and humanity and nature as one. Traditionally, this has been the case in Japan, a country of dedicated nature travelers.

For centuries, signs of the changing seasons—cherry blossom in spring, snow and ice in winter—have been greeted with festivities. The essence of Shinto, Japan's native religion, is harmony with nature. Throughout the country there are Shinto shrines at sacred spots to which people make pilgrimages. When Buddhism came to Japan in the sixth century, many monasteries were built in the mountains. People would (and still do) climb these sacred mountains, not to conquer but to commune with nature.

Japan's greatest poet, Matsuo Basho, lived in the seventeenth century. In the tradition of wandering philosopher-poets, he walked huge distances to visit sacred places. "What brush could show or words describe this wondrous creation of nature?" he wrote about islands bathed in moonlight, in his book *The Narrow Road to the Deep North.*

KEGON FALLS *by Eisen (1790–1848).*

MODERN ECOTOURISM

Numerous organizations, from government bodies to international conservation groups and ecotour operators, are involved in ecotourism planning.

The concept that nature travel could be used as a conservation tool began to evolve during the 1980s as academics, conservationists, economists, and representatives from both the public and private sectors began to meet and discuss its enormous financial potential.

Ecotourism became officially established by 1990, warranting its own annual international symposium as well as a nonprofit organization devoted to promoting it. The Ecotourism Society, based in Washington, DC, serves as a center for research, information, and policy development. The society directs its programs and policies toward building regional networks and promoting local participation.

Other organizations provide scientific research and planning assistance to help identify fragile areas around the globe as potential ecotourism sites. Part of the planning process involves identifying wilderness areas where low-impact ecotourism may help finance protection for the region, as well as locating places where ecotourism can be substituted for more damaging forms of traditional tourism. These organizations include the World Wide Fund for Nature, the World Resources Institute, the IUCN (World Conservation Union), and UNESCO.

UNESCO operates two major programs that benefit natural areas around the world. Under its Man and the Biosphere (MAB) program, set up in 1971, areas deemed to include key ecosystems are designated biosphere reserves. A central aim of the program is to demonstrate that conservation objectives can be balanced with sustainable development. UNESCO's World Heritage Convention Committee awards World Heritage status to natural areas that are considered to be of exceptional interest and universal value. Signatories to the convention pledge to protect such sites within their borders. In return, they receive significant financial and scientific assistance from the international community.

CONSERVATION ORGANIZATIONS

Conservation groups are at the forefront of planning. The World Wildlife Fund (WWF) conducts important research, including surveys to help determine the potential for ecotourism in developing nations. The WWF also funds many ecotourism

THE WORLD WILDLIFE FUND
sponsors numerous conservation projects as well as services for ecotravelers, such as this information kiosk in Greece (right). The WWF logo (above right). A Galápagos hawk perches on a park sign in the Galápagos National Park (top).

ORANG-UTANS *at Bohorok Rehabilitation Station in Sumatra.*

projects. One is Bohorok Rehabilitation Station in Sumatra where ecotourists can observe once-captive orang-utans being returned to the wild. Entrance and guide fees help finance the project and provide a source of income for local people. This helps encourage their support of habitat protection.

The Nature Conservancy operates an extensive system of private wildlife preserves in the United States and South America, all of which are open to visitors. The Conservancy also sponsors ecotours to other natural areas around the world, as does the National Audubon Society. Both organizations plan their trips so that a percentage of the fees paid by ecotourists funds conservation projects in the countries where the tours take place.

ELEVATED WALKWAYS, *such as this one in the Manú Biosphere Reserve in Iquitos, Peru (right), allow visitors to view the jungle canopy without damaging habitat. Ecotourism can encourage local people to protect wildlife. This Papuan child (far right) is holding a katydid.*

Many private tour operators use the same formula. For example, Birdquest of Stonyhurst, Lancashire, England, raises funds for bird-oriented conservation projects in such countries as Madagascar and Poland, and International Expeditions, of Birmingham, Alabama, USA, runs a nonprofit foundation to fund conservation in Peru's Manú Biosphere Reserve.

PUBLIC AWARENESS

Academic institutions also play an active role by sponsoring research and fieldwork. Many universities practice ecotourism by leading nature study tours, as do museums and zoological societies. The Smithsonian Institution in Washington, DC, offers nearly 200 study programs around the world that raise awareness about conservation issues.

Governments have embraced ecotourism by enacting policies and establishing agencies to carry them out. Canada and Belize have created special departments or advisory councils on ecotourism through their ministries of tourism. Costa Rica's democratically elected government made ecotourism a key plank in its party platform. In the United States, agencies such as the Environmental Protection Agency and the Fish and Wildlife Service have developed programs addressing ecotourism.

Public acceptance of ecotourism is widespread. A recent survey of 500 travelers conducted by the World Wildlife Fund found that 46 percent had been to a region specifically to visit protected wilderness areas.

CONSERVATION MANAGEMENT

For ecotourism to be successful, management strategies must be based on the specific requirements of the region set aside for conservation.

L ike the ecosystems it serves to protect, eco-tourism takes many forms. Management strategies that are effective in New England do not necessarily work in Papua New Guinea. However, despite varied approaches, nearly all are concerned with the issues of carrying capacity, revenue return, and local involvement.

Costa Rica is a showcase of ecotourism management. A fine example is Rara Avis, a private reserve in the mountains near Braulio Carrillo National Park. The preserve is home to jaguars, monkeys, and countless tropical birds. Small groups of visitors are brought in by jeep from San José. Nearly all the food and supplies they require are purchased in a local village, Horquetas. Visitors stay at a locally owned and operated lodge and villagers are hired to serve as guides. Because ecotourism has become such an important source of income for the village, the local people work hard to keep the preserve from being harmed by poachers, loggers, and settlers. As a result, rain forest has been protected, money made, and visitors educated and enthralled.

ACCESS AND FUNDING
In some cases, sites are managed to limit visitors rather than encourage them. Natural areas are inherently fragile and too many nature lovers can, at times, literally love nature to death. This was almost the situation at the Waitomo Caves in New Zealand, a unique subterranean maze of caves where glow worms hang from the ceilings. Tourists reach the caves by small power boat. In 1979, site managers discovered that

CONTROLLING ACCESS to ecotourism sites such as Rara Avis Reserve in Costa Rica (left) and Waitomo Caves in New Zealand (below) protects their fragile environments.

the glowing insect larvae were dying because the large number of visitors on each tour was causing a significant rise in carbon dioxide levels within the caves. To ensure the site's sustainability, visits were limited to smaller, less frequent tours. The plan worked: glow worms still glow and visitors still visit.

Ecotourism cannot be effective if the authorities fail to invest revenues in the resources that earned them. This

PROTECTED SPECIES An Australian road sign (top). If the African black rhino (left) is to survive in the wild, the species must be protected from poachers.

was the case in Kenya where, for many years, only 2 percent of the money earned by the country's parks was put back into running them. Low wages for guards and inadequate funding for proper management resulted in many problems, including widespread poaching.

In 1989, Kenya's president moved to improve the situation, giving the Kenya Wildlife Service greater independence and authority to manage park areas. In addition, park entrance fees were raised and the level of funding increased, with the goal of returning 20 percent of revenues to the areas from which they came. This has resulted in more effective resource management, regular training for guards, and antipoaching measures.

PLANNING FOR ECOTOURISTS

Without proper development plans and an infrastructure to support them, lands set aside to protect wildlife and attract ecotourists are preserves in name only. Indonesia produced a promising national conservation plan in the 1980s

that led to the creation of dozens of national parks and reserves totaling some 54,000 square miles (140,000 km²). However, lack of national will to devote resources to manage them has resulted in the parks, and thus their continued attraction as ecotourism destinations, being threatened by poaching, illegal logging and mining, and agricultural encroachment.

The tiny Central American nation of Belize, on the other hand, has taken an aggressive stand toward managing its natural areas. This approach is turning it into a major ecotourism destination. One program entails a zoning scheme that regulates use of perhaps the country's most important attraction—one of the largest coral barrier reefs in the world. Not surprisingly, one of the models for this was a scheme developed in Australia by the Great Barrier Reef Marine Park Authority.

Part of Australia's reef ecotourism program is based on the theory that the more people know about a place, the more they are likely to care about it and want to protect it. Most ecotours to the Great Barrier Reef are accompanied by qualified marine biologists who help visitors acquire an understanding of marine ecology, reef biology and botany, oceanography, and natural resource management. The experiences are designed to be fun as well as educational.

A WORLD PARK

An ambitious plan for ecotourism is being considered for Antarctica. "The Ice" is particularly vulnerable to human impact, and controlling human activities has been difficult because the continent's sovereignty is claimed by a number of nations and no laws exist to govern tourism. A solution proposed by the General Assembly of the United Nations would make Antarctica a World Park. Funded by tourism, the park would protect the region from further mining, oil drilling, and waste disposal, and turn the continent into a haven for wildlife.

DESTINATIONS

From studying beetles in a local park to viewing howler monkeys

in the depths of the Amazonian rain forest, ecotourism

offers travelers a wealth of memorable experiences.

Ecotravel can be as adventurous as you wish to make it, or as comfortable. It can take you to a neighborhood park or to the ends of the Earth; from the arctic chill of Alaska's remote Brooks Range to the blazing sands of Australia's Simpson Desert; from the bamboo forests of China to the quiet lagoons of Baja California.

People ecotravel in search of experiences that are becoming as rare in everyday life as some of the species of wildlife they hope to see. Ecotravel is a philosophical approach to traveling, whether you're birding in Florida's Everglades or hiking through the Himalayas.

For the ecotraveler, no vacation at a highrise hotel overlooking a crowded beach can equal the joy of watching sea turtles lay their eggs on a remote island protected from development. No shopping spree in one of the world's great cities can provide the sense of accomplishment that comes on reaching a mountain peak after having helped reconstruct the trail leading to it. No visit to an amusement park can compete with the excitement of looking for tigers in a sanctuary funded by entrance fees paid by like-minded ecotravelers.

RARE EXPERIENCES *A jewel beetle (top). A hiker savors the sense of exhilaration after scaling a Himalayan peak (left). Scarlet macaws at a clay lick in Peru (above). Scientists are not sure whether macaws eat clay to supplement their diet with minerals or to detoxify the seeds that they consume.*

NUMEROUS ALTERNATIVES

There are differing approaches to ecotravel. Some people are looking for comfortable ways to experience nature, such as visiting a responsibly designed lodge such as Chan-Chich in Belize that features all the comforts of home along with wildlife right outside the veranda. Others want rugged adventure, such as taking a whitewater rafting trip down the Urubamba River in Peru or trekking across the Darien Gap in Panama.

Either approach can lead to once-in-a-lifetime experiences, such as finding a wildflower that blooms nowhere else, or seeing a flock of scarlet macaws gather at a natural mineral lick along the Amazon. Both allow the traveler to understand that nature is not only still flourishing, but we are a part of it, no matter how remote it may seem from the often artificial environment of our own lives.

*Let us permit nature
to have her way. She
understands her business
better than we do.*

Essays,
MICHEL DE MONTAIGNE (1533–92),
French essayist

Natural areas sought out by ecotravelers can range from tiny preserves protecting rare species, such as The Nature Conservancy's 5 acre (2 ha) tract in Connecticut for endangered tiger beetles, to a huge biosphere covering several ecosystems and crossing multiple international boundaries, such as the 5 million acre (2 million ha) Maya Peace Park in Central America.

For many ecotravelers, the cultural resources of a destination are as important as its natural resources. The experience of traveling to the highlands of New Guinea, for example, is enriched by visiting the local tribes whose culture revolves around their environment. Ecotourists must treat indigenous peoples with respect and sensitivity. It is as essential to tread lightly when visiting traditional cultures as it is in natural areas.

DIFFERENT STROKES *While some ecotourists prefer the comforts of a game lodge such as the Ark in the Aberdares, Kenya (above), others enjoy the challenge of camping in the Himalayas (right).*

OFF-LIMITS
While the range of ecotravel experiences on offer is vast, there are some parts of the world that, for one reason or another, remain off-limits.

Some areas are just too fragile for humans to set foot in, however sensitively they behave. In some cases, wildlife is adversely affected by human intrusion. Studies at Kenya's Amboseli National Park suggest that a decline in the cheetah population there is due to an increase in the number of tourists. Some areas of the park have therefore been declared off-limits to visitors.

Other regions remain inaccessible, despite the efficiency of modern transport. In Siberia, for instance, there are vast tracts of wilderness that would undoubtedly be appreciated by ecotravelers. Yet, with no way to reach them, their potential remains untapped.

Political instability sometimes prevents ecotravel to areas that would otherwise be prime destinations. Rwanda, for instance, once boasted a popular and successful ecotourism site. People came from around the world to the Virunga Mountains to see rare and endangered mountain gorillas. However, when a protracted civil war broke out, the political situation brought ecotourism to an end.

THE HUMAN IMPACT
Increased visitation to Kenya's Amboseli National Park may have caused a decline in the park's cheetah population.

This world, after all our science and sciences, is still a miracle; wonderful, inscrutable, magical and more, to whosoever will think of it.

On Heroes, Hero-Worship and the Heroic in History,
THOMAS CARLYLE (1795–1881), Scottish historian

CHAPTER TWO

PLANNING *an* ECOTOUR

CHOOSING *a* TRIP

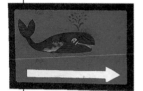

With such a wide choice of natural areas to visit and so many ways to experience them, the biggest challenge of ecotravel can be deciding where, when, and how to go.

The keys to unlocking the gates to a rewarding ecotour are self-awareness, research, and planning. Only you can decide exactly what you want to see and do. To find out what sort of trip will suit you best, ask yourself some basic questions:
• What particularly interests you about nature?
• What kind of environment do you want to see?
• Where can you see it?
• What do you hope to learn from your experience?
• How can you help protect the Earth by traveling?
• How much do you want to spend?
• When can you go and for how long?
• How is your health?
• How adventurous are you?
• Do you want to travel alone or with a group?
• Do you want to take your children?
• How do you want to get there?

CONDUCT RESEARCH
Research comes next. Ask your friends and colleagues where they've been and find out what they've seen and done. Read up on the destinations that grab your attention: study their natural habitats, their ecosystems, and their environmental problems. Most countries have tourism offices, so write to the relevant ones for information about their natural areas. Many conservation organizations and academic institutions sponsor nature trips. Contact the ones that look promising, plus a number of travel agents and commercial tour operators. Find out which destinations they travel to and the kinds of trip they offer. Study their brochures and call them with questions.

There are many issues to consider when deciding between destinations and itineraries. What level of physical activity is required? Are you ready to trek through the rain forest for 10 days or would you be more comfortable seeing the view from the deck of a passing cruise ship? Operators typically grade their trips. Treks are identified as easy, moderate, or strenuous; raft trips are rated from Class I to Class V, depending on the rapids. What type of terrain

ON LAND AND SEA *A signpost in Baja California, Mexico (top). Cruising the waters of Antarctica (below). A rain-forest trail on Lord Howe Island, Australia (right).*

RESEARCH *the environments and activities you are interested in carefully. A strenuous, high-altitude hike (below) is not for everyone.*

area. Travel guides and field guides will teach independent travelers a certain amount about a place, but they won't supply the in-depth knowledge of habitats and wildlife or the cultural insights that the local guides and professional naturalists employed by tour operators will provide.

Organized tours also offer companionship. When you travel on an ecotour, you're accompanied by like-minded people. There are plenty of opportunities to discover and discuss shared interests. Each night, over dinner, you're able to swap travelers' tales and review the day's events.

will you be visiting? If a trek involves a climb and you suffer from altitude sickness (see p. 48), you'll need to know how high you'll be going beforehand. When is the best season to visit? There's more to seasonality than the weather. You wouldn't want to visit the arctic tundra in winter if it's birding you're after. Finally, how much will the trip cost? What should your daily budget be?

INDEPENDENT OR TOUR?

Another major consideration is whether to travel on your own or with a group. Independent travel allows you the freedom to organize your own trip and to spend as much time in a place as you want. You can ensure that your travel will help protect the environment by following the same practices as the "green" ecotour operators do. These include staying in locally owned accommodation, eating in local cafes or markets, hiring native guides, and packing out all your trash.

There are shortcomings to independent travel, however. The first is expense. It's hard to match the economies of scale achieved by large companies. Because they make block bookings, tour operators can obtain discounts that they then pass on to their clients.

Another advantage of organized travel concerns access to protected areas. Many national parks and private reserves restrict access, and tour groups are often admitted ahead of independent travelers. In some places, independent travel is forbidden. Galápagos National Park, for example, requires all visitors to be accompanied by licensed guides. Other destinations lack the infrastructure or transportation to accommodate visitors traveling on their own. You'll find it hard enough to get to Antarctica independently, much less travel around.

A further trade-off concerns the knowledge you can expect to gain about a natural

PLAN AHEAD

Finally, plan ahead when choosing an ecotour. It can save time and money, not to mention aggravation. Start planning as early as you can. Ecotourist destinations are chosen with small groups in mind, which means there will be competition for the most popular sites and tours. Bookings for the best ecolodges in Costa Rica at Christmas time, for example, are taken one year in advance. Planning early will not only improve your chances of going on the trip you want, it can also help you take advantage of advance-booking discounts and other savings.

A BUYER'S MARKET *Purchasing your food in local markets, such as this one in Guatemala, supports local communities.*

JANUARY	FEBRUARY	MARCH	APRIL	MAY	JUNE

The Everglades, USA: An incredible array of nesting wetland birds

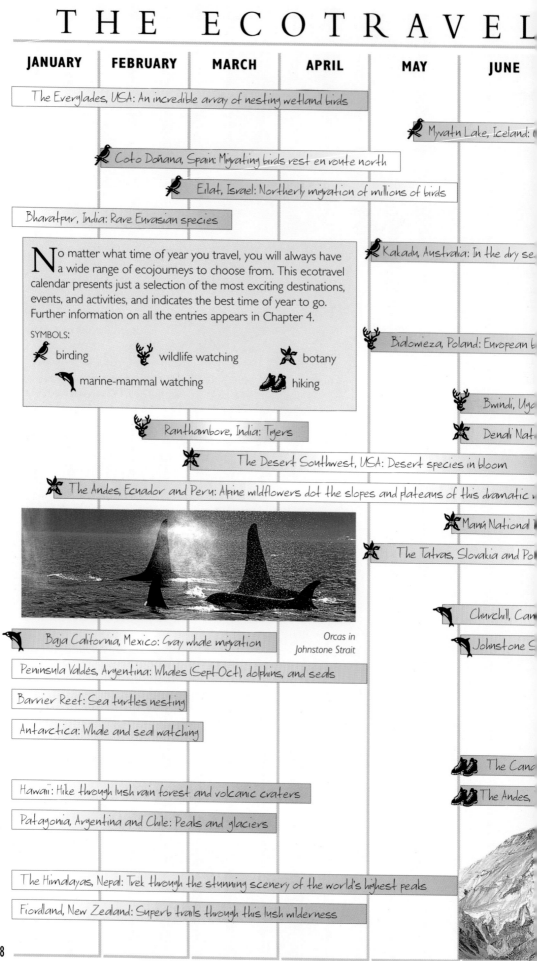

🐦 Myvatn Lake, Iceland:

🐦 Coto Doñana, Spain: Migrating birds rest en route north

🐦 Eilat, Israel: Northerly migration of millions of birds

Bharatpur, India: Rare Eurasian species

N o matter what time of year you travel, you will always have a wide range of ecojourneys to choose from. This ecotravel calendar presents just a selection of the most exciting destinations, events, and activities, and indicates the best time of year to go. Further information on all the entries appears in Chapter 4.

SYMBOLS:

🐦 birding   🦌 wildlife watching   🌸 botany

🐬 marine-mammal watching   🥾 hiking

🐦 Kakadu, Australia: In the dry se

🦌 Bialowieza, Poland: European b

🦌 Bwindi, Uga

🌸 Denali Nati

🦌 Ranthambore, India: Tigers

🌸 The Desert Southwest, USA: Desert species in bloom

🌸 The Andes, Ecuador and Peru: Alpine wildflowers dot the slopes and plateaus of this dramatic

🌸 Manú National

🌸 The Tatras, Slovakia and Po

🐧 Churchill, Can

🐬 Baja California, Mexico: Gray whale migration

Orcas in
Johnstone Strait

🐧 Johnstone S

Peninsula Valdés, Argentina: Whales (Sept-Oct), dolphins, and seals

Barrier Reef: Sea turtles nesting

Antarctica: Whale and seal watching

🥾 The Cana

🥾 The Andes,

Hawaii: Hike through lush rain forest and volcanic craters

Patagonia, Argentina and Chile: Peaks and glaciers

The Himalayas, Nepal: Trek through the stunning scenery of the world's highest peaks

Fiordland, New Zealand: Superb trails through this lush wilderness

YEAR PLANNER

JULY	AUGUST	SEPTEMBER	OCTOBER	NOVEMBER	DECEMBER

The Pantanal, Brazil: Over 600 colorful species

The Everglades

00 nesting ducks of 16 different species

Coto Doñana, Spain: Southerly migrations

Eilat, Israel: Birds and their young return south

Bharatpur, India: Spectacular heronry and rare Eurasian species

A wood stork in the Everglades

ns of waterbirds gather at contracting wetlands

Northern Alaska, USA: Caribou migration

Churchill, Canada: Polar bear migration

ning Europe's last remaining area of virgin forest

sai Mara, Kenya: Wildebeest migration

Masai Mara: Wildebeest return south

tain gorillas

, Alaska, USA: Wildflowers abound on the tundra

: Amazonian rain-forest plants

Migrating wildebeest in Masai Mara

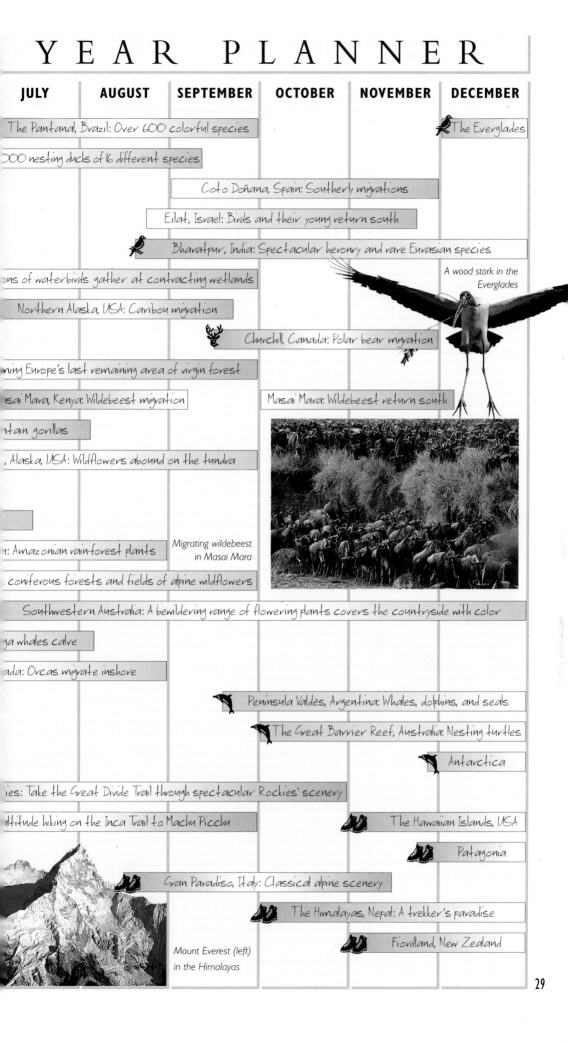

coniferous forests and fields of alpine wildflowers

Southwestern Australia: A bewildering range of flowering plants covers the countryside with color

ga whales calve

ada: Orcas migrate inshore

Peninsula Valdés, Argentina: Whales, dolphins, and seals

The Great Barrier Reef, Australia: Nesting turtles

Antarctica

ies: Take the Great Divide Trail through spectacular Rockies' scenery

altitude hiking on the Inca Trail to Machu Picchu

The Hawaiian Islands, USA

Patagonia

Gran Paradiso, Italy: Classical alpine scenery

The Himalayas, Nepal: A trekker's paradise

Fiordland, New Zealand

Mount Everest (left) in the Himalayas

29

CHOOSING *an* OPERATOR

To ensure a quality trip at a reasonable price, and one that's environmentally responsible, you must ask your tour operator some pointed questions.

The popularity of ecotourism has created a blossoming ecotravel industry. Under the banner of ecotravel you will be offered everything from low-impact camping tours to holidays in ecologically sensitive jungle lodges, with destinations ranging from Arizona to Zaire.

OPERATOR QUALITIES

Experience, environmental commitment, customer support, and competent on-site staff are the main qualities you should look for in any environmentally responsible operator.

It is essential that the tour operator has long experience of running tours to the area you are interested in. Countries in the developing world are often politically unstable, their infrastructures are limited, and their amenities for travelers are highly variable. Tour operators must therefore possess an insider's knowledge of a region in order to make alternative

plans when things change abruptly. The experienced tour operator can turn a hiatus into an opportunity.

Be wary of companies that subcontract their trips to other operators. It is unlikely that they will be able to maintain sufficiently tight control over the quality and environmental commitment of the tour. On the other hand, many fund-raising trips run by nonprofit organizations do rely on professional tour operators. That does not mean you should rule them out. Just make sure that their subcontractors are operating in an environmentally responsible manner.

Any enterprise offering trips to natural areas must be environmentally committed. If they aren't willing to tell you how, then take your business elsewhere. This is particularly important when the operator is a profit-driven company.

Ask operators how they support the environment. Conscientious companies restrict the size of their tours in order to minimize their impact on the environment. Normally, a tour group should have no more than 12 participants.

Give preference to tour companies that include tax-deductible contributions to environmental organizations or conservation programs as part of the tour cost. Choose a trip where the guides promote conservation by raising their clients' environmental awareness. Favor operators that employ local guides and service companies and that use local products. The best companies also use locally owned lodges rather than large, foreign-owned hotels. All of this will help support the host country's economy and create incentives for the local people to protect their natural areas.

BROCHURES *(above) should be studied carefully. Give preference to companies that employ local guides, such as these Sherpas in Nepal (right).*

SOFT OPTIONS *Even in remote areas, tour operators can provide many home comforts. The luxury cruise boat* Sepik Spirit *accommodates visitors to the Sepik River in Papua New Guinea.*

CUSTOMER SUPPORT

Customer support should begin with your first contact with the tour operator. When you called, did the booking agent have the answers to your questions? Did he or she take the time to describe the trip in detail and volunteer information about how the company supports conservation? If not, perhaps you should look elsewhere. After all, travel isn't cheap; you have a right to know what to expect before you buy.

If you will be traveling with small children, make sure the trip you choose is appropriate. Most commercial outfitters note which tours are suitable for families in their brochures. Be sure to check.

Once you book, the company should provide you with a comprehensive briefing package containing information on the kind of equipment you'll need, a reading list, natural history overviews, and general travel information. Ideally, your tour operator will also provide you with insights into the host country's indigenous cultures and the attitude of its people to

foreign visitors. The operator should instruct participants before departure on inoffensive and low-impact behavior. The amount of pre-trip preparation the operator supplies is a good indication of the level of service you can expect throughout the trip.

TOUR LEADERS

On-site staff provides the best indication of the quality of a tour operator. In the field, the person you will rely on most is your guide. He or she must not only be thoroughly knowledgeable about the sites you are visiting and the wildlife you are seeing, but be able to educate and inspire you as well. The best guides will have lived in the area for some time, know its inhabitants, and speak the local

language fluently. They will be well informed about local conservation issues and be concerned about them.

So, before you sign up for a tour, ask the operator about their trip leaders. How experienced are they? What are their qualifications? How long have they been with the company?

One of the best ways to decide on an operator is to speak with people who have already traveled with them. Bona fide operators willingly provide potential clients with references. After all, they know that the best possible advertisement is a personal recommendation from a satisfied customer.

A DUAL PURPOSE *Nature observation and sporting activities can go hand in hand. For example, a trip to the Isle of Skye in Scotland (right) could combine superb birding with challenging hiking.*

HEALTH MATTERS

By taking a number of basic precautions and equipping yourself with a simple medical kit, you can minimize the health risks that travel to far-flung destinations inevitably involves.

Nature travel can expose you to health risks you'd never encounter back home. This is especially true in developing countries where vaccination programs and public sanitation and hygiene are often rudimentary. You can help reduce your risk of contracting a disease by taking the necessary precautions and exercising common sense. At a minimum, follow these basic rules:
• Avoid drinking tap water (and avoid ice cubes in drinks). Use bottled water; if none is available, purify water by boiling it, filtering it, or treating it with purification tablets. Use bottled or purified water for cleaning your teeth and be careful not to accidentally drink water while bathing.
• Avoid raw foods, such as fresh vegetables and fruit, unless you can clean and peel them yourself. Avoid dairy products unless they have been pasteurized. Foods that

MODERN WATER FILTERS *are extremely compact. They can be especially valuable in remote areas where bottled water may not be available.*

have been well cooked are generally safer, but do not eat anything that looks as though it has been on display for some time.
• Protect yourself against insect bites. The best way to avoid getting malaria and other insect-borne diseases is to avoid being bitten. Apply insect repellent and minimize skin exposure by wearing long sleeves, long trousers, and adequate footwear. Sleep under a mosquito net or in an air-conditioned room with the windows closed.
• Treat cuts and abrasions quickly and aggressively. If you do have to have medical treatment, try to avoid injections or blood transfusions. (It's a good idea to carry your own syringes and suture kit.)
• Never practice unsafe sex.

VACCINATIONS

Immunization can offer protection from several major diseases and should not be neglected. Regulations and recommendations for each country change from time to time, so make sure you find out what vaccinations you need at least eight weeks before departure. You can obtain up-to-date information on international health matters through specialist travelers' medical centers and government public health offices (see p. 276).

Most doctors and travelers' medical centers strongly advise travelers to developing

MEDICAL FACILITIES *in many developing countries can be rudimentary, so it pays to have a health and dental checkup before you set off.*

countries to be vaccinated against diseases such as polio, tetanus, hepatitis A, typhoid, and, depending on the risk factors, hepatitis B, rabies, tuberculosis, meningitis, and other less well-known diseases. Recent developments have resulted in these vaccines being more effective and having fewer side effects.

Travelers to sub-Saharan Africa or northern South America must be vaccinated against yellow fever. If you have traveled through yellow-fever-infected areas, you may be required to show proof of vaccination when entering other countries. Officially, cholera vaccination is no longer compulsory. However, in some areas, notably Africa, border guards demand to see cholera vaccination certificates, so some doctors recom-

mend obtaining a certificate for this reason.

Malaria is widespread in developing countries and travelers should be vigilant in protecting themselves. Instructions regarding anti-malarial medication should be followed strictly. Courses of medication normally begin at least one week before departure. If you experience any flu-like symptoms while, or just after, traveling in malaria-infected areas, you should consult a doctor as soon as possible. Malaria is treatable but can be fatal if symptoms are ignored.

Make sure you have the types and dates of your vac-

KEEP A RECORD *of your vaccinations on an International Health Certificate.*

cinations entered on an International Health Certificate to take with you. Even if you've undergone a full course of immunization, don't assume further precautions are unnecessary. Not all vaccinations offer 100 percent protection.

FINDING A DOCTOR

In most major cities in the world, you can find an English-speaking doctor. Often the best way to locate one is to go to one of the upscale tourist hotels. The addresses of organizations that provide the names of English-speaking physicians throughout the world are in the Resources Directory (see p. 276). Another approach is to contact your embassy or consulate in the country you're visiting. They can provide you with a list of local doctors and dentists.

MEDICAL KITS

On any trip to a developing country or wilderness area, you should carry a medical kit that includes the following items:

• **Your regular medication** Carry copies of your prescriptions with your travel documents. Take a detailed, up-to-date record of your medical history. Obtain two supplies of each prescription drug and pack one in your carry-on bag and one in your luggage. Keep them in their original containers, but ask your pharmacist for plastic rather than glass bottles. Don't put unidentified pills in unmarked containers as this could lead to trouble with customs officers. Avoid buying medicines in markets abroad: many countries have problems with counterfeit drugs that contain chalk or talcum powder instead of active ingredients.

• **Over-the-counter items** Pack sunscreen, insect repellent, painkillers, decongestants, antihistamines for allergies, indigestion tablets, and other products. Finding such basic items is not always easy in developing countries. Leave them in their original containers.

• **First-aid kit** Include bandages, antiseptic, and dressings for minor cuts and scrapes. You should also take packets of rehydration mixture; Immodium or Lomotil for diarrhea; Flagyl or Fasigyn for giardia; antibiotics; and a pack of disposable syringes.

In many countries you remember your meals, while in other—and I think more interesting—places, you remember your illnesses.

PAUL THEROUX (b. 1941), American writer

MONEY *and* SECURITY MATTERS

Whether you're using dollars, dinars, or Deutsch marks,

make sure you have enough money of the right kind when ecotraveling.

The most common forms of paying for expenses when traveling are credit cards and traveler's checks. Both relieve the necessity of carrying large amounts of cash, which makes for greater peace of mind.

Credit cards are widely accepted throughout the world. They have the advantage of offering a better rate of exchange than if you change your money locally or cash traveler's checks. That's because credit-card conversions are usually made at an exchange rate just one percentage point above what is called the international wholesale rate—the best rate available to financial institutions on currency transactions.

You can also use your bank card at most automated teller machines (ATMs) around the world. The machines give you local currency and the amount is automatically converted and debited from your account. Most banks

charge a nominal transaction fee for using machines outside their own network of ATMs. Bear in mind that you are not going to find ATMs away from the larger towns.

Traveler's checks can be cashed for the local currency at banks and many hotels. Ones issued by lesser-known banks can be a problem because banks in remote areas are often suspicious of them and won't change them. They are also often unwilling to change checks that are not in US dollars.

Obtain a small amount of the currency of your destination before you depart. This will come in handy if you arrive late at night or need to pay for transportation to your hotel. If there isn't a currency exchange near you, ask your local bank to arrange this. They can usually obtain some of the currency for you, but give them advance notice.

A SMALL AMOUNT
of the currency of your destination should be purchased before you depart.

TRAVELER'S CHECKS
are the safest way to carry money because you can normally obtain a refund in the event of them being lost or stolen.

Take a reserve of US dollars along with you, too. Small bills come in handy when you find yourself making an unexpected layover in a jungle village, or having to cover an unforeseen park fee or departure tax. In many developing countries, US currency is preferred to the local currency.

Invest in a money pouch to hang around your neck or a money belt to wear under your shirt. It's not a good idea to keep valuables in a fanny pack as the pack can be easily removed by a smart operator with a knife or a pair of scissors.

PASSPORTS AND VISAS

A valid passport is required for entry to most countries. Passports are issued at agencies in most cities and at some major post offices. It's a good idea to photocopy the pages in your passport that bear your picture, name, and passport number and carry this separately when traveling. This will help should you need to replace a stolen or lost passport when abroad.

Over half the countries in the world require that visitors also obtain a visa—official government approval for the bearer to enter and exit the country. Visas are issued for a specific period, typically 15 days, 30 days, or six months. While some countries will issue a temporary visa at the border, it's best to obtain one prior to entry.

Your travel agent or tour operator should be able to advise you on visa requirements for the country or countries you plan to visit. Visas are normally issued by foreign embassies, consulates, or tourism offices. Some countries supply visas free, others charge a fee. Most require you to send an application form along with your passport and one or more passport-style photos. Phone some time ahead to find out how long it takes for a visa to be issued: some embassies take only a day or two, others take weeks.

MOST COUNTRIES
require visitors to hold a valid passport and many have further visa requirements. Check with your travel agent for details.

In some places, private companies can help you get visas quickly. These companies will charge a handling fee on top of the regular visa fees.

IS IT SAFE?

Before embarking on a trip to any foreign destination, especially the world's political hot spots, it's a good idea to check whether a "travel advisory" has been issued by your government. For US travelers, the US State Department operates a 24-hour travel advisory hotline (see p. 276). It bases its recommendations on such factors as political instability, war, terrorism, epidemics, and crime. Information is also available on the World Wide Web at http://www.stolaf.edu/network/travel-advisories.html.

TRAVEL INSURANCE

Before buying travel insurance, make sure you aren't already covered under your existing homeowner, automobile, and/or health insurance policies. Many credit card companies offer free travel insurance when you book your holiday using their card.

A wide variety of travel insurance policies is available and your travel agent or tour operator will make recommendations. A good policy will cover theft, loss, and medical treatment. Make sure you are covered for ambulances and an emergency flight home. Check the small print to see whether "dangerous activities" such as scuba diving are excluded.

A trip-cancellation policy (generally included with other travel insurance, but also available separately) will reimburse you if you have to cancel or interrupt a trip and would lose a substantial prepayment.

A MONEY BELT *like this one is light and comfortable, and can easily be concealed beneath clothing.*

It's a good place to carry your travel documents as well as cash and traveler's checks.

BACKGROUND BRIEFING

Just as you should tone up physically before embarking on an extensive hike, so should you bone up mentally before leaving on an ecotour.

Whether it's watching wildlife, climbing mountains, identifying wildflowers, or visiting a remote jungle camp, traveling in the world's natural areas will challenge your mind as much as your muscles.

Contact a government tourism office, a tour operator, or a travel agent about possible destinations and itineraries, and your mailbox will quickly overflow with colorful brochures. While these will give you a taste of what lies ahead, you will need to dig deeper if you want to make the most of your trip.

Start gathering background information and begin reading it while you're planning your trip. This will prove as valuable as a road map, guiding you to the places that you don't want to miss and answering many of your questions. If you hold off doing your background reading until you're at your destination, you'll spend most of your time trying to figure out what it was you just saw

THE LAY OF THE LAND *Studying detailed maps of the areas you will be visiting on your ecotour (right) will help you get your bearings once you arrive.*

rather than appreciating what you're seeing. Purchase a good, detailed map and trace your itinerary on it. This will help counter the disorientation that comes with long-distance travel.

The best tour operators will supply you with comprehensive information kits once you sign up. These should include itineraries and scientific material about the area's landscape, natural history, and key environmental features.

You'll need to augment these backgrounders with other materials. Ask your outfitter for a reading and reference list. Head for your local bookstore or library and check out some of their recommendations. While you are there, undertake a literature search of your own. Ask the bookseller or librarian for assistance.

Check indexes to geography, conservation, and wildlife magazines for features on your destination's natural history and environmental issues.

VIDEOS

There is a number of stunning videos devoted to travel and natural history topics, and you may well find some of these at your local library or video rental store. Ones to look for include any of the "Nature" series and those produced by National Geographic and the Audubon Society. They cover a wide range of subjects, from orcas to rain forests. You'll also find videos on such subjects as field identification of birds and mountaineering.

Keep an eye on television listings too. Nature documentaries are very popular, especially on the public broadcast stations. Watching these will

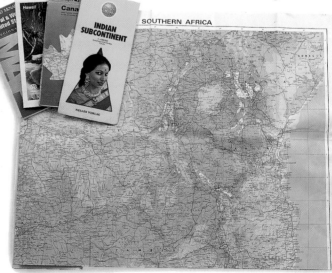

FIELD GUIDES and travel guides are
available for almost every environment.
Browsing through these and watching
wildlife videos (opposite) will help you
hone your identification skills.

hotels, airline schedules,
and weather. You can use
magazine, reference, and
newspaper databases to
conduct online searches for
articles on selected topics.

The World Wide Web on
the Internet offers a wealth of
information for ecotravelers.
Many national parks and
reserves have their own web
sites, as do many conservation
organizations. For example,
you can obtain a map of the
Smoky Mountains region at
http://www.nando.net/
smokies/smokies.html or
peruse articles on travel by
elephant in Thailand at
http://nearnet.gnn.com/
gnn/meta/travel/mkt/focus/
index.html. Check out an
Internet directory for details
of other sites (see p. 277).

increase your understanding
of nature and enhance your
appreciation of it.

Museums and academic
institutions often sponsor talks
and slideshows on travel and
natural history topics. These
are also good ways to learn
more about your destination.
You might want to check
with your local college or
museum to see if they are
offering any classes that might
prove beneficial to your
travels, such as a language
course. Contact your local
conservation organizations,
too. Some, such as local
Audubon chapters, offer birding and other field identification classes. Also check
with your local bookstore.
Many host audiovisual presentations by travel writers
and guidebook authors.

FIELD GUIDES

True, field guides are useful
once you arrive, and you
should definitely carry some
with you, but consider studying them before you go.
You'll then know what to
expect and be able to recognize the most common species
when you see them. There are
field guides for nearly everything that grows and lives in
the wild, from birds and
butterflies to seashells and
mushrooms. The Collins
Eyewitness, Audubon Society,
and Peterson field guides are

among the most popular. You
also might want to purchase
an audiotape of birdcalls and
spend time listening to it
before you go. This can prove
especially valuable in rain
forests where you generally
hear the birds in the dense
foliage rather than see them.

PERSONAL COMPUTERS

You can also research your
travel destination through
your personal computer using
online information services.
CompuServe, for example,
has user forums on various
travel topics and
destinations, such as
the Travel Forum,
Adventures in
Travel, and France
Info USA. You'll
also find useful
information on

THE INTERNET is an
excellent source of travel
information. Numerous
national parks, reserves,
and World Heritage
Areas are covered by of-
ficial and unofficial World
Wide Web sites, such as this
guide to Grand Canyon
National Park (http://
www.kbt.com/gc/).

THE PRACTICALITIES
of PACKING

When it comes to packing for an ecotour, the best advice is to

keep it light and don't take anything you can't replace.

For most ecotours, you should limit your luggage to a small personal carry-on—which can also double as your day pack—and only one piece of baggage. Soft-sided luggage made of lightweight, water-repellent, durable material such as Gore-Tex is ideal. Your bag should be light enough for you to be able to hoist onto the roof of a vehicle without dislocating your shoulder and rugged enough to be stowed in the bow of a dugout canoe. (For information on backpacks, see p. 41.)

CUSTOM GEAR *Choose clothing that is appropriate for your destination's weather and for the type of activities you will be participating in. Pack everything into one soft but sturdy travel bag (right) and attach a strong identification tag (above).*

THE ESSENTIALS

Most outfitters and tour operators will supply you with a list of suggested clothing and gear to take on your type of trip. You should follow it closely and augment it with any items that you particularly need.

While what you choose will vary depending on the destination, a nature traveler's basic kit should include:

- sunglasses
- hat
- swimwear
- 1 washcloth and small towel
- 1 pair of walking shoes or lightweight hiking boots
- 1 pair of casual shoes
- socks and undergarments for 3 to 4 days

- sleepwear
- 3 shirts or blouses
- 1 pair of shorts
- 2 pairs of pants/2 skirts
- 1 sweater or fleece pullover
- 1 waterproof jacket or 1 raincape that will also cover your backpack
- toiletry kit
- basic first-aid kit (see p. 33)
- day pack (see p. 40)
- Swiss-Army-type pocket knife
- small flashlight
- camera
- folding umbrella
- wallet and travel documents.

Choose garments carefully. Lightweight, supple materials—cotton, jerseys, silk knits, synthetic fibers, and blends—take up less space and fold more easily than, say, heavy wools and stiff linens. Keep in mind your destination's weather, however.

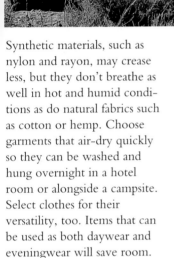

TRAVELING LIGHT *You may not be the only one that's thankful if you keep your luggage to a minimum. Loading up camels in the Suriqwat Valley, China, en route to K2 (left). Yaks (below) are used to carry hikers' gear along many of the trails in the Himalayas.*

When you arrive at your destination, transfer your passport and other valuables to a pouch that you can wear around your neck or a money belt that can be concealed beneath your shirt. Keep a small amount of currency for your immediate needs in a buttoned pocket or a fanny pack.

Flying? I've been to almost as many places as my luggage.

BOB HOPE (b. 1903)
American actor and comedian

Synthetic materials, such as nylon and rayon, may crease less, but they don't breathe as well in hot and humid conditions as do natural fabrics such as cotton or hemp. Choose garments that air-dry quickly so they can be washed and hung overnight in a hotel room or alongside a campsite. Select clothes for their versatility, too. Items that can be used as both daywear and eveningwear will save room.

PACKING TIPS

When packing, put slightly less in your bag than you can actually fit. Not only will this prevent zipper or clasp strain, it will leave room for souvenirs and purchases made abroad.

Remember, consolidation is the key; use all the available space. Stuff socks and underwear into shoes, place small items in empty corners. Unwrap things that come in boxes. Replace glass jars and bottles with plastic ones. Place any containers holding liquids in sealed plastic bags. Carry extra plastic bags for wet bathing suits and dirty laundry.

Check with your tour operator regarding luggage allowances on flights. While these may be fairly generous on international flights, domestic carriers and, in particular, small bush planes may have much more restrictive limits.

Tape your name, address, and phone number inside your bag in addition to securing a name tag on the outside. Have two sets of prescription drugs and eyeglasses and pack one set in your luggage and the other in your carry-on, along with your camera, money, and travel documents.

PACKING FOR KIDS

You can smooth even the roughest of journeys by packing "a little bit of home" into your children's bags. Bringing along their favorite sleepwear, stuffed animal, and story book helps out at bedtime in strange hotel rooms.

For long journeys, each child should have their own carry-on. Pack it with snacks and extra clothes, along with a couple of small toys and paper and colored crayons.

For nature walks and wildlife safaris, supply your children with their own binoculars. It's hard to share. Buy them a field guide or two, particularly on subjects they have already shown an interest in. Children quickly learn to use these and will soon be identifying species on their own. These relatively inexpensive pieces of equipment will hold your children's interest and allow them to satisfy their natural curiosity.

ECOTRAVEL EQUIPMENT

*Certain items of equipment will enhance any nature trip,
whereas the usefulness of others will depend on the environment
you will be visiting and your planned activities.*

A good pair of binoculars is essential for any trip and will add greatly to your enjoyment of nature. They will provide you with a close-up view of birds and animals, and, when turned upside down, will magnify the hidden world of plants and bugs.

When choosing binoculars, you need to consider magnification, brightness, focus, durability, weight, and price. All binoculars have two sets of numbers on them, such as 10 x 40. The first number, 10, refers to the magnification, meaning that the image will look 10 times larger than it appears to the naked eye. The second number, 40, is the diameter of the objective (front) lenses in millimeters. The larger the lenses are, the more light will enter and the brighter the image will be, which can be highly significant at dawn and dusk when there is little light, and birds and animals are at their most active. Magnification of between 7 and 10 times and objective lenses of between 30 and 40 are recommended for nature study. A ratio of 1:5 between the two numbers normally provides the right balance between magnification and clarity.

Try several pairs of binoculars before making your selection. Rubber-coated ones tend to be more durable and water-resistant, and make sense for travelers embarking on birding and whale-watching tours.

CAMERA EQUIPMENT

You'll also want equipment to record your ecotour. A basic setup for the field includes a quality 35 mm camera, a zoom lens or several fixed lenses, film, lens cloth, carrying case, notepad, pen, and ziplock bags to keep everything dry.

FOR EASY ACCESS, *carry your notebooks and pencils for taking field notes (left) in a fanny pack (above).*

When selecting a camera, pick one that allows you to focus and select your shutter speeds manually as well as change lenses. Ideally, take a 55 mm lens as your basic lens, a macro for plants and insects, a 200 to 500 mm telephoto for wildlife, and a wide-angle for landscapes. Buy film with a range of different speeds, and always purchase more rolls than you think you will need.

If taking a video camera, make sure you pack all the tapes you will need. Lightweight cameras with powerful zoom lenses are best. Take a voltage transformer so that you can recharge your batteries. (See also p. 46.)

DAY PACKS

Unless you're on an extended trek, a day pack will usually see you through a day's worth of ecotouring. Choose one that is made of lightweight fabric such as Cordura. It should distribute the weight evenly

BINOCULARS *(above) are essential for any trip. A powerful telephoto lens (left) will allow you to obtain close-up views of animals and birds without disturbing them*

A ROOM WITH A VIEW *Campers in Torres del Paine National Park, Chile.*

with two padded shoulder straps, be reinforced at the bottom, have compartments for easy access, and be roomy enough to carry your gear.

When packing for a day trip, consider including the following: hat, rain jacket or poncho, additional layer of clothing, binoculars, notepad and pencil, field guide, energy food, pocket knife, sunscreen lotion, insect repellent, first-aid kit, camera, and film.

OUTDOOR CLOTHING

You need the right clothes if you are to enjoy the outdoors. Specialty clothes for nature trips are functional. Naturalist's vests are available with pockets for your binoculars, field guide, sunscreen lotion, and so on. Neutral colors, such as olive, tan, or a camouflage pattern, will help you blend into your surroundings and get closer to wild creatures.

In hot weather, wearing fewer clothes doesn't necessarily mean being cooler. Loose-fitting, long-sleeved shirts and long pants will keep you cooler than shorts and a T-shirt, and will protect you from the sun and bugs. Don't forget sun-glasses and a wide-brimmed hat.

DRESSED FOR SUCCESS *Layering clothes (right) is the best way of coping with cold weather. An internal frame backpack (above).*

In cold weather, you need to wear three layers to keep warm and dry. The thin inner layer, such as long underwear, should be made from a combination of fibers that will wick moisture away from your body. Synthetic fleece pullovers and pants are ideal for the middle layer. The outer layer, or shell, should be made of water-repellent and windproof material such as Gore-Tex.

BACKPACKING AND CAMPING

Backpacks with internal frames are most suitable for cross-country and active travel; ones with external frames are best for hiking in hot weather and carrying large loads. Try on several different loaded packs to find the one that fits you best. Most of the weight should rest on the padded hip belt, not on your shoulders.

If you plan to camp, choose your equipment carefully. You want gear that is comfortable, lightweight, and durable. Consider the range of temperatures and the types of environment where you're going. You don't need a sleeping bag rated for below freezing if you're headed for the tropics. Likewise, if your destination is Patagonia you'll want a sturdy tent that can hold up in the wind rather than a flimsy tarp.

Responsible ecotravelers cook on camp stoves rather than campfires as they are less polluting and don't strip an area of its trees and twigs. Make sure your stove works with fuel that is available locally, as fuel cannot be transported by air. Take a compact water filter and bring garbage bags along so you can pack out what you pack in.

Other items that come in handy on camping trips include an inflatable raft, tarp, portable shower, and headlamps, which provide light while leaving your hands free. (For further information, see p. 50.)

The World, we are told, was made especially for man—
a presumption not supported by all the facts ...
Why should man value himself as more than a small
part of the one great unit of creation?

JOHN MUIR (1838–1914),
Scottish-born American naturalist and writer

CHAPTER THREE
RESPONSIBLE TRAVELING

ECOTRAVEL ETHICS

If we are to preserve the world's wild lands and give their people, animals, and plants the respect that are their due, we must develop and adhere to a new code of ethics.

When you venture out into the natural world, remember that you are making your way through the homes of animals and plants. Behave the way you'd wish visitors to behave in your home. Think how you'd feel if a group of people barged into your place unannounced and grabbed everything in sight, threw their trash around, and made loud noises, then tried to view your every action, from eating your dinner to going to the bathroom, to breeding, bearing, and rearing your young.

You should therefore adhere to these simple rules when traveling in protected areas:
• Do not pick flowers or collect sea shells, eggs, or rocks. If you want a souvenir or a specimen, take a photograph.
• Never touch, disturb, or harass wildlife, even if it means foregoing a close-up view of a species you've traveled a long way to see. Approaching animals and birds closely places them under unnecessary strain.
• Always stay on designated trails. Delicate surfaces and vegetation may take

DO NOT DISTURB *Never remove plants, sea shells, or rocks. Always remember that little by little these activities deplete the environment.*

decades to recover from the impact of a traveler's boots.
• Make sure that any waste you create is disposed of properly, and that you leave no trace of your visit.
• Make every visit to a natural area an experience that will heighten your awareness and appreciation of nature and a tool to further its protection.
• Never buy souvenirs and products that encourage activities detrimental to the environment and wildlife.
• Never support a tour company that does not adhere to a strict code of environmental ethics.

PROTECTING CULTURAL RESOURCES

Being an ecotourist also means being committed to traveling in a way that

LOCAL KNOWLEDGE *Make the most of your involvement with local people by taking the time to learn about their culture, language, and lifestyle. Tourists with a local boat operator on the Sepik River in Papua New Guinea (above). A Yemeni woman in traditional costume (below right).*

protects cultural resources. Many native cultures, as well as rare plants and animals, are threatened with extinction. The spread of western music, movies, and satellite TV is eroding many of the cultural differences that give the world its richness and diversity.

It's important, then, to respect the cultural values of the communities you visit and to minimize your impact on them. Be aware of native peoples' customs, beliefs, and attitudes. This will help you to avoid offending

Please leave the flowers growing here for others to enjoy

LIMITED RESOURCES *Communities around the world are becoming increasingly aware that their natural resources are limited, as these signs from Nepal (right) and India (below right) show.*

MIND HOW MUCH TIME DOES IT TAKE TO GROW A TREE AND HOW MANY OF THEM YOU NEED. ACAP

AXE ON THE TREE DANGER TO MEN & EXISTENCE

them and spare you possible problems and embarrassment. It can also improve the quality of your visit by opening lines of communication.

The best advice is to learn before you leave. Study the culture as well as the ecology of a place when planning your trip. If you're taking an organized tour, ask for background information on local religious beliefs, ceremonial practices, dress codes, language, and politics. You can obtain additional information from books and by contacting the country's office of tourism.

Keep cultural differences in mind when packing. Remember that certain types of dress are considered offensive in many parts of the world. Learn some of the local language before you go. Although English is the official tongue of 426 million people in 40 countries, you'll be amazed at how appreciative people are when they hear a foreign visitor say "please" and "thank you" in the native language. Carry a phrase book with you.

When you arrive, be sensitive to the inhabitants' needs and feelings. You can learn a good deal by observing body language. In turn, be careful about your own body movement, especially when it comes to greeting or touching another person. Hand gestures take on different meanings from country to country. Always ask for permission before taking a photo or using a video camera.

The best general rule? When in any doubt, ask your tour guide.

GUIDELINES FOR CULTURALLY SENSITIVE TRAVEL

The following guidelines, developed by the Ecumenical Coalition on Third World Tourism, should be adhered to by all travelers:

- Travel in a spirit of humility and with a genuine desire to meet and talk with local people.
- Be aware of the feelings of other people, thus preventing what might be offensive behavior. Remember this especially with photography.
- Cultivate the habit of listening and observing, rather than merely hearing and seeing.
- Realize that people in the country you visit often have time concepts and thought patterns that differ from your own. Not inferior, just different.
- Discover the enrichment that comes from seeing another way of life, rather than looking for the "beach paradise" of the tourist posters.
- Acquaint yourself with the local customs and respect them. People will be happy to help you.
- Cultivate the habit of asking questions instead of knowing all the answers.
- Remember that you are one of thousands of visiting tourists. Do not expect special privileges.
- Spend wisely. Remember when shopping that the bargain you obtain is only possible because of the low wages paid to the maker.
- Make no promises to local people unless you are certain you can fulfill them.
- Reflect daily on your experiences; seek to deepen your understanding. What enriches you may rob or violate others.

ECOFRIENDLY SOUVENIRS

For some of us, souvenirs are an important part of a trip, but think twice before you buy. Even seemingly innocuous mementos may have cost the life of an animal or a plant.

That colorful headdress you see in a Papua New Guinea market-place could be made with the feathers of endangered birds. How many butterflies were killed for those framed collections being sold on the streets of Cuzco? Products made from hides, feathers, shells, teeth, tortoiseshell, coral, and ivory not only encourage destruction of wildlife, but, in many cases, are illegal. In addition, in some countries you risk government seizure of your souvenirs upon return and may face substantial fines.

Ecotravelers should do all they can to avoid purchasing goods that are made from animal parts (particularly endangered species) or rare plants. When purchasing souvenirs, stick to handmade crafts such as cloth goods, weavings, pottery, baskets, and paintings. If you wish to buy carvings, first determine the source and type of wood being used. Ask your tour guide or naturalist rather than the vendor.

PHOTOGRAPHY

A more environmentally friendly way to remember your trip is through photographs or videos.

When you come upon a scene that catches your attention, take a moment to study it before snapping away. Amateur nature photographers often miss good shots because they are too overwhelmed by the subject. Begin by looking for an original point of view.

TAKE ONLY PICTURES
Photographs are without doubt the most eco-friendly mementos and some animals are only too happy to get in the picture. However, you should never harass wildlife just to obtain a photograph.

PLAY SAFE *when purchasing souvenirs. Choose handmade items such as fabrics (above) and pottery. Most customs departments publish lists of products that you should avoid buying (top left).*

Experiment with framing the scene and adjusting your angle. You'll find that every new angle creates a different shot.

Lighting allows you to control the image. Predawn, dawn, and early morning light soften images. Full sun usually makes them harsh. The easiest forms of natural light to shoot in are overcast or drizzly conditions and diffuse shade.

Use rechargeable batteries whenever possible. Never dispose of batteries improperly as they are hazardous waste. For information on selecting still camera and video equipment, see p. 40.

MAKING A VIDEO

When making a video, try to relate each shot to the next. Give your video a beginning, a middle, and an end so that it tells a story. Use establishing shots and provide transition scenes between locations. Don't overdo pans and zooms. Shoot activities and concentrate on motion. When taping people, make sure they're doing something. Put yourself into the picture occasionally.

When videotaping wildlife, shoot an establishing shot, then zoom in on a specific

animal. If the animals are on the move, try to anticipate their direction. Aim the camera at their heads so you can better follow them.

PICTURE ETHICS

Find out how local people feel about being photographed and always ask permission first. Some people consider it a personal affront to be photographed. If someone asks you to take their picture, get their

address and send them a print after you return home.

If you are using a video camera, don't assume that this permits you to be first in line when viewing wildlife.

Exercise restraint when photographing wildlife. Overzealous shutterbugs can place animals under a great deal of stress. Never throw rocks or make loud noises to make an animal move or react. Avoid lingering near nesting sites. Never get between animal parents and their young or between marine mammals and the water's edge. Let your telephoto lens do your stalking for you.

BUYER BEWARE

Do not purchase:
- products made from animal skins, particularly crocodile, lizard, and snake skins (watchbands, handbags, shoes, boots, belts); or from turtle shells (combs, hair clips)
- birds (live or mounted); products made from bird skins and feathers
- ivory from elephants, whales, walruses, and narwhals

- furs and fur products, particularly from spotted cats (jaguar, leopard, snow leopard, tiger, ocelot), marine mammals, and polar bears
- coral jewelry and ornaments
- rare and exotic plants

AVOID *products such as these ivory carvings from Tanzania (below) and this Siamese crocodile key-ring (above).*

A clear breeze has no price,

The bright moon no owner.

SONG HON (1535–98), Korean poet

HIKING

Walking on designated trails is the way to get the most

out of a nature trip while causing the least harm.

You're part of nature when your feet are on the ground.

Walking is the best way to experience almost any environment. You can enjoy your surroundings at an unhurried pace and stop whenever you like for a close look at interesting flora and fauna. Furthermore, you make little noise, create no pollution, and, if you stay on trails, cause no damage to the habitat you are passing through.

PLANNING A ROUTE

Even short hikes require careful planning. Deciding where to go depends on what you want to see, your physical ability, your budget, and the time available. A detailed map of the area you have chosen will help you plan your route. A topographical map is necessary to determine altitude gain and loss—a key consideration. Two miles through the Tallgrass Prairie Preserve in Oklahoma is hardly the same as a trail of similar length in the Swiss Alps.

ON THE TRAIL *In order to minimize habitat damage, always remain on designated trails, such as this one in Joshua Tree National Park, USA (right). In areas where there are few trails, such as Torres del Paine National Park in Chile (above), keep off delicate vegetation.*

Plan for an unhurried pace so that you can linger where you want. Plot your course on a map, choosing viewpoints and campsites carefully. Just as it's more pleasurable to eat lunch while taking in a fantastic view, it's also more enjoyable overnighting in a sheltered spot with an adequate supply of water.

Take into account your physical fitness and that of your companions. Be honest: the wilderness is no place for ego. Undertake a physical training regimen before you set off. You'll enjoy yourself more

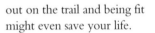
EXTENDED HIKES *may involve crossing difficult terrain. Make sure you know what's expected of you before you set off.*

out on the trail and being fit might even save your life.

Always use common sense and adhere to safety rules. Check the weather conditions, dress appropriately, and carry protective clothing. Use proper hiking, camping, and climbing equipment (see p. 40).

Be especially alert for altitude sickness in high country. Symptoms include headache, shortness of breath, and nausea. If you experience any of these rest for a couple of days and let your body become accustomed to reduced amounts of oxygen. If the symptoms persist or worsen, or if you begin to cough up blood, descend immediately. A good rule of thumb is to

BE PREPARED *Make sure you have the right gear for the environment you will be visiting. If you are hiking in New Zealand's South Island, for example, you'll need warm, waterproof clothing.*

allow a recovery day for each 1,000 feet (300 m) you climb above 10,000 feet (3,000 m).

Travel with a companion and leave your route and itinerary with someone back at base. Tell them when you expect to return and make sure they know who to contact should you be late.

TREADING LIGHTLY
Always stay on the trail and follow markers, both for your own safety and to preserve the habitat. In open, untracked areas, spread out, so that the steps of a number of people cause the minimum impact. Walk on rocks and hard ground wherever possible and hike around sensitive groundcover and marshy areas. Never take shortcuts between switchbacks as it will accelerate erosion. Keep your voices down.

LOCAL GUIDES
Using guides and porters makes sense in places such as in the Himalayas and the Andes. Not only can they lead you to the best sites and sights, they'll help carry your load, set up your camp, and prevent you from getting lost. Furthermore, by employing them, you'll be contributing to the local economy.

When hiring a guide, be sure you both understand what you expect of each other before setting out. It's vital, too, to give your guide an accurate picture of your physical abilities before agreeing upon a route. Trace the trek on a map together. Double-check food and gear. This will help prevent misunderstandings later on.

TOP HIKES

The Great Divide Trail, Canadian Rockies 300 miles (480 km) of dramatic Rocky Mountain scenery (p. 84)
The Pacific Crest Trail, USA 2,600 miles (4,200 km) from the Canadian border to Mexico via the Cascade and Sierra Nevada ranges (p. 90)
The Appalachian Trail, USA 2,100 miles (3,400 km) through the Appalachian Mountains and 14 states (p. 98)
The Inca Trail, Peru An ancient Incan footpath covering the mountainous 20 miles (33 km) between Cuzco and Machu Picchu in the Central Andes (p. 134)
The Magistrale, the High Tatras National Park, Slovakia A five-day hike through the pine forests and granite peaks of the High Tatras. Stunning alpine scenery (p. 160)
Annapurna Sanctuary, Nepal A two-week trek from Pokhara to the heart of the Himalayas (p. 214)
Kamikochi, the Japan Alps A challenging three-day (24 mile [38 km]) hike that ascends Mount Yari and Mount Hotaka (p. 226)
The Overland Track, Tasmania, Australia 50 miles (80 km) of alpine meadows, forested valleys, and rugged mountains (p. 262)
The Milford Track, Fiordland National Park, New Zealand Four day's hiking (33 miles [53 km]) through a lush, mountainous, and often rainy wilderness (p. 264)

CAMPING

There's no better way of feeling part of the great outdoors than going camping, but you must take steps to keep your impact on your surroundings to a minimum.

Whether you're spending the night at a car-camping site or are miles down a wilderness trail, always aim to leave as few traces of your visit as possible, and make sure you're well prepared. The essential ingredients of any overnight trip in the outdoors are a tent, a sleeping bag, an insulation pad, a flashlight, food and water, and a stove.

SLEEPING BAGS

Sleeping bags have been around for decades, but the heavy, canvas-sided bags that campers once used are very much a thing of the past.

The most versatile bags are now made with synthetic fill and are covered with a material such as Gore-Tex that is water-repellent but also lets air in and out. They are light and maintain their loft when damp. They are also less expensive than the goose-down bags that previously dominated the market. Down bags are still popular for use in extremely cold environments, but they tend to lose their insulation value when wet.

Using an insulating pad and ground cloth between the sleeping bag and the ground is essential if you want to stay warm and comfortable. Insulation pads come in a variety of materials, from waffled polyurethane foam mats to self-inflating mattresses covered in waterproof nylon. Never break off tree branches or collect vegetation to use as a mattress.

BACKCOUNTRY CAMPING *is a wonderful way to get close to nature. A good sleeping bag (left) is essential, while a headlamp (above left) will come in handy on most trips.*

TENTS

While little beats sleeping under the stars, nothing is worse than having to spend a night outside in the pouring rain. It's always a good idea to take some form of shelter, and the most dependable is a strong, lightweight tent.

There are many styles and sizes of tent from which to choose. Large, family-size ones will be heavier than two-person, backpacking ones. Buy a tent that is easy to erect and suits the environment that you intend to use it in. You'll need one with a rain fly for rainy climates and one with large openings covered in netting for where it's hot. Choose one with a low profile for use in windy areas.

Practice erecting your tent before you set off. It will help should you have to set it up in the dark, and you can check for tears in the fabric.

Night's center deepening.

Cry of wild geese.

I watch the moon

along the sky.

Attr. KAKINOMOTO NO
HITOMARO (c. 700),
Japanese poet

After a camping trip, always hang the tent out to dry before storing it. If you roll it up and put it away while it's wet, it will become mildewed and could be ruined.

STOVES AND LIGHTS

When purchasing a camp stove, opt for a liquid-fuel model that's refillable over one that uses butane or propane cartridges. This will save on waste. You should also take matches rather than plastic lighters as they are more environmentally friendly. Carry the matches in a waterproof container, or dip their heads in wax to keep them dry.

Headlamps are useful when it comes to working at night, or while reading. Always use rechargeable batteries for electrical items.

GREEN CAMPING

There are many other things you can do to lessen your impact on the environment when camping. Begin by choosing a durable campsite over one that's fragile. Look at the ground carefully and avoid setting up on wildflowers and small plants. Choose thick forest duff (leaf litter), rock, or gravel bars instead.

In popular camping areas, use an existing site rather than creating a new one. It has been found that repeated use of a site causes little additional deterioration. Don't dig drainage trenches or try to level out sloping ground. Never uproot plants that are making it awkward for you to pitch your tent.

CAMPING OPTIONS *Permanent camps (above) may be more comfortable, but carrying a tent enables you to camp almost anywhere (below). A liquid-fuel stove with a refillable tank (right).*

You can lighten both the load on your shoulders and your impact on the environment by keeping food packaging to a minimum. When buying food, choose items that come with minimal or recyclable packaging. Some food, such as pasta, granola, and dried fruit, can be bought in bulk and repackaged in reusable bags. Buy the rugged plastic freezer bags as you can wash them and reuse them.

Always pack out what you pack in. Don't burn trash. Avoid using soap: even biodegradable soap is alien to the environment. Clean bodies and dishes and dispose of dirty water at least 150 feet (45 m) from any water

source to avoid pollution. Use sand as a pot scourer.

When it comes to body waste, check with the land management agency regarding the most appropriate disposal method. If toilet facilities are provided, use them. If they aren't, use single-use latrines dug about 6 inches (15 cm) deep, located at least 150 feet (45 m) from any water source.

Pack out toilet paper, tampons, and diapers in ziplock bags. To kill germs and odors, add a tiny piece of ammonia-soaked sponge.

CYCLING

Traveling by bicycle is an excellent, ecofriendly way to explore the world, providing you restrict your pedaling to roads or designated bike trails.

In many countries, bicycles are still the principal mode of transport. There are 800 million of them worldwide, twice the number of cars. On a bike, you can follow paths reserved for two-wheelers, pedal along endless miles of quiet country lanes and dirt roads, or go off-road (providing you stay on designated bike trails).

Organized bicycle tours in natural areas are becoming increasingly popular. They range from luxurious inn-to-inn tours accompanied by support vehicles that carry your luggage and spare gear (and sometimes pick up a weary rider), to rugged adventure treks on mountain bikes in seldom-visited areas where you carry your own gear and sleep under the stars.

You need to be reasonably fit for a bicycle tour. You will be expected to ride between 20 and 100 miles (30 and 160 km) a day, depending on the nature of the tour and the terrain. Most tour operators supply bikes for you to rent, or you can take your own. Airlines generally include bikes in your baggage allowance.

If you're planning to go bike touring without joining an organized group and don't want to take your own bike, you will usually be able to rent or buy one at your departure point. Call ahead to make sure you can obtain the size and style you need.

EQUIPMENT

There are three basic styles of bicycle to consider when planning a trip: road, cross, and mountain. Road bikes are restricted to paved surfaces. Their wheels are quite narrow and their tires thin. Mountain bikes have wide, knobby tires for off-road terrain and specialized suspension to help take the bumps out of the trail. Cross bikes are a blend of both.

Dress for biking as you would for hiking; in other words, layer your clothes to facilitate thermal adjustment (see p. 40). You can carry your gear in specially designed bags called panniers that fit on the bike frame. They're typically made of lightweight, durable nylon or waterproof Gore-Tex. Always wear a helmet and carry a pump

OFF-ROAD BIKING *can cause considerable damage, particularly in areas prone to erosion, such as the desert southwest of the United States.*

PEDAL POWER *is the most economical and ecofriendly way to get about, whether you're touring or busy with your day-to-day affairs.*

and tool kit. A dynamo lighting system is essential. Gloves and specialized footwear ease the strain.

LOW-IMPACT CYCLING

While mountain bikes offer freedom for the rider, they also pose risks to the environment and are banned from going off-road in all designated wilderness areas and many parks. Cyclists must be mindful of the damage their tires can cause.

First of all, check to see if mountain bikes are allowed in the region where you plan to ride. Respect the rights of walkers to peace and safety and approach corners in the expectation that there could be someone just out of sight. Always stay on the track or within the designated off-road area and never take shortcuts. If possible, ride in existing ruts.

Care for the trail as you go by clearing fallen branches so that later riders won't be tempted to ride off–trail. Don't remove partially buried logs or rocks, however, as these help hold the trail together. Avoid soft, loose soil. Stick to hard surfaces wherever possible. When riding on trails along creeks, stay as far from the banks as you can.

On steep slopes, slightly deflate your tires to give the bike better traction. If you start to skid while going downhill, get off and walk. Avoid riding straight up and down slopes as this accelerates damage by erosion.

As when hiking, always travel with a companion in remote areas, and before you leave base tell someone where you're going and when you plan to be back.

TOP CYCLE TOURS

The Canadian Rockies See Banff and Jasper national parks by taking the wide-shouldered Icefield Parkway (p. 84)
Costa Rica Tough, rewarding mountain biking along coastal trails and through lush mountain rain forests (p.120)
The Scottish Highlands Pedal on little-used roads through heather-covered moorland, past lochs and mountains (p. 156)
Hell's Gate National Park, Kenya One of the few parks in Africa where you can cycle (or walk). Enjoy abundant wildlife amid the dramatic scenery of the Great Rift Valley (p. 184)
Tasmania, Australia Pastoral landscapes and rugged wilderness areas where the wildlife is wonderful (p. 262)
The South Island, New Zealand See the great Southern Alps, rain forests, and lakes in extensive national parks (p. 264)

INLAND WATERS

Cruising along a tranquil river or riding thundering rapids can be the thrill of a lifetime and can take you closer to wildlife than you've ever been before.

Animal activity and the abundance of wildlife increase the closer you are to water. Rivers are therefore among the most biologically alive of all habitats, and a trip along an inland waterway can provide the ecotraveler with a feast of everchanging scenery and wildlife.

Almost every ecotravel destination has its great rivers and a range of outfitters offering to take you down them. When planning a river trip, think carefully about the type of experience you're looking for. Do you want to paddle yourself or have a guide row for you? Do you want to travel along flat water or white water? Do you want to take a cruise, perhaps living on board for a few days? What kind of habitat do you want to explore: desert, tropical, forest, or mountain? Are sunbathing, swimming, and time out for hikes important?

WILD RIVERS *Much of the Tasmanian Wilderness in Australia can only be reached by boat (right). Safety equipment (left) is essential on all river trips.*

Work out your answers to these questions before contacting an outfitter. If you are interested in white-water rafting or canoeing, be sure to say how experienced you are. Ask for an estimate of the river's volume for the time you'll be there as this will affect the size of the rapids and the speed of the trip. It can change dramatically, depending on the rainfall and season.

Water volume is measured in cubic feet per second (CFS). The higher the CFS, the faster and bigger the flow of the river. Rapids are measured in degree of difficulty, with class I being very easy and class VI unrunnable.

TOP RIVER TRIPS

Tatshenshini and Alsek rivers, Alaska and Yukon, USA and Canada Raft two of North America's most exciting rivers, where bald eagles, moose, and grizzly bears abound (pp. 74, 78)

Tuolumne River, California, USA Tough white-water rafting on class III and IV rapids at the edge of the Sierra Nevada (p. 90)

Colorado River, Arizona, USA Trips of up to 225 miles (360 km) taking in up to 70 rapids provide a unique experience of the magnificent Grand Canyon (p. 92)

Pacuare River, Costa Rica A favorite river among rafters and kayakers in a region rich in tropical wildlife (p. 120)

Amazon River, Brazil A cruise through the rain forest from Manaus is one of the best ways to experience the Amazon (p. 130)

Zambezi River, Zimbabwe and Zambia Kayak the rapids below Victoria Falls or view the wildlife on a tranquil cruise (p. 192)

Sun Kosi River, Nepal Exhilarating river running from the Himalayas to the vast Gangetic Plain (p. 214)

Alas River, Sumatra, Indonesia Run the rapids and float through the gorges and lush forests of Gunung Leuser National Park (p. 232)

Sepik River, Papua New Guinea Enjoy a few days aboard a cruise boat or houseboat in the exotic Sepik wetlands (p. 246)

Franklin River, Tasmania, Australia A demanding white-water trip through the Tasmanian Wilderness (p. 262)

BIRDING BY BOAT *Ecotravelers on the lookout for birds along the Ariau River, west of Manaus in Brazil.*

LIGHTWEIGHT KAYAKS
allow you to reach remote areas (left). White-water rafting trips can involve a good deal of teamwork (below).

EQUIPMENT

River rafts range from two-person inflatables to large motorized boats that carry 16 people. Those most commonly used on ecotravel trips hold five or six people. They're usually equipped with oars for the guide and a paddle for each passenger. Rafts are ideal for long trips since there is plenty of room for camping gear.

Today's canoes are more durable than traditional canoes and spray skirts and removable air bags make them more reliable in big water. Kayaks are the speedy acrobats of

Under the wavering water

shine the stones,

rounded in ruby-colours

and clouded white.

Beside the Creek,
JUDITH WRIGHT (b. 1915),
Australian poet

the river-running set. They are maneuverable and portable—a big advantage when you have to portage around unrunnable rapids.

SAFETY ON THE WATER

Shooting the rapids in a raft, canoe, or kayak involves some risks. First-time kayakers and canoeists require training before attempting rapids on their own. Even with an experienced rafter at the helm, passengers embarking on an inflatable raft trip should know exactly what to do in case of a flip or being thrown out of the boat.

Equipment such as personal flotation devices, helmets, and, depending on the season, neoprene clothing and wet suits are essential. Always check river conditions with local authorities before setting off.

RIVER PROTECTION

Carry out all that you bring in; on many heavily used rivers that means human waste, too. Check

with land management officials for proper disposal guidelines.

While on the river, never intentionally dislodge boulders or alter the current. Be careful when pulling ashore: avoid landing on fragile riverbanks or in marshy areas. Don't use overhanging branches for rope swings as it can damage the tree. Always practice minimum-impact camping (see p. 50) on overnight trips.

OCEAN WATERS

You can view the oceans from a sea kayak, take a luxury nature cruise, or explore the underwater world by going snorkeling or scuba diving.

Exploring the oceans has long been synonymous with adventure and scientific discovery. The oceans account for nearly three-quarters of the planet's surface and a wondrous array of life forms lives in their waters.

There are many ways you can explore the marine environment. You'll need to ask yourself a few questions to decide which kind of trip will suit you. What kind of marine system do you wish to experience: tropical, arctic, or temperate? Do you want to go snorkeling, scuba diving, paddle yourself in a sea kayak, or ride in an ocean liner? Do you want to spend days and nights on an ocean crossing, or do you want to stay within sight of land and make frequent visits ashore? Are onboard lectures important?

SEA KAYAKING

Sea kayaking has become one of the most popular ways to experience the marine environment. Larger and more stable than their white-water cousins, sea kayaks enable paddlers to reach places no ship can get close to, such as rocky coves and small islets. They are easy to carry and highly maneuverable. Being quiet and having a low profile, they are well-suited for observing wildlife.

When kayaking near wildlife, keep your distance and behave respectfully. Don't try to touch whales and other marine mammals, no matter how close to your craft they surface.

CRUISING *the waters of the Nerofjord in Norway (above). A sea kayaker in Baja California, Mexico (above left).*

NATURE CRUISES

Today's cruise ships catering to nature travelers are much smaller than the great ocean liners of old, usually carrying from 80 to 100 passengers. They feature onboard naturalists and guides, guest lecturers, and itineraries that are designed to make the most of wildlife viewing opportunities and onshore nature excursions.

Many nature cruises now combine recreational travel with scientific pursuits. For example, most antarctic cruises accommodate research scientists who double as lecturers and onboard experts. They are available to answer your questions, and may even invite you to help with their studies, such as carrying out wildlife population surveys.

MARINE MAMMALS, *such as this humpback whale, can be your companions in ocean waters.*

Before you buy your ticket, ask the cruise company representative about its environmental practices. Make sure waste isn't dumped at sea but carried back to port for proper disposal. What are the company's anchorage practices? Ships should never drop anchor on sensitive sea bottoms, such as coral reefs.

DIVING

Snorkeling and scuba diving open up a whole new world for nature lovers. For snorkeling, all you need is a mask, snorkel, and flippers. Although scuba diving is a good deal more technical, it doesn't take long to master the basic skills required and there are numerous courses on offer.

SCUBA DIVING opens up a whole new world. Take care not to touch the coral and never harass sea life.

When selecting a dive-boat excursion, always choose a well-equipped vessel over one that has cut back on equipment to keep the price down. Also make sure before you buy your ticket that the boat carries its waste back to port for proper disposal and does not anchor on reefs.

A good dive boat will feature reserve tanks and an onboard compressor to facilitate speedier refills. Easy-to-board vessels with open gear-donning areas are another plus. Always insist on certified divemasters.

When picking an itinerary, look for locations where the boat visits at least two dive sites a day. Choose locales where there is plenty to see above 45 feet (14 m). Visibility will be better in these areas and your air supply will last longer because the deeper you dive, the more air you use.

TOP SEA SPOTS

Prince William Sound, Alaska, USA Cruises and sea kayaking in a land of fiords, glaciers, and abundant marine life (p. 74)

Johnstone Strait, British Columbia, Canada Boat and kayak trips allow you to view huge numbers of migrating orcas (p. 82)

Gulf of California, Baja California, Mexico Cruise or sea kayak among gray whales and a rich variety of other marine life (p. 110)

Barrier Reef, Belize, Travel by sea kayak or glass-bottom boat among coral islands, or go snorkeling and scuba diving (p. 118)

Galápagos Islands, Ecuador View sea lions, marine iguanas, giant tortoises, and bluefooted boobies on motorized yacht and sailboat cruises among these volcanic islands (p. 126)

Svalbard, Norway As you cruise the coastline of these arctic islands, you'll see glaciers, seals, seabirds, and possibly polar bears (p. 148)

The Red Sea, Egypt and Israel Snorkeling and scuba diving among corals close to the shore (p. 180)

Palau, Micronesia The top diving destination among the myriad islands of the western Pacific's Micronesian chain (p. 244)

The Great Barrier Reef, Australia Glorious coral reefs provide superb snorkeling and scuba diving (p. 254)

Kaikoura, New Zealand Here you can go whale-watching and dive with dolphins and seals year-round (p. 267)

Antarctica Cruise ships from South America or New Zealand visit this vast, chilly world of icebergs, whales, and penguins (pp. 268, 270)

ON ICE *Emperor penguins and antarctic cruise ship (right).*

NATURALIST-LED TOURS

Organized nature tours are a wonderful way to familiarize yourself with the natural world. If you're a curious ecotourist, nothing beats being with an expert.

A huge range of naturalist-led tours is available. You can choose a tour that focuses on a particular area of interest, say, botany, butterflies, or vulcanism, or you can look for one that's more generalized.

What distinguishes any tour is the person serving as your window to the world—your naturalist and guide. The most rewarding tours are ones led by experts who not only take you to memorable sites but contribute to your understanding and appreciation of the places you visit.

On a birding trip, for example, the naturalist must be an expert in field identification. He or she should be able to point out the different bird species for you as well as teach you about their behavior and the various roles they play in the ecosystem.

PLANNING AND CHOOSING

Plan carefully before you choose a tour. Are you only interested in wildflowers, or do you also want to learn about an area's geology? Special-focus trips tend to be frustrating for people who want a more general introduction to an area's wildlife and natural features. You'll find this especially true on birding trips, for determined birders tend to be interested in nothing but birds.

AN EXPERT AT HAND *A naturalist guide with his tour group in the Galápagos (above). Birders in southern Europe and Africa are likely to come across the European bee-eater (top left).*

Find out who will be running the tour and ask for a biography of the principal naturalist. Determine whether there will be any guest experts accompanying the trip.

Some of the large tour companies subcontract their trips to smaller outfitters that specialize in particular regions or areas of interest. Always ask for information about the subcontractor and be alert for last-minute guide substitutions.

SPECIAL FOCUS

Make sure the tour matches your needs and interests. If photographing wildlife is your prime focus, you'll be better off on a specialized photo safari than on a straightforward nature tour. An expert photographer will accompany you

and you won't have to worry about keeping the rest of the tour members waiting while you take one last shot.

Another advantage of taking a specialized tour is that you'll be joining travelers whose interests will be similar to your own. You'll have more to talk about and will be in a position to learn from one another.

Birding tours are among the most popular special-focus trips. A typical birding trip will involve long days in the field, usually from dawn till dusk, and will move at a considerable pace in order to

ON SAFARI *Tourists on a naturalist-led trip in Kenya (left). A scientist explains the properties of a medicinal plant in India (below). A birder on the job (bottom).*

take in as many locations and hence as many birds as possible.

One of the newest types of specialty trip is the butterfly tour. Wildflower tours are also becoming increasingly popular.

NATURE STUDY TRAVEL

Naturalist-led tours are offered by a variety of institutions, including colleges, universities, conservation groups, museums of natural history, and zoological societies.

While a trip such as an Oceanic Society-sponsored whale-watching tour to Baja California will offer both adventure and relaxation, its

main objective will be to educate you in the natural history of the region and relevant environmental issues. Nature study tours such as this are also a terrific way for travelers who are concerned about the environment to contribute to conservation projects, as these programs are conducted primarily for fundraising purposes. Before booking, check where the money raised is going to be spent and how the organization ensures that its programs are environmentally responsible.

Taking part in a university-sponsored field study can be a rewarding experience. Not only do scientists and naturalists typically lead these tours, but the programs usually include lectures, discussions, and multimedia presentations. On some trips, participants may even qualify for college credits.

TOP BIRDING SITES

The Everglades, USA Subtropical wetlands rich in birdlife, including spoonbills, frigatebirds, pelicans, and gallinules; Dec–Apr (p.100)
Costa Rica Colorful tropicals such as tanangers, jacamars, macaws, and toucans; year-round (p. 120)
The Galápagos Islands, Ecuador Darwin's finches and seabirds, including boobies and tropicbirds; year-round (p. 126)
The Pantanal, Brazil Throngs of ibises, herons, storks, and brilliantly colored tropical birds such as toucans and macaws; July–Sept (p. 138)
The West Estonian Archipelago Biosphere Reserve, Estonia Wetland stopover for migrating waterfowl; Apr–May (p. 154)
Estremadura, Spain Numerous bird-of-prey species and black storks in Mediterranean forest and scrubland; year-round (p. 166)
The Great Rift Valley, Kenya Lakes pink with flamingos, and migrations of storks, birds of prey, and shorebirds; June–Feb (p. 184)
Bharatpur (Keoladeo Ghana National Park), India An impressive heronry and many rare Asian species; Aug–Feb (p. 220)
Kakadu National Park, Australia A tropical river system that's home to many of the country's 700 species; May–Sept (p. 250)
The Antarctic Peninsula, Antarctica Penguins and seabirds in profusion in an icy world; Dec–Feb (p. 268)

VOLUNTEER VACATIONS

You can lend a hand in caring for the natural world by planning your vacation as a volunteer on a research expedition or a service trip.

Opportunities abound both at home and abroad for ecotourists who are willing to roll up their sleeves and join the volunteer workforce, whether it involves rebuilding a hiking trail or helping with a rhino census.

Why pay for a vacation on which you're expected to work? The answer lies in the satisfaction you'll feel having helped the environment and the wildlife that depends on it for survival. Volunteer vacations enable ordinary citizens to join a scientific team in field research. Trips are usually to beautiful natural areas, and your experience will differ so much from your daily routine that it'll be something you'll never forget.

Volunteer vacations with an emphasis on nature and the environment fall into two categories: research expeditions and service trips.

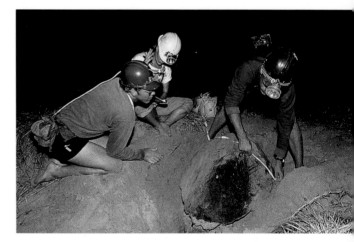

RESEARCH EXPEDITIONS

On a research trip, you assist scientists in the field. Research expeditions cover a wide range of academic disciplines, from archeology to entomology. You can board a ship researching whales in the South Pacific, conduct wildlife surveys in the national parks of Kenya, search for rare monkeys in Peru, map coral reefs off Belize, or inventory flora in Nebraska.

Many universities, zoological societies, museums, and conservation organizations sponsor these types of trip, often with other nonprofit organizations acting as intermediaries, see p. 30.

When you join a research expedition, you become part of the labor force and a funding source for conservation all in one. You don't need to be a scientist in order to sign on, just a willing participant, although certain trips require particular qualifications, such as scuba certification.

Typically, you pay a share-of-cost contribution that covers your meals, lodging, and ground transportation, and provides for the chief researcher's expenses, including

CONDUCTING SURVEYS *Sea turtle research being undertaken in the Pacific (above). Volunteers in Jamaica working on a vegetation survey (left). Tools for fossil examination (top left).*

OCEAN RESEARCH *Researchers studying the reef at Heron Island, Queensland, Australia (left). A zoologist approaching a southern right whale and calf in Argentinian waters (below).*

equipment and supplies. In exchange, you are given an opportunity to experience the natural world as few nature tourists ever do. There is plenty of time for you to travel on your own and visit the area, usually at a cost far below what you would pay if you were on an organized tour. What's more, most trips of this sort are nonprofit and therefore tax-exempt.

Normally, you must arrange and pay for your transportation to and from the site, though the sponsoring agency will usually arrange transportation from a staging area to the final location on projects where the site is remote. Meals and shelter are usually provided, but check to make sure.

To determine which expedition is best for you, contact the various organizations that sponsor trips (see p. 278) and find out what is available. Match the study focus of the trips to your own interests and the locations to the places you would like to visit. Most projects are conducted over a period of years so other volunteers will probably have already worked on them. Get in touch with a few of these people and ask them about their experiences. Contact the lead scientists and question them about field conditions and what will be expected of you. If you have special skills, mention them.

RESTORING HABITAT

Hiking clubs, conservation organizations, and government agencies all organize service trips that range from building trails to eradicating invasive, non-native plants. The work is generally performed in parks, forests, and wilderness areas. You pay a small registration fee that helps cover administration costs and insurance. The sponsoring organizations (hiking clubs, conservation groups, and so on) typically provide food and shelter while a cooperating agency (a government agency) will supply tools and equipment. Though the work can be hard, you will have time to explore on your own.

Many service trips require participants to be in good physical condition. Read the trip description thoroughly and make sure you know what is expected of you before you enlist. The organization should supply you with a detailed equipment list.

Come forth into the light

of things,

Let Nature be your

teacher.

The Tables Turned,
WILLIAM WORDSWORTH
(1770–1850),
English poet

CARE FOR THE WILD *Trail maintenance is one of the many tasks that volunteers are involved in on service trips.*

ANIMAL-SUPPORTED TRAVEL

In many parts of the world, domesticated animals offer enjoyable and ecofriendly ways to travel through wilderness.

Sure-footed and low-impact, animals can take the strain out of backcountry treks and provide unique ecotravel experiences. In Nepal, you can search for tigers and rhinos while riding on the back of an elephant. The high perch provides a bird's-eye view and also offers a measure of protection from the tigers. In Kenya, you can experience the awesome scenery and extraordinary wildlife of the Great Rift Valley on a one-week horse safari. Llamas will carry your gear for you on a day-hike through the peaks of Rocky Mountain National Park in Colorado, USA.

If you're looking for an animal-supported trip, as with selecting any ecotour, do your homework and ask plenty of questions. Do all you can to check that the animals are well

treated. Consider whether you want to ride, or walk while animals carry your gear. If you're going on an equestrian trip, find out if the horses are gentle or high spirited. What kind of saddlery is used: English (a small saddle without a horn or raised back) or Western (larger, with a horn and more pronounced seat)? Western is generally better for people who are new to riding. What level of experience is required? Who will be handling the animals?

On any type of trip, it pays to get in shape. When it comes to riding, no matter how physically fit you are, you'll find you'll use muscles you never even thought you had. You need to spend some time in the saddle to prepare your bones and butt for a long ride. If you've never ridden before, take a few lessons. Make sure you break in your jeans and boots and do some stretching exercises before you mount up.

SPECIAL EQUIPMENT

When horseback riding, hard-soled shoes or boots with a pronounced heel are essential as they give you better bite in the stirrups. Take a pair of gloves along and wear a bandanna around your neck. You can use it to cover your mouth and

FOUR-LEGGED FRIENDS
Horse trekking in Abruzzo National Park, Italy (above). In Grand Canyon National Park in Arizona, USA, mules take visitors into the canyon (left). In Australia, camels (right)—descendants of animals brought by early explorers —take travelers on desert tours. If you find animals are being ill treated, notify the appropriate authorities.

RHINOS CROSSING *Visitors on an elephant safari in Chitwan National Park, Nepal, pause to watch an Indian rhinoceros and its calf walking past.*

nose on dusty trails. If you bring a hat, make sure it fits snugly on your head. A tie or chin strap will keep it from blowing off. A loose hat on the trail can spook the horses behind you.

Odds are you'll be traveling with an outfitter who will serve as head wrangler and packer. Packing a horse requires skill and special equipment. You can make it easier by bringing your personal belongings in an internal frame rucksack or duffle bag rather than a hard-sided suitcase. Put items you'd normally carry in a day-pack—camera, water bottle, sunscreen, insect repellent—in specially designed pannier bags that strap to your saddle.

ENVIRONMENTAL CONSIDERATIONS

No matter what type of animal-supported trip you're taking, make sure the outfitter is committed to environ-mentally responsible travel. Animals can cause considerable damage to fragile ecosystems if care isn't taken to minimize their impact.

Pack animals should always be restricted to trails. While soft-footed animals such as llamas are relatively easy on the environment, a string of mules or packhorses can des-troy delicate vegetation with their hooves and dislodge rocks, causing erosion.

Prevent animals from defecating in or near water. Avoid tying animals directly to trees and bushes or in grassy areas as they'll paw and trample root systems. This can kill trees in heavily used sites. Construct a picket line on bare or rocky ground instead. When breaking camp, scatter whatever manure there is around the picket area. It dries and decays faster that way and attracts fewer flies. Fill in any holes dug by pawing animals. Pack out all garbage.

TOP ANIMAL-SUPPORTED TRIPS

Rocky Mountain National Park, Colorado, USA Let llamas carry your gear on day-hikes along mountain trails (p. 88)
Yosemite National Park, California, USA Week-long High Sierra saddle trips through this mountain wilderness are so popular that you need to apply at least a year in advance (p. 90)
Grand Canyon National Park, Arizona, USA Travel the switch-backs that lead to the canyon floor on the back of a burro (p. 92)
Iceland Ride Icelandic ponies and stay at mountain huts in the uninhabited heart of this land of volcanoes (p. 150)
The Great Rift Valley, Kenya Five-day horse safaris take travelers across the Athi Plains, through the Ngong Hills, and into the Great Rift Valley. Highlights of the tour include Hell's Gate National Park and Lake Naivasha (p. 184)
The Okavango Delta, Botswana View these magnificent wetlands while riding elephants rescued from culling operations in South Africa and zoos in North America (p. 196)
Royal Chitwan National Park, Nepal Track elusive tigers and rare rhinos from atop trained elephants (p. 218)
The Red Center, Australia Camel tours through the MacDonnell Ranges allow you to experience the outback's wildlife, its spec-tacular gorges and water holes, and Aboriginal rock art (p. 260)

We ... had come to study ... fossils and glaciers,
the ebb and flow of seasons, wind and albatrosses,
metropolises of penguins ... We were pilgrims in the
last new land on Earth.

The Crystal Desert: Summers in Antarctica, DAVID CAMPBELL,
American scientist and author

CHAPTER FOUR

ECOJOURNEYS

HOW *to* USE ECOJOURNEYS

Whether you dream of rafting the rapids of the Zambezi River or tracking tigers in Indian jungle, this guide to some of the world's great natural areas is the ideal place to start planning your next ecojourney.

The following pages will take you from the glaciers of Alaska to the rain forests of Amazonia, from the grasslands of the Serengeti to the coral reefs of coastal Queensland. Ecojourneys features 68 natural areas arranged under the six geographical headings listed opposite. Each section begins with an introduction that includes a map of the region and a list of the featured destinations. Each entry incorporates the features shown here.

Maps show the locations of the parks and preserves, and main access routes to the area. Heavy black lines indicate principal roads (relative to others in the region). Bear in mind that a highway in East Africa may not be quite the same as a highway in North America.

Key to symbols

birding	wildlife watching	botany
marine-mammal watching	geology and landscape	
hiking	boating and kayaking	scuba diving
cycling	animal-assisted treks	cultural sites

Asia

Oceania and Antarctica

The Red Center
Australia

From above, the center of Australia spreads in a panorama of red soil speckled with dusty vegetation, rows of brown mountain ranges and pencil-thin roads. Much of the history of this ancient landscape is in its rocks, some of them nearly two billion years old.

Compared with most arid areas, Central Australia is rich in vegetation and wildlife. All sorts of marsupials, from rock wallabies to the mouse-like hairy footed dunnart, leave their footprints in the sand, as do dingos, and many birds, rodents, frogs, and lizards. This country is home to the world's second-largest lizard, the perentie, which grows to 8 feet (2.5 m), and the bizarre thorny devil, a small, slow-moving lizard that is covered with spines.

The richest natural areas lie deep within gorges that were formed by ancient rivers, where cool water holes give life to a profusion of plants and creatures. There are any number of secluded gorges in the MacDonnell Ranges, which are only a day trip from the town of Alice Springs. The closest is Simpsons Gap, which can be reached along a 10 mile (16 km) bicycle path from the Alice. Energetic walkers can do the completed sections of the Larapinta Trail, which will eventually run for 132 miles (213 km) from Alice Springs west along the backbone of the West MacDonnell Ranges.

Palm Valley in the Finke Gorge National Park, 90 miles (145 km) from Alice Springs, is an oasis where hundreds of red cabbage palms grow. It's a jolting four-wheel-drive trip to the valley, but you are rewarded

Uluru (Ayers Rock) rises 1,050 feet (340 m) from the desert floor (left). A red kangaroo (right).

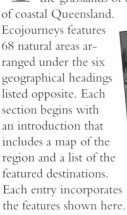

Glen Helen G near Kata Tju lizard eats th

with an a including contrasti

Austr Rock), the broa Uluru a Olgas) Uluru owned here how t ment view scape

260

Accurate and evocative color illustrations of the destination's flora and fauna.

The **illustrated banding** identifies the region in which the destination is located. See the key on the right.

Vivid **color photographs** have been carefully selected to show the best of the region's scenery, typical habitats, and characteristic flora and fauna.

Sarawak and Sabah

e Red Center

the 6 mile (9.5 km) trail around Uluru, to see its changing rock forms, the water holes, and various caves containing Aboriginal art. Visitors are drawn to climb the rock but the local people regard this as disrespectful.

their greenery
' burning red.
luru (Ayers
at rises from
lden spinifex.
a Tjuta (the
age listed
which is
who have lived
eir tours describe
harsh environ-
e Aboriginal
n sees the land-
ing deep spiritual
You can walk

BACK ROADS
For a drive that encompasses the Center's unique features, take the Mereenie Loop Road from Alice Springs to Yulara, the resort near Uluru. The road links Glen Helen, Kings Canyon, and Yulara, returning to Alice Springs via the Lasseter and Stuart highways. Side roads lead to the chasms and waterholes of Simpsons Gap, Standley Chasm, Ellery Creek Big Hole, Serpentine Gorge, and Ormiston Gorge. You should allow five days for the trip, to have plenty of time for swimming and walking.

Mount
nwhile.
s have
s, and
earby.
ll,
alk,
d
3 feet
o spot
r.
ear
t
lere
e

the forefront of the anti-logging efforts, leading blockades and standing before bulldozers. Many have been arrested over and over again, but refuse to give up the struggle to save their forest home for generations to come.

HORNBILLS

With their long, down-curved beaks, often with a prominent casque on top, hornbills are easy to recognize. However, you are likely to hear them first: they make great honks and laughter-like whoops, and the air passing through their wings as they fly sounds like a locomotive.

There are some 45 species of hornbill spread across Africa and Southeast Asia. At least 10 inhabit Borneo, and almost all of them can be found in Gunung Mulu National Park. Few animals mean more to the people of the Borneo rain forest than these great birds, which often appear in the legends, dances, and art of the Iban, Kenyah, Ngaju, and other tribes.

Hornbills have a unique way of nesting. The female builds a nest in a tree cavity, plasters the hole shut, and stays there for the entire incubation period and beyond. A narrow, vertical opening is left, through which she and the brood are fed by the male.

TRAVELER'S NOTES

Access Domestic flights from capital cities to Alice Springs. Coach and 4WD tours from Alice Springs, where 4WD vehicles and campervans can be rented. Uluru is 288 miles (480 km) from Alice Springs, 45 minutes by air

When to visit Year-round. Hot during the day; coolest Apr–Sept. Cold at night

Information Central Australian Regional Tourism Association.

Cnr Gregory Tce and Hartley St, Alice Springs NT 0871, Australia; tel. (089) 525-199, fax (089) 530-295

Accommodation Hotels, motels, hostels, campsites in Alice Springs and Yulara; hotel, hostel, campsites at Kings Canyon; motel, campsites at Glen Helen; campsites in national parks

Notes Carry water on all walks; 8 pints (4 l) per person per day. Register with rangers before going on long hikes

261

Traveler's Notes contains practical information on travel, accommodation, when to visit, and where to obtain information locally. The symbols (see the key opposite) indicate activities for which the region is renowned.

The **box features** supply detailed information on associated topics, such as local environmental issues, significant conservation projects, the lifestyles of indigenous peoples, and notable flora and fauna.

North
America
68

Central
and South
America
104

Europe
142

Africa
172

Asia
208

Oceania
and
Antarctica
238

North America

ECOTRAVEL *in* NORTH AMERICA

North America has the most extensive system of parks, wildlife refuges, and wilderness areas in the world.

The remarkable national parks system in the United States is the result of the foresight and efforts of such early conservationists as John Muir, Theodore Roosevelt, Aldo Leopold, and Bob Marshall. Beginning with the creation of Yellowstone National Park in 1872, the United States developed a land conservation system that has been copied by countries around the world. Today, the National Park Service administers 53 parks, 76 monuments, 10 seashores, and 12 preserves, totaling more than 109,000 square miles (280,000 km²). It is the foundation of a booming nature travel industry.

The federal government also oversees millions of acres of other public lands in the form of national forests, wildlife refuges, and grazing lands. Another 82,800 square miles (214,500 km²) of natural areas are protected by state agencies. These lands are often considerably less crowded than the national parks.

Vast areas of Canada are protected by its

SCENIC WONDERS *Akaka Falls Park in the Hawaiian Islands (above). Clouds of steam from the geyser, Old Faithful, in Yellowstone National Park (right). Newly opened leaves and flowers of the white oak, in North Carolina (top left).*

34 national parks, 1.5 million square miles (3.9 million km²) of national forests, 46 national wildlife areas, and 101 national bird sanctuaries. Canada's low population density and huge areas of wilderness make for an abundance of outdoor recreation opportunities.

North America also offers an array of private preserves, such as the more than 1,100 reserves in the United States operated by The Nature Conservancy and the 80 reserves and wildlife sanctuaries managed by the National Audubon Society. These sites rely on

THE BALD EAGLE *Once endangered, this species is now making a comeback, thanks to protection of its habitat.*

volunteers to help manage them, thus providing a way for nature lovers to practice ecotourism in the field.

THE HAWAIIAN ISLANDS
The Hawaiian Islands, located about 2,500 miles (4,000 km) southwest of the United States, are the most isolated bits of land on the planet. This makes for a collection of some of the most unusual wildlife species found anywhere.

A sophisticated tourist infrastructure and an efficient inter-island air service make travel easy. Haleakala and Hawaii Volcanoes national parks on the islands of Maui and Hawaii are not to be missed, but you should also make time to visit lesser-known areas, such as the

Huleia National Wildlife Refuge Complex on Kauai and Kakahaia National Wildlife Refuge on Molokai, both of which protect large numbers of waterfowl and shorebirds.

THE NORTHWEST

Despite the remoteness of many of Alaska's parks and wilderness areas, and the distances between them, you can still explore several of the state's natural areas in the space of a two-week visit. One option is to base yourself in Anchorage and tour the mainland preserves. Another is to explore the fiords and rain forests of southeastern Alaska—the panhandle—by taking the state-run ferry that travels through the Inside Passage. Ferries depart from as far south as Seattle, allowing the traveler to experience coastal British Columbia before continuing north.

Hawaiian Islands
(not to scale)

IN THE WEST *Temperate rain forest in Olympic National Park, Washington State (right). A bull moose shedding velvet from its antlers (below). The vast granite form of Half Dome in Yosemite National Park, California (bottom).*

Misty Fjords National Monument and Glacier Bay National Park are among the parks of the panhandle.

More temperate rain forests can be explored to the south in the Pacific Northwest states of Washington and Oregon, where Olympic, Mount Rainier, and North Cascades national parks can be combined in one short trip.

Check out the various national wildlife refuges in the region, as well. Coastal wetlands and estuaries are prime stopovers for the millions of waterfowl that travel up and down the migration route known as the Pacific Flyway each year. At Washington's Willapa Bay, for example, you can see countless thousands of shorebirds, including dunlins, avocets, sanderlings, plovers, and curlews.

CALIFORNIA

In California alone, scientists have identified nearly 400 distinct types of habitat that, overall, are home to 7,850 kinds of plant, 30,000 species of insect, and 2,300 different vertebrate species. Nearly half the state is owned and managed by government agencies. There are six national parks, ranging from the primeval forests of Redwood National Park in the north to the desert wonderland of Joshua Tree National Park in the south.

The Sierra Nevada, the granite backbone of the state, boasts some of the most scenic landscapes found anywhere: few places on Earth can match the beauty and majesty of Yosemite National Park.

THE ROCKIES

The Rocky Mountains run down the length of North America like a stegosaurus' spine. Towering peaks, vast ice fields, jewel-like lakes, wildflower-dappled alpine meadows, and thick forests— these are the scenes you can expect to find when you explore the high country along the Continental Divide.

Four national parks in the United States and four in Canada provide perfect settings in which to learn about the Rockies' unique environment and their wildlife. Species such as wolf and grizzly bear that once tottered on the brink of extinction have been given a renewed lease on life, thanks to reintroduction projects and public education. By visiting these parks, you play a part in their protection.

THE SOUTHWEST

To the early European pioneers, the deserts of the Southwest appeared to be lifeless, inhospitable terrain, good-for-nothing places where nothing could survive. Today, this corner of North America has become one of the most popular nature destinations of all.

Several of this region's most famous parks can be seen by following a clockwise route through Utah and

NORTH TO SOUTH *Capitol Reef National Park, Utah (right). A curious polar bear near Churchill, in Canada. (below left). Punting through a cypress swamp in South Carolina (bottom).*

Arizona on a two-week-long visit to Zion, Bryce Canyon, Capitol Reef, Canyonlands, Arches, and Grand Canyon national parks. Unfortunately, the desert's fragile environment—a hiker wandering off the trail can cause damage that will last decades—is threatened by the vast numbers of visitors heading to these areas. Many ecotravelers are therefore seeking out equally beautiful but less visited destinations such as the Escalante Wilderness in southeastern Utah, Bosque Del Apache National Wildlife Refuge in New Mexico, and Coronado National Forest in Arizona.

THE PRAIRIES AND THE GREAT LAKES

Harrows have turned the vast midsection of North America into one giant breadbasket, plowing under what was once a shimmering sea of prairie grasses. Though little remains of this important ecosystem, nature travelers can still find remnants in such places as the Tallgrass Prairie Preserve in Oklahoma. In North Dakota's badlands, Theodore Roosevelt National Park provides a safe haven for descendants of the approximately 25 million bison that once roamed the prairies.

There are other wildlife strongholds in the Midwest, as well. In Minnesota, you can paddle a canoe through Voyageurs National Park, a 340 square mile (880 km²) patch of forested, watery wilderness that straddles the United States–Canada border. The park is home to wolves, moose, black bears, bald eagles, river otters, and waterfowl. You may well hear the eerie cry of the common loon—the sound of the North Woods.

THE EAST

While the East may not have the vast areas of designated wilderness found in the West, there are still plenty of natural areas where you can leave civilization far behind. In Florida, you can look for alligators and waterfowl in the swamps of the Everglades. Red wolves howl and black bears hunt for berries in Great Smoky Mountains National Park, a 780 square mile (2,000 km²) patch of wilderness that straddles the North Carolina–Tennessee border. In the Appalachian Mountains, a contiguous stretch of back-country, large areas have changed little since the days of the Pilgrims.

In Canada, you can take an ecotour to see polar bears at Churchill, Manitoba, or to see seals at Magdalen Island in the Gulf of St Lawrence. Such tours are typical of the ways in which ecotravelers can experience wildlife while supporting the economy, thus protecting the local ecosystem.
DH

BROWN PELICANS *abound in Everglades National Park.*

Hooks and fishing line injure Pelicans
NO FISHING in marina area during daylight hours

Please do not feed the pelicans

Alaska

United States of America

Alaska is immensely rich in wildlife and remarkably diverse. Its coastline stretches over 5,000 miles (8,000 km), from the panhandle in the southeast, site of one of the world's few remaining temperate rain forests, to the bold cliffs and thundering surf of the outer coast, and north to the arctic waters of the Beaufort and Chukchi seas.

The interior—expansive in scope and extreme in climate—holds its own enchantment: in summer the birds, flowers, and insects run riot in the forests and across the tundra, but in winter the land withdraws into frigid, silent darkness. Few places remain in the world where this kind of wildness exists.

Alaska's national parks and wildlife refuges offer a superb introduction to these environments. Visiting just a few provides a taste of Alaska's varied grandeur.

ISLANDS AND FORESTS

Only a few hours' drive south of Anchorage, at the northern limit of the temperate rain forest, Prince William Sound is an explorer's paradise. The sound can be accessed from Seward, Cordova, Whittier, and Valdez. At each of these centers, tour operators offer sightseeing flights and boat trips, and kayaks can be hired.

This is a place of verdant islands and massive glaciers, a wonderland of channels and backwaters, home to otters, Sitka black-tailed deer, brown bears, black bears, and foxes.

The waters of the sound support salmon runs and rich stocks of halibut and sablefish. Harbor seals and northern sea lions feed on fish such as capelin and herring. Endangered populations of fin and humpback whales pass through seasonally, as do gray whales, recently taken off the endangered species list. Five pods of orcas, comprising about 90 animals, are resident here.

A frozen river in the Alaskan interior (top). A bald eagle on an iceberg in Kenai Fjords National Park (left)

To the east, the Copper River Delta provides a staging ground for phenomenal flocks of dunlins and western sandpipers. Sandhill cranes, trumpeter swans, and Aleutian terns all use these remote breeding grounds. The sound is home to over 3,000 bald eagles (surpassing the entire population of the lower 48 states), as well as to shearwaters, kittiwakes, puffins, and marbled murrelets.

FJORDS AND GLACIERS

Nearby Kenai Fjords National Park presents the savage beauty of a land fresh from the carving forces of glaciers and the relentless pounding of the sea. The 300 square mile (780 km²) Harding Ice Field sits atop the southern Kenai Peninsula,

A breaching humpback whale in Prince William Sound (left). The horned puffin (below) is one of the most common birds along the coast.

its tremendous expanse of ice resulting from up to 600 inches (15,000 mm) of snow annually. Thirty glaciers flow seaward from the ice field, eight reaching the ocean. Many of these rivers of ice can be viewed on boat tours and hiking trips operating out of Seward.

In the late 1700s, a bountiful population of sea otters brought Russian and Aleut hunters here. Driven to the edge of extinction, the otters have now made a comeback. Kittiwakes, puffins, murres, and countless other seabirds fill the skies, while Steller's sea lions, harbor seals, whales, and an armada of fish enliven the sea.

TRAVELER'S NOTES

Access International flights to Anchorage. Car or bus to mainland towns, Denali. Prince William Sound: boat or plane from Seward, Valdez, Cordova, Whittier. Kenai Fjords: boat or plane from Seward. Gates of the Arctic, ANWR: plane from Fairbanks

When to visit June–Sept. May for shorebird migrations

Information Alaska Public Lands Information Center, 605 W. 4th Ave, Suite 105 Anchorage, AK 99501, USA; tel. (907) 271-2737.

Also APLC, 250 Cushman, Fairbanks, AK 99701, USA; tel. (907) 451-7352

Accommodation Hotels in towns. Lodges and campsites in parks

Note Plan trips carefully. Glaciers can be dangerous; watch out for bears in northern parks. Insect repellent essential

75

MOUNTAINS AND TUNDRA

Nowhere provides a better introduction to Alaska's rugged interior than Denali National Park and Preserve. The crowning glory of the park's 9,400 square miles (24,300 km²) is Mount McKinley, known as Denali, or "the high one", to the local Athapascan people. At 20,320 feet (6,200 m), this is the highest peak in North America. From the road, which runs east–west for 91 miles (147 km), 37 species of mammal and 159 species of bird can be seen. Cars are permitted up to the Savage River Bridge, beyond which only park buses may travel. Hikers may disembark from the bus at their discretion and board later for the return.

The park contains caribou, Dall sheep, foxes, grizzly bears, wolves, and wolverines. Golden eagles nest here in the greatest density per square mile known anywhere, and are joined by 17 other species of owl, hawk, and falcon. White and black spruce predominate in the forests, interspersed with cottonwood, birch, and aspen. In summer, the tundra explodes with flowers and berries.

Denali National Park (top), home of the willow ptarmigan (above). Grizzlies at play (right). A Dall sheep ram (left).

THE BROOKS RANGE

Hardy adventurers seeking a more extreme backcountry experience should head farther north, beyond the Arctic Circle, to the wilderness that surrounds the Brooks Range.

Gates of the Arctic National Park and Preserve, a rugged, roadless park covering over 1,300 square miles (3,400 km²), is named for the wide pass that lies between the peaks of Boreal Mountain and Frigid Crags. Six wild rivers provide rafting opportunities, and the hiking is excellent, though no established trails exist.

The ecosystem here is a fragile one. Dwarf willow may take decades to rise a foot above the soil. Spruce and birch may be hundreds of years old but only inches in girth. Granite itself becomes brittle from repeated freezing and

thawing. Grizzlies each require 100 square miles (259 km²) of territory. Herds of caribou, numbering close to a quarter of a million animals, winter to the south and calve farther north. Grizzly and black bears, caribou, Dall sheep, and wolves are also found here.

OIL: THE THREAT TO WILDLIFE

Oil is Alaska's biggest industry. From Prudhoe Bay on the north coast to drilling platforms in Cook Inlet near Anchorage, Alaska's precious oil reserves are sought after and exploited. Oil brings prosperity—but at a cost. Spills occur with alarming frequency and can be devastating. The 11-million-gallon (49.5 million l) 1989 Exxon Valdez oil spill in Prince William Sound resulted in the deaths of at least 3,500 sea otters and 350,000 seabirds, plus countless numbers of fish.

The preservation of wilderness areas is also threatened by pressure from the oil industry to develop new areas for exploration. The industry is pushing hard to open the ANWR to exploratory drilling, but environmentalists (and the Native Gwich'in people) are adamantly opposed. Oil company representatives claim that Prudhoe Bay is a success story, with caribou and oil facilities existing in harmony with one another. Biologists, however, point to a 23 percent decline in herd numbers since 1992.

To the northeast, lies the sprawling Arctic National Wildlife Refuge (ANWR), the United States' largest refuge. Its 30,000 square miles (78,000 km²) encompass three geographical regions—the wide coastal plain, studded with marshes and lagoons; the eastern Brooks Range; and the boreal forest to the south.

About 135 bird species are to be found on the coastal plain. It also provides denning habitat for polar bears and arctic foxes, and is the calving ground for the 163,000-strong Porcupine caribou herd. The caribou migrate south to the forested lowlands of Canada for the winter.

There are seven great mountain ranges within the refuge. About 800 grizzly bears and 10,000 Dall sheep share this territory with large numbers of moose and wolves. Several rivers flow down the southern slopes of the mountains and through the forests, including the Sheenjek, the Coleen, and the Porcupine.

Visitors must take a bush plane to the ANWR and then hike and camp in the backcountry. There are no roads or marked trails in the refuge, but the river rafting is unparalleled. DS

A herd of caribou in the Arctic National Wildlife Refuge (top). Gray wolves (above) are common in Gates of the Arctic and the ANWR. An oil-covered bird receiving treatment after the Exxon Valdez oil spill (left).

77

The Yukon

Canada

Canada embraces seemingly endless wilderness, much of it flat country laced with lakes and ponds. The Yukon Territory, however, is a land of towering mountains and legendary gold discoveries. One of the most striking sights in all of North America is the massive ice field high in the remote northwest, lying across the great arc of coastal mountains that joins Alaska and Canada. Apart from Greenland, this is the greatest nonpolar ice field in the world.

Kluane National Park was established in 1972 to protect 8,500 square miles (22,000 km²) of this

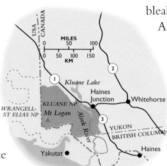

bleak, beautiful country. On the Alaskan side, these magnificent mountains and glaciers have been protected in the Wrangell-St Elias National Park and Preserve. Together, these parks make up the largest area of protected wilderness in the world.

This is a land of violent geological forces. Ash from a volcanic eruption 1,200 years ago lies 3 feet (1 m) thick atop Kluane's Klutlan Glacier. Eskers and hoodoos (gravel ridges and rock columns sculpted by glaciers) are still being formed. High cirques and the faces of hanging valleys ring with the sounds of summer waterfalls.

At the heart of Kluane stands Mount Logan, Canada's highest peak at 19,341 feet (5,900 m). Climbers come from far and wide to tackle its slopes, and those of nearby peaks.

GLACIER COUNTRY

Over 2,000 glaciers spill from the ice field, 60 of which are ones that move dramatically (advances of 2 miles [3.2 km] per year have been recorded). Such glaciers sometimes

A grizzly bear feeding on salmon.

Kluane National Park (above) safeguards vast glaciers and mountains in Canada's northwest. Bearberry on the tundra (right).

dam rivers, forming lakes. When the glacier weakens, the lake breaks through and carves a new river. About 200 years ago, the Lowell Glacier dammed the Alsek River, submerging the Haines Junction area. Raft remains have been found high on the mountain, which would have been the high-water mark. In 1850, the ice-dam broke, sending a wall of water roaring down the valley. The Southern Tutcheone Indians still tell stories of this devastating inundation.

The Alaska Highway runs along the northeastern boundary of Kluane and, on a clear day, snow-capped peaks dominate the landscape to the west. To the east is Kluane Lake, which lies outside the boundary of the park. For visitors who would love to see the glaciers but are not up to the climb, bush pilots based at Kluane Lake offer inspiring sightseeing trips.

Kluane's verdant fringe is accessible from the highway and there are over 300 miles (500 km) of trails. In the lower elevations, forests of spruce, quaking aspen, and balsam predominate. The densest concentration of grizzlies in Canada is found here, as well as black bears, caribou, coyotes, moose, and wolves. Higher up, the forest gives way to meadows. In spring and summer, these are bright with the colors of moss campion, arctic poppies, fireweed, and lupine—just some of the 1,300 plant species that grow here. Higher yet, Dall sheep seek refuge from predators on precipitous slopes.

Over 105 species of bird have been recorded in Kluane. These include the golden eagle, the peregrine falcon, and many songbirds. DS

The howl of the coyote is a familiar, chilling call of the wild. The coyote is frequently mistaken for a wolf.

TRAVELER'S NOTES

Access International flights to Anchorage. Drive from Anchorage (12–14 hours) or take domestic flight to Whitehorse via Juneau. Car or bus from Whitehorse (1½ hrs)

When to visit May–Sept

Information Kluane NP, Box 5495, Haines Junction, Yukon Territory YOB-ILO, Canada; tel. (403) 634-2251

Accommodation Campground in park at Kathleen Lake, hotels in Haines Junction

Notes This is remote country. Plan trips carefully and advise park rangers of your intentions

Churchill

Canada

The history of Canada features tales of a vast wilderness exploited by both British and French fur traders. Located on the banks of Hudson Bay in Manitoba, the town that is now Churchill was established by the Hudson's Bay Company in 1684. Many of the furs bound for Europe went through the town. Modern technology has cut the distances between major cities and many of Canada's outposts, but you are in little doubt when you step onto the tundra at Churchill that you are at the edge of the Earth.

The fur traders who settled here would scarcely have imagined that people might one day come to Churchill from around the world to view the most feared of arctic predators, the polar bear. From mid-October to early November, the town lies on a migratory pathway that (in the days before bear-proof garbage containers) once led bears right through town.

BEARWATCHING

Polar bears hunt seals—almost their only source of nutrition—on the sea ice of Hudson Bay from late fall until around May when temperatures rise and the ice floes break up. They are then forced onto land along the coast. Family groups and young bears move inland, while adult males tend to remain near the bay. The bears live off their fat stores during summer, feeding on carrion, and occasionally invading garbage dumps for food. As fall approaches, the bears make their way along the coast toward Cape Churchill, waiting for the freeze-up. As the water begins to freeze, they move onto the ice again. (Up to 90 percent of Hudson Bay is covered in pack ice until spring.)

Beluga whales (left). Warning signs (right).

In fall, polar bears (above) are Churchill's main attraction, but in winter you will see the wonders of the northern lights (right).

Hunting of polar bears is banned. Because the bears have no fear of people, they sometimes wander into Churchill, and the residents are always on the lookout for them. If a bear poses a threat, wildlife officials will subdue it with tranquilizers and place it in a holding facility until it can be safely released.

Most people who visit Churchill book a trip on one of the specially designed wildlife-viewing vehicles that journey from the town out to Hudson Bay. Visitors sit inside glass cabins that provide superb visibility and protect them from harmful encounters. To minimize impact on the tundra, the vehicles stay on special roads, then drive onto the pack ice.

Polar bears are not the only attraction around Churchill. Arctic foxes and a small caribou herd also wander through the area and during the short northern summer the tundra is ablaze with wildflowers such as Venus slipper, arctic aven, purple saxifrage, and bog orchid.

A pair of Ross's gulls (left) nests near Churchill, the only ones known to nest outside Siberia.

Beluga whales are often seen offshore and in the mouth of the Churchill River. You can go on a whale-watching boat to take a closer look. The river's warmer waters and abundant fish stocks make it an ideal place for the females to calve.

June is the best month for birding. Gyrfalcons, ivory gulls, snowy owls, plovers, and many kinds of duck and goose congregate here, plus a nesting pair of Ross's gulls that is thought to be the only pair in North America.

In winter, Churchill is an ideal place for watching the magnificent displays of the aurora borealis, or northern lights. ST

TRAVELER'S NOTES

Access International flights to Winnipeg, domestic flights or train to Churchill. There is no paved road to the town

When to visit Oct–Nov polar bear migration; March northern lights; June–July wildflowers, beluga whales

Information The Churchill Visitor Center, Churchill, MB R0B-0E0, Canada; tel. (204) 675-8863

Accommodation Hotels and guesthouses

Notes Hiking to see the bears is dangerous; tours in specially designed vehicles are the best way to see them. Reservations recommended

Johnstone Strait

Canada

The coastline of British Columbia and southeastern Alaska is indented by a maze of inlets and channels, bordered by islands, known as the Inside Passage. This vast marine highway extends from Seattle, in Washington State, all the way to Skagway, in Alaska. Cruise ships and ferries ply these waters, carrying visitors who come to see the stupendous scenery, the totem poles in Tlingit and Kwakiutl villages, and the orca migrations in Johnstone Strait. Despite the cool, moist summers, the only thing likely to dampen your spirits is the visual blight of areas of clear-cut logging.

MILES
0   10   20
0   15   30
KM

Port Hardy

Alert Bay

Port McNeil

Telegraph Cove

Johnstone Strait

ROBSON BIGHT
RESERVE

LITTLE HUSTAN
CAVES PARK

Tsitika R.

19

MIGRATING ORCAS

These waters are protected from tempestuous north Pacific storms by a huge archipelago of barrier islands that includes Vancouver Island, the largest island on the west coast of North America. The waters off the northeastern shore of Vancouver Island are the setting for one of this region's most dramatic events.

Each summer, pods of orcas—the most intelligent and acrobatic of marine mammals—migrate out of the vastness of the North Pacific to feed on schools of sockeye salmon returning to their spawning grounds in the rivers and streams of southwestern British Columbia. At Johnstone Strait, the salmon are pinched into a deep, narrow passageway. Since the whales can swim much faster than the salmon, the whales end their migration here and simply

River otters (left) can be seen along the coastline.
A totem pole in Alert Bay, Vancouver (right).

82

A pod of orcas in Johnstone Strait
(above). When spawning, male
sockeye salmon turn bright red (left).

wait for the salmon to swim through. Northbound pods of orcas from the Washington and Oregon coasts occasionally swim as far north as Johnstone Strait, creating a "super pod" of over 200 feeding and frolicking whales.

At a shallow indentation in the coast, known as Robson Bight, whales pursue salmon spawning at the mouth of the Tsitika River, swimming to the shore and rubbing their bellies on the smooth stones that form the seabed. This "rubbing beach" has been protected as the Robson Bight Ecological Reserve, and there are strict viewing guidelines for visitors. Stands of old-growth forest grow down to the shore. Once slated for logging, the valley is now protected and acts as a buffer zone for the bight. Land access is prohibited.

Porpoises and seals are often seen in the Johnstone Strait area, and occasionally even gray whales. Bald eagles perch on tree snags, or swoop down to feed on the salmon. Black-tailed deer and elk emerge from the woods now and then to forage along the estuaries, and mink and river otter may be seen prowling around shoreline driftwood.

Many ecotourists who come to Johnstone Strait seek out the orca by sea-kayak, a modern version of the *baidarka* boat once used by aboriginals of the

Aleutian Islands to harpoon whales and seals in the Bering Strait. Guided sea-kayaking trips into the strait are available in summer, and independent groups can paddle here as well, although previous kayaking experience is necessary if you undertake such a trip on your own. Fishing boats follow the salmon, and cruise ships, freighters, and logging tugs also voyage up and down the strait on a regular basis.

In winter, Queen Charlotte Sound and Broughton Strait are favored by scuba divers because of the stunning clarity of the deep waters.

On shore, the limestone karst topography of northern Vancouver Island has produced some striking caves. Fine examples can be seen in Little Hustan Caves Provincial Park at Nimpkish. ST

TRAVELER'S NOTES

Access International flights to Vancouver, Victoria, and Seattle. Ferries from Bellingham (50 miles [80 km] south of Vancouver) to Ketchikan, Alaska, once a week; from Port Hardy to Prince Rupert every other day in summer. Ferries daily from Ketchikan for points farther north, such as Petersburg, Sitka, Juneau, and Skagway. Cruises from Vancouver and Seattle. Bus service from Victoria and Nanaimo to Port Hardy. Daily and weekly boat and kayak tours into Johnstone Strait from Port McNeill and Telegraph Cove

When to visit Apr–June cool and wet. July–Sept warmer but crowded. Late June to Aug orca migration

Information Port Hardy and District Chamber of Commerce, Box 249, Port Hardy, BC VON-2PO, Canada; tel. (604) 949-7622, fax (604) 949-6653

Accommodation Hotels and motels in Port Hardy, Port McNeill; camping in Telegraph Cove

The Canadian Rockies

Canada

The jagged spine of the North American Continental Divide that runs from the Mexican border to northeastern British Columbia is at its most spectacular in the Canadian Rockies. The tilted layers of rock that make up these awesome summits are the product of a dramatic overlap of tectonic plates in the Earth's crust.

Curiously, it was the curative powers of the hot springs of Sulphur Mountain, not the majesty of the mountains, that was behind the establishment of Banff (the Canadian Rockies' best-known showpiece) as Canada's first national park in 1885.

In the ensuing century, 8,000 square miles (20,700 km²) have been protected in four national parks (Banff, Jasper, Yoho, and Kootenay), whose contiguous boundaries straddle the mountains separating Alberta from British Columbia.

The Canadian Rockies form a large, complex ecosystem that is home to a vast array of plants and animals. Marshy lowlands favored by moose, elk, and beavers lie barely 4,000 feet (1,200 m) above sea level, while glacier-clad summits top out at 12,000 feet (3,700 m). Moose and elk forage in the aspen stands in the valleys close to the Banff and Jasper townsites, while more reclusive wolves, black bears, grizzly bears, and mountain goats favor the grassy, flowering meadows and rocky cliffs of the subalpine and alpine zones.

While the fragile ecosystems in these parks have been protected

Herds of elk (left) forage in the marshy lowlands. A beaver busy on top of its lodge (right).

The still waters of Moraine Lake in Banff National Park (above). Numerous trails depart from here, allowing the visitor to escape the crowds. A moose and her calf feeding on water plants (right).

from the ravages of logging, mining, and fossil-fuel exploitation that are so evident elsewhere in the Rockies, they are threatened by growing numbers of people coming to visit or live in the area. Golf courses, ski-area developments, hiking and biking trails, huts and campgrounds, highway upgrades, and expanding communities within the parks' boundaries are taking a major toll.

BACKCOUNTRY WILDERNESS

Luckily for the ecotourist, fewer than 5 per-cent of visitors ever venture off the beaten track, leaving the vast backcountry wilderness untouched. The trailheads of hundreds of miles of hiking routes can be reached from highways crisscrossing the parks. Intrepid hikers can take the Great Divide Trail that runs from Palliser Pass at the south end of Banff National Park all the way to Mount Robson, over 300 miles (480 km) distant. By mid-November, the blazing

wildflower meadows and turquoise lakes enjoyed by hikers in the brief alpine summer are buried in snow, becoming a ski-touring paradise.

If your time is limited, it's well worth going to Lake Louise, Emerald Lake, Maligne Canyon, and the Columbia Icefields. These world-famous beauty spots live up to their billing. To beat the crowds, time your visit near sunrise or sunset and explore some of the trails that lead into the back-country. Here, in the dense conifer forests and alpine meadows, the true spirit of this inspiring and ever-changing landscape reveals itself. ST

TRAVELER'S NOTES

Access International flights to Calgary and Edmonton; bus, train, or car to Banff or Jasper

When to visit June, Sept–Oct best for hiking and few crowds. Nov–Mar excellent backcountry skiing. July–Aug crowded but best chance of sunshine

Information Dept of Canadian Heritage, Publications Section, Room 10H2, 25 Eddy St, Hull, PQ K1A–0M5, Canada;

tel. (809) 997-0055

Accommodation Hotels and motels in Banff, Lake Louise, and Jasper. Campgrounds in parks. Backcountry lodges require reservation in advance

Notes When hiking the backcountry, be prepared for a wide variety of weather conditions: snow a possibility at higher elevations, even in midsummer

85

The Pacific Northwest

United States of America

A landscape of glacier-clad volcanoes, vast forests, wilderness waterways, and jagged mountain ranges, the Pacific Northwest is prime wildlife habitat. There are stunning sights to see, ranging from orcas cruising in the sounds and spawning salmon jostling their way upriver, to black bears foraging for berries.

These natural riches are the cause of considerable conflict between conservationists seeking to preserve and protect them and those who wish to exploit them financially. Visitors will undoubtedly encounter debate on perennial environmental issues such as logging, fisheries, and the impact of development on wildlife.

Two of North America's finest national parks are located in this region: Mount Rainier and Olympic. Both of them are in Washington State, within a few hours' drive of Seattle.

MOUNT RAINIER NATIONAL PARK

Mount Rainier rises regally from a shroud of forest in the southwest of the state. The highest peak in the Cascade Range, the mountain is

visible from some 200 miles (320 km) away on a clear day—a rare occurrence in this rainy part of the country.

The mountain dominates Mount Rainier National Park, created in 1899 to protect this magnificent region of old-growth forest, waterfalls, and ice fields. Formed by volcanic eruptions that began less than a million years ago, Rainier is a sleeping giant, expected to erupt again within the next 500 years. An average of more than 50 feet (15 m) of snow falls each winter on its heavily forested western slope. The eastern slope, in the mountain's rain shadow, is much drier and the vegetation sparser.

Three hundred miles (480 km) of trails cover a variety of terrain. The Wonderland Trail, a 93 mile (150 km) loop, circles the mountain's flanks, passing through alpine meadows and valley forests to give views of 26 glaciers—the largest

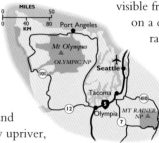

Red-tailed hawks (left) hunt in the high country. The Olympic marmot (opposite) is unique to the Olympic Peninsula.

Mount Rainier (above) is the highest peak in the Cascade Range. Many of the valleys in Olympic National Park are filled with lush, temperate rain forest (left), the result of the region's abundant rainfall.

collection on one peak in the lower 48 states. You're likely to see mountain goats and Roosevelt elk in the high country, but black bears tend to stay hidden. The park supports more than 150 bird species, and 100 wildflower species bloom in its woods and meadows.

OLYMPIC NATIONAL PARK

Olympic National Park encompasses a 57 mile (90 km) stretch of fog-shrouded coastline plus vast tracts of old-growth forest and glacier-draped mountains. The mountains rise steeply from the shore and Pacific storms dump about 200 inches (5,100 mm) of rain and snow on them annually. Along the coast, Sitka spruce and western hemlock dominate the temperate rain forest. As you head inland and the elevation increases, you'll find a succession of habitats: lowland forest, montane forest, subalpine forest, and, finally, alpine meadows.

During the ice age, the peninsula was ice-bound, resulting in the evolution of several species that are found nowhere else. These include the snow vole, the Olympic marmot, the Olympic chipmunk, and Flett's violet.

Most visitors sample Olympic on foot, taking to the hiking trails. The coast is a wonderful place to explore: check out the sea anemones and the crabs in the pools at low tide and look for shorebirds at the water's edge. Harbor seals are common and you may see a river otter.

Great blue herons stalk in the coastal wetlands, while bald eagles, red-tailed hawks, and other raptors soar over higher ground. In summer, alpine wildflowers bloom in profusion. BD

TRAVELER'S NOTES

Access International flights to Seattle, then rent a car. Olympic is a 3-hour drive, Mt Rainier is a 2½-hour drive

When to visit June–Aug best but also busiest

Information Olympic NP, 600 East Park Ave, Port Angeles, WA 98362, USA; tel. (206) 452-4501.

Mt Rainier NP, Tahoma Woods, Star Route, Ashford, WA 98304, USA; tel. (206) 569-2211

Accommodation Lodges, cabins, and campgrounds in both parks. Motels and inns in nearby towns

The United States Rockies

United States of America

The Rocky Mountains, North America's premier mountain range, are aptly called "the crown of the continent". They stretch 2,000 miles (3,000 km) from Canada to Arizona, connecting with the Alaska Range in the north and the Sierra Madre in Mexico. Mountain-making in the Rockies occurred over a period of 20 million years, some 60 million years ago, and about 15,000 years ago nomadic hunter-gatherers came to the region. Blackfoot, Crow, Shoshone, and Ute Indians were living in the Rockies when white explorers arrived in the late eighteenth century. Yellowstone—an extraordinary world of mud pots, geysers, and hot springs—became the world's first national park in 1872. Today, these mountains act as a magnet for the city-worn, with their glorious snow-capped peaks, alpine meadows, glacier-carved valleys, sapphire lakes, vast forests, and abundant wildlife.

There are four major national parks in the United States Rockies. Each is worthy of at least a week-long visit, or you can take a three-week car trip to visit them all, heading west from Denver to Rocky Mountain National Park, and then north. Grand Teton and Yellowstone lie at the heart of the Rockies in northwestern Wyoming, and Glacier, which joins Waterton Lakes National Park at the border with Canada, is in northern Montana.

The Rockies afford a wide variety of activities throughout the seasons. They make their own weather, with frequent rain storms in summer and blizzards in winter. Summer is the best time for hiking, birding, and camping but spring and

Bighorn sheep (far left) graze in the meadows of the high country. Algae around a hot pool in Yellowstone National Park (left).

The jagged peaks of the Tetons, in Wyoming (above). Trumpeter swans (right), so named because of their booming calls, are found in Grand Teton National Park.

fall are also delightful, having the added benefit of few visitors. Cross-country skiing and snowshoeing are great ways to explore the mountains in winter.

THE TETONS

Grand Teton National Park combines some of the finest scenery in the Rockies with plentiful wildlife. The peaks of the Tetons are awesome. The largest, Grand Teton, rises 7,500 feet (2,500 m) above the broad valley of Jackson Hole, through which the Snake River runs.

Large herds of elk and pronghorn roam the sagebrush plains, while at higher levels black and grizzly bears live in the spruce and pine forests. Along the banks of the Snake River, bald eagles, and ospreys hunt for fish. Jenny Lake is a major

trailhead, offering walks to lakes where beaver live, and 200 miles (320 km) of rugged back-country trails for hikers and climbers.

From spring to fall, the river flats and meadows are bright with almost 900 species of wildflower. Of the park's 305 bird species, perhaps the endangered trumpeter swan is the most treasured.

Sadly, the parks in the Rockies are being loved to death—Grand Teton alone receives over 3 million visitors a year and housing developments around Jackson Hole are right on the park's boundary. Park programs show visitors how to minimize their impact on the environment. Local communities are being taught the value of reintroducing wolves to control growing elk and deer populations. SM

TRAVELER'S NOTES

Access International flights to Denver; domestic flights to Jackson, Wyoming, and Bozeman, Montana. The best way to visit is by car

When to visit June–Aug hiking and wildflowers (high season); Nov–Mar snowshoeing and skiing

Information Rocky Mountain NP, Estes Park, CO 80517, USA; tel. (303) 586-1206, fax (303) 586-1310.

Grand Teton NP, Drawer 170, Moose, WY 83012, USA; tel. (307) 739-3300, fax (307) 739-3438. Yellowstone NP, PO Box 168, WY 82190, USA; tel. (307) 344-7381, fax (307) 344-2323. Glacier NP, West Glacier, MT 59936, USA; tel. (406) 888-5441, fax (406) 888-5581

Accommodation Lodges, cabins in parks and environs; camping in parks

The Sierra Nevada

United States of America

A 430 mile (690 km) long range of lofty granite mountains, the Sierra Nevada is set between California's Central Valley and its vast eastern desert. It is a place of incomparable beauty: towering peaks, glacier-carved valleys backed by cliffs, ancient groves of giant sequoias, lush alpine meadows, lake-dotted backcountry, misty waterfalls, and wilderness rivers.

Large areas of the range are protected in three national parks. Kings Canyon and Sequoia provide spectacular examples of such scenery and excellent opportunities for hiking and wildlife-watching. But to see the best of the range in one trip, the ecotraveler can do no better than to visit Yosemite National Park.

It was the lobbying of John Muir that led to the eventual establishment of a national park here in 1890. By the mid-nineteenth century, when Yosemite's Native

American inhabitants had been all but driven out, the Yosemite Valley had already become a tourist attraction and protection was needed to prevent overdevelopment. By the 1940s, over 500,000 visitors were coming to the park each year and today that number has swollen to over 4 million. Most people go to the 7 mile (11 km) long Yosemite Valley, which comprises less than 1 percent of the 1,200 square mile (3,000 km²) park. This is resulting in severe congestion and associated environmental problems, and park officials are considering limiting the number of visitors.

YOSEMITE'S TREASURES
Yosemite Valley and its overlooks are, however, must-sees, especially for the views of El Capitan, a sheer granite wall rising nearly 4,000 feet (1,220 m) above the valley floor; Half Dome, a massive granite monolith; and Yosemite Falls, the highest waterfall in North America. Other dramatic waterfalls include Vernal, Bridalveil, and Nevada falls. In spring, following the snow-melt, they are at their most dramatic.

There are over 750 trails in the park, providing an easy escape from the crowds. The high

A pika gathering grass which it will dry and store to eat in winter.

Yosemite Falls in Yosemite National Park (above). Giant sequoias (right) grow on the Sierra Nevada's western slopes.

country offers exhilarating, truly wilderness experiences. Alpine meadows, remote lakes, and wondrous glacier-carved granite landscapes can be reached from numerous trailheads along the Tioga Road which runs over Tioga Pass and across the park. At Tuolumne Meadows you can join the John Muir Trail, which begins at Vernal Falls and ends 212 miles (340 km) to the south at Mount Whitney in Sequoia National Park. This forms part of the Pacific Crest Trail that runs all the way from the Canadian border to Mexico.

Yosemite supports 37 species of tree, including forests of pine and fir, and groves of giant sequoias, which are among the largest and oldest plants on Earth. Some of these trees are almost 3,000 years old and average 250 feet (75 m) in height and 20 to 25 feet (6 to 7.5 m) in diameter. Some 1,400 species of flowering plant grow here, including shooting star, monkey-flower, larkspur, and Indian paintbrush, decorating the alpine meadows in spring and summer.

The park's animal residents include mule deer and raccoons in the valley, and black bears, coyotes, gray foxes, marmots, badgers, and pikas in the high country. Over 220 bird species are found in the park. Steller's jays, flickers, and meadowlarks frequent the lower elevations; nutcrackers, and chickadees are common in the higher regions. Golden eagles are sometimes seen soaring above the valley. Rarities include white-headed woodpeckers, great gray owls, and peregrine falcons. BD

In summer, mountain bluebirds are found in the alpine meadows in the high country. As winter closes in, they descend to the valleys and fly south.

TRAVELER'S NOTES

Access International flights to San Francisco, then rent a car. Yosemite is 4–5 hour's drive. Kings Canyon is 4 hours from Yosemite, Sequoia 5 hours

When to visit Valleys year-round, avoiding major holiday weekends. High country mid-May to mid-Oct

Information Box 577, Yosemite National Park, CA 95389, USA; tel. (209) 372-0200. Kings Canyon and Sequoia National Parks, Three Rivers, CA 93271, USA; tel. (209) 565-3134

Accommodation Campgrounds and lodges in the parks, hotels in nearby towns

91

The Desert Southwest

United States of America

America's southwestern deserts are an other-wordly region of vast, cactus-studded plains; deep, river-cut canyons; high, forested plateaus; and expanses of colorful sandstone cut and carved by wind and water. Despite scorching heat and bitter cold, these deserts harbor an abundance of animal and plant communities.

The heart of America's desert country is southern Utah and northern Arizona. Three national parks in this region—Bryce Canyon, Zion, and Grand Canyon—are all within a day's drive of each other and provide a bountiful sampling of the desert's splendors.

CANYONS OF COLOR

Bryce Canyon is a remarkable amphitheater of red rock pinnacles, spires, and eroded canyon walls, rimmed by forest. The towering limestone spires (called hoodoos), arches, and bizarre rock formations of Bryce's canyons have been created by countless years of rain and snow, freezing and thawing. Some 50 miles (80 km) of trails lead along the canyon rim or down in among the hoodoos and chasms. For a spectacular overview, hike the Rim Trail at sunrise, when the canyon glows gold, red, and purple.

Among the 160 species of bird that inhabit the park are swifts, swallows, nighthawks, northern flickers, eagles, and owls. Green-leaf manzanita carpets the ground beneath the tall ponderosa pines along the rim and bristlecone pines are found in high, exposed regions. In spring, the vegetation is bright with wildflowers, including sego lilies (Utah's state flower), star lilies, bellflowers, asters, penstemons, evening primrose, and wild iris. In all, over 400 plant species

The diamondback rattlesnake feeds on small mammals.

Moonrise over Bryce Canyon (above).
In spring, Indian paintbrush (right)
blooms in the sand among the rocks.

are found in the park. The animals you are most likely to see include mule deer, porcupines, skunks, chipmunks, and ground squirrels.

Bryce Canyon occupies only 55 square miles (140 km²) and can be busy in summer. An alternative is to visit during winter, when the park is blanketed in snow. The roads are closed, visitors are few, and you can explore this wonderful, fragile world on snowshoes or cross-country skis.

HIKING THROUGH ZION

Zion National Park offers yet more brilliantly colored geological wonders. The park's central feature is Zion Canyon, cut by the Virgin River. A scenic drive runs parallel to the river, snaking between the canyon's walls that glow in shades of crimson, tan, and orange, and form massive rock monoliths. Cottonwood, box elder, willow, and ash grow alongside the river, their foliage a delicate, shimmering green in spring and summer, turning gold in fall. The park boasts nearly 800 species of plant which thrive in a variety of habitats.

The Zion–Mount Carmel Highway takes you to the park's higher elevations—a landscape of Navajo sandstone plateaus and massive petrified sand dunes. One such is the Checkerboard Mesa, the gridlike markings on its surface formed by vertical cracks across its horizontal strata.

Short hikes from the main road lead to waterfalls and pools that create microclimates nourishing wildflowers, ferns, and mosses. The 2 mile (3 km) round-trip Riverside Walk leads to the Narrows, where the canyon's walls begin to close in. At times, along the 16 mile (26 km) route that leads on from the Narrows, the walls are but a hallway width apart, and you may have to wade through thigh-deep sections of the river.

TRAVELER'S NOTES

Access International flights to Las Vegas. From Las Vegas, it's a 3-hour drive to Zion, another 3 to Bryce, and 3 to the North Rim of the Grand Canyon

When to visit Apr–Oct

Information Bryce Canyon NP, UT 84717, USA; tel. (801) 834-5322. Zion NP, Springdale, UT 84767, USA; tel. (801) 772-3256. Grand Canyon NP, PO Box 129, Grand Canyon, AZ 86023, USA; tel. (602) 638-7888

Accommodation Hotels and motels around parks; lodges and campgrounds within parks

Notes South Rim of Grand Canyon open year-round. North Rim closed mid-Nov to mid-May because of snow. Hikers must register at visitor centers. Permits required for overnight backcountry trips. River-rafting trips must be booked at least 6 months in advance

A northern flicker.

During spring runoff, and following summer storms, the river turns into a raging torrent and the route is closed.

Kolob Canyons and Lava Point, in the northwest of the park, have relatively few visitors. Kolob Canyons Road winds 5 miles (8 km) into red-rock "finger" canyons, where the lower slopes are forested with bigtooth maple, and pinyon and juniper grow on the plateaus. A demanding but rewarding 14 mile (23 km) round trip takes hikers to Kolob Arch, which, with a span of 310 feet (95 m), is one of the largest natural arches in the world.

Zion currently attracts over 2 million visitors a year, and automobile congestion and the associated noise and pollution have become significant problems. To help alleviate matters, guided tram tours of the canyon are available and there are bike paths to encourage two-wheeled exploration. The National Park Service is also developing a shuttle bus system.

The Virgin River in Zion (top). Broadtailed hummingbirds (above) breed throughout the Southwest. Mule riders on the South Kaibab Trail (right).

In addition to these popular parks, Southern Utah offers less well-known but equally magnificent wilderness areas, such as Capitol Reef National Park and the Escalante region. Travel in these areas requires careful preparation.

GRAND VISTAS

Millennia of erosion by the Colorado River carved northern Arizona's magnificent Grand Canyon, a chasm whose dimensions—285 miles (460 km) long, 18 miles (30 km) wide, and over a mile (1.6 km) deep—boggle the imagination.

Five million visitors throng the park each year, most heading to the canyon's South Rim, over 200 miles (320 km) by car from the more remote North Rim, which attracts a mere 400,000 visitors. Travelers who also visit Zion and Bryce national parks will fortunately be much closer to the North Rim.

Lining the North Rim are forests of yellow and ponderosa pine, blue spruce and quaking aspen, and mountain meadows bright with wildflowers in spring. Mule deer and woodpeckers live in these forests, as does the rare Kaibab tassel-eared squirrel—a white-tailed relative of the Abert's squirrel found on the South Rim.

Grand vistas can be seen from points along the rim, but to really experience the canyon you must descend its precipitous walls on foot or by mule. From the North Rim, the 14 mile (23 km) North Kaibab Trail, recommended for experienced backpackers only, leads down to Phantom Ranch and the Colorado River. As you descend, you pass from present-day topsoil to Vishnu schist—a layer of 2-billion-year-old rock on the canyon floor. The round trip takes three days, or you can continue across the canyon floor and up to the South Rim.

On the North Rim, the Transept Trail from Grand Canyon Lodge and the Cliff Springs Trail from Cape Royal are shorter, easier walks. As you descend into the canyon, plants such as cacti, agave, and creosote bush become more plentiful. During the day, when temperatures can be over 100°F (38°C), golden eagles and ravens circle overhead, and warblers and hummingbirds flit about seeps. At dawn and dusk, many animals come out of hiding, including deer, chuckwallas, bighorn sheep, and rarely seen mountain lions.

Running the Colorado River in a raft is a wonderful experience. There are more than 70 rapids in the canyon and innumerable beaches and side-canyons. More than a dozen park-regulated companies offer raft trips through the Grand Canyon, taking you to regions that are otherwise inaccessible. BD

GRAND CANYON CONCERNS

Over the years, the Grand Canyon has faced a variety of environmental threats. From the late 1920s to the early 1980s, a burgeoning, non-native wild burro population caused extensive damage, until it was brought under control through culling and, later, airlifting the animals out of the canyon. More recent major environmental concerns include air pollution from nearby coal-burning power plants and uranium mines, excessive numbers of visitors, and aircraft noise from scenic flights.

The Colorado River itself is being studied to determine the long-term environmental impact of the Glen Canyon Dam, which was completed in 1964. The river, once muddy brown and prone to flooding that would regularly strip vegetation from riverbanks, now runs clear and maintains a regulated flow rate. This has allowed plants, such as cattail and arrowweed to flourish on the shoreline. The waters, which now issue from the bottom of Lake Powell (the lake created by the dam), are also much colder than before the dam was built. This has upset the breeding patterns of the seven native fish species that inhabit the river.

Bright Angel Point on the North Rim of the Grand Canyon (top). The Abert's squirrel (above) inhabits the South Rim. A mountain lion and her cub (left). 95

The North Woods

United States of America

When the glaciers retreated from North America some 11,000 years ago, they excavated five gigantic basins that filled with water to form the Great Lakes—a freshwater inland sea. As plants and animals colonized the surrounding land, the North Woods were formed. Modestly mountainous, the terrain is a medley of conifers and hardwood trees laced by cobalt-blue skies, surging rivers, silvery creeks, and a rich array of fauna and flora.

SLEEPING BEAR DUNES

One of the best places to experience this country is in Michigan. Sleeping Bear Dunes National Lakeshore lies on the east of Lake Michigan, west of Traverse City. Running for 33 miles (53 km), the park is the site of massive sand dunes. As a result of unrelenting winds, these graceful mounds are always in flux. The park includes two large offshore islands: North Manitou, with 25 square miles (65 km²) of wilderness, and South Manitou, featuring a stand of colossal old white cedars.

Tahquamenon Falls State Park is situated north of Traverse City. Among old-growth hardwoods, the Upper Falls spread across a 200 foot (60 m) precipice, thousands of gallons of water per second cascading 50 feet (15 m) to form huge islands of foam.

Traveling westward, Pictured Rocks National Lakeshore extends 42 miles (68 km) along the shores of Lake Superior. The park is named for the 15 mile (24 km) stretch of sandstone bluffs that looms above the lake. Wind, waves, and ice have refined the stone into grottos, arches, and

The Big Carp River in Porcupine Mountains Wilderness State Park.

Chapel Beach at Pictured Rocks (above). A beaver (left). The unearthly call of the common loon (below) is a hallmark of Isle Royale.

various other formations. Miner's Castle, a monolith as tall as a nine-story building, is edged by rocky ramparts. On Battleship Row, the prows of a flotilla seem to emerge from the cliffs. Caves dot the walls in Beaver Basin. Over the years, minerals have stained the cliffs red, orange, black, and white. Through the day, the changing light sends shades of the colors dancing across the stone.

Farther west along the rugged coast, Porcupine Mountains Wilderness State Park offers 90 miles (145 km) of trails. Within this forest of hemlocks and northern hardwoods you'll find rivers, lakes, black bears, and nearly 200 bird species.

ISLE ROYALE

Roadless Isle Royale National Park, which is 99 percent federally designated wilderness, sits in Lake Superior. It consists of many small islands and one large one that is 45 miles (70 km) long and 9 miles (15 km) wide at its widest.

The island's mountain ridges are blanketed by forest: white spruce and balsam fir mingled with hardwoods. Bogs and lakes open up here and there. Wildflowers run rampant. The island harbors about 700 plant species, including 32 kinds of orchid, 12 plants native to western states, and 32 common to arctic tundra.

Isle Royale is best known for its moose and gray wolves, both of which are thought to have migrated here from the mainland after 1900. Moose are fairly easy to see but wolves are not. Sometimes you'll hear their howls. Beavers, red squirrels, and snowshoe hares are also common.

The park's 226 bird species include peregrine falcon and bald eagle. Twenty-four duck species bob on the water, and the woods are filled with woodpeckers and songbirds. EW

TRAVELER'S NOTES

Access International flights to Detroit or Chicago, flights to Lansing, then by car. Isle Royale accessible by boat from Houghton or Copper Harbor and Grand Portage, plus plane from Houghton

When to visit May–Oct. Bird migrations: late Apr to May, Aug, Sept

Information Travel Bureau, Dept of Commerce, PO Box 30226, Lansing, MI 48909, USA; tel. (800) 5432-YES

Accommodation Campgrounds in parks; permits required for backcountry camping. Cabins in Porcupine and Isle Royale, and lodge on Isle Royale. Hotels, motels, campgrounds in nearby towns

Notes Weather can be cold year-round. Bring warm clothing and insect repellent. Isle Royale accessible mid-May to mid-Oct. Book lodge and transport in advance

The Appalachian Mountains

United States of America

The Appalachian Mountains, which comprise the great mountain ranges of the east, extend some 1,600 miles (2,600 km) from southeastern Quebec through the eastern United States down to Alabama's coastal plain.

HIKING THE TRAIL

Running through these ranges is the Appalachian Trail, which, at 2,157 miles (3,473 km) is the world's longest unbroken hiking path. It crosses 14 states from its origins in Springer Mountain, Georgia, to its grand finish in Mount Katahdin, Maine.

Along the way, the trail winds through eight national forests and two national parks. Conceived in 1921 by Benton MacKaye, a forester and planner, the trail was com-

Red wolves, once hunted almost to extinction, are now being returned to the wild through captive breeding programs.

pleted in 1937 and designated a national scenic trail in 1968.

Many hikers dream of walking the entire trail, planning their five- to six-month journeys meticulously. But there are over 500 access points along the way for short-term visitors, some of which take you into three of the country's best parks.

Take the Great Smoky Mountains National Park, for example, situated on the Tennessee–North Carolina border. Its abundant rainfall has resulted in great biodiversity.

From the lowest elevations, you pass through hardwood forests, up to where pine and oak grow, then to slopes of northern hardwoods. Above these forests, many of the mountain ridges bear grassy, open areas known as balds. Higher still, you'll find spruce and fir forests.

Maple and tulip trees dominate the park's flora, but you will also see luxurious growths of evergreen trees and rhododendrons, plus delicate orchids, columbines, and painted trilliums.

Great Smoky is a haven for rare creatures, such as the red wolf, which was reintroduced to the park in 1991, and the river otter. Other wildlife, from wild turkeys to white-tailed deer,

Fall foliage along the Appalachian Trail in Vermont (above). A white-tailed deer buck, polishing its antlers (left).

is more abundant, and black bear sightings are common.

To the north, the trail runs through Shenandoah National Park, a strip along the Blue Ridge of the Appalachians that is thickly forested with hemlock, hickory, and oak. Hikers come from the nearby Washington DC area, as do numerous day-trippers in cars, drawn to Skyline Drive, which runs the length of the park. Visitors come in spring to see the waterfalls and the azaleas that color the forest glades; in summer to enjoy the meadows bright with wildflowers; and for fiery foliage colors in fall. Along the trail, away from the crowds, you may see pink lady's-slipper orchids blooming in the forest, white-tailed deer feeding, and peregrine falcons wheeling overhead.

NORTHERN APPALACHIA

Continuing north, you leave the thick stands of azaleas and rhododendrons behind as you enter forests of beech, birch,

Black bears are abundant in Great Smoky.

maple, and cherry. Over 1,000 miles (1,600 km) later, the walk ends among the evergreens, ferns, and scrubby blueberry bushes of Baxter State Park in northern Maine. Here, Mount Katahdin rises 5,267 feet (1,606 m) amid thick pine forests. In summer, its windswept heights are carpeted with wildflowers growing in the alpine tundra. Moose feed in the marshy lowlands and there are beavers about, although you'll seldom see them. Bald eagles, black bears, and coyotes are common, and the cry of the loon is a constant refrain.

Maintenance of the trail by volunteers keeps it in top condition and minimizes environmental damage. Hikers can help by packing out trash and keeping to the trail to reduce erosion. EP

TRAVELER'S NOTES

Access Great Smoky: Gatlinburg, Tennessee, ½ hour from Knoxville. Shenandoah: Luray, Virginia, 1½ hours from Washington, DC. Baxter: Millinocket, Maine, 5 hours north of Portland. All these cities have international airports. Onward travel by car

When to visit Great Smoky and Shenandoah: Apr–Oct. Baxter: June–Oct (Maine winters severe)

Information Appalachian Trail Conference, PO Box 807, Harpers Ferry, WV 25425, USA; tel. (304) 535-6331, fax (304) 535-2667

Accommodation Campgrounds, simple lodges every 10 miles (16 km) along trail. Lodges and hotels in nearby towns. Camping permits required in Great Smoky, Shenandoah, and Baxter

The Everglades

United States of America

From Lake Okeechobee in southern Florida, a sheet of water only 6 inches (15 cm) deep fans out 50 miles (80 km) wide over limestone, flowing slowly southward for 100 miles (160 km) until it spills into Florida Bay, where the Gulf of Mexico meets the Atlantic. This is the Everglades, a wetland wilderness where the tropics blend richly with the temperate zone. Most of the finest portion remaining (after encroachment by farming and human settlement) lies in Everglades National Park, which covers more than 2,350 square miles (6,000 km²).

Much of the park is covered by great sweeps of sawgrass, a sharply barbed sedge that stands up to 15 feet (4.5 m) above the water. The sawgrass "prairie" is dotted with low islands (hammocks) supporting hardwoods, such as mahogany, gumbo-limbo, and strangler fig. Ferns and epiphytes drape the tree limbs.

As well, there are islands formed by willows that support plants such as dahoon holly and sweet bay. These willowheads form in sloughs—twisting channels of deeper water. Water-loving cypress trees also create islands in these waters.

SLASH PINES AND MANGROVES

Groves of slash pines grow in sandy, dry areas and these pinelands support 30 species of plant that exist only in the Everglades. Mangroves form a belt along the coast, extending prop roots into the brackish water. These thickets abound with wildlife, especially nesting birds such as roseate spoonbills—large, paddle-beaked, shell-pink wading birds.

Manatees, gentle aquatic mammals, are found in the waters around the Ten Thousand Islands.

A great blue heron standing in Taylor Slough in Everglades National Park (above). American crocodiles (right) inhabit salt-water areas in the south of the park. A roseate spoonbill (below).

Habitat diversity fosters wildlife diversity. To most people, the Glades means alligators and the rarer American crocodile. The mammals range from mangrove fox squirrels to black bears. There are numerous fish species and invertebrates of every kind fly, crawl, and swim all over the place.

The park's greatest glory is its 347 bird species. The range is enough to make a birder swoon: bald eagles and brown pelicans; kites swooping through the skies; seven heron species; three kinds of egret; gallinules stepping over lily pads; black vultures and frigatebirds soaring.

There are many ways to sample the Glades. Trails, trams, and tour boats explore the mangrove swamps and Florida Bay, where you may see crocodiles and sea turtles. Boats also cruise among the Ten Thousand Islands.

Big Cypress National Preserve is a vast swamp that lies along the park's northwestern border. Cypress trees cover a third of the area and there are a few giants up to 700 years old, their massive, flaring trunks bedecked with orchids and bromeliads.

Near Naples is the Corkscrew Swamp Sanctuary, created by the National Audubon Society. It is home to the country's largest surviving nesting colony of wood storks.

Extensive development in the region has resulted in water levels in the Glades dropping severely and a high level of agricultural pollution. Steps are being taken to curb pollution and restore water flow but the entire ecosystem is at risk. EW

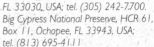

An anhinga, consuming a fish.

TRAVELER'S NOTES

Access International flights to Miami then by car to any of three entrances to park. Main visitor center is about 1 hour's drive from Miami

When to visit Mid-Dec to mid-Apr balmy weather. Rest of year rainy and hot. May–Oct hurricane season

Information Everglades National Park, PO Box 279, Homestead, FL 33030, USA; tel. (305) 242-7,700. Big Cypress National Preserve, HCR 61, Box 11, Ochopee, FL 33943, USA; tel. (813) 695-4111

Accommodation Campgrounds in parks. Hotels, motels, and private campgrounds in nearby towns

The Hawaiian Islands

United States of America

The Hawaiian Islands lie in the North Pacific Ocean, some 2,500 miles (4,000 km) from the nearest continent. Created from volcanic eruptions on the ocean floor, the islands were gradually colonized by plants and animals brought by air and ocean currents, and by migratory birds. Over 90 percent of the islands' native flora and fauna is found nowhere else.

From just a few pioneers, numerous species came into existence. A few hundred plants evolved into a thousand and 15 bird species became 70. Since AD 750, when Hawaii's first human inhabitants—the Polynesians—arrived, non-native species have

An iiwi, a native honey-creeper.

wrought havoc on these endemics, leading to countless extinctions and threatening the existence of many others.

There are few better places to observe Hawaii's fascinating geology and native flora and fauna than Haleakala National Park on Maui and Hawaii Volcanoes National Park on the Big Island (Hawaii).

HOUSE OF THE SUN

Rising 10,023 feet (3,057 m) above sea level, Haleakala volcano (Hawaiian for "House of the Sun") is an immense crater at the top of a great mountain of lava. Although it is considered still active, Haleakala last erupted in 1790.

A road leads 40 miles (65 km) from the coast to the top of the volcano, a transition from lush coastal plains to a bizarre landscape of cliffs, cinder cones, and lava flows. En route is the Hosmer Grove, a collection of exotic trees planted in 1910. Trails lead through the grove which is inhabited by colorful native birds such as the iiwi and the apapane.

Winding on toward the crater rim, the road reaches the trailhead for the Halemauu Trail—a two-day round trip into the crater. At Kalahaku

Kilauea erupting (above), lava pouring down its slopes. One of the cinder cones in Haleakala National Park (right).

Overlook, where the views are wonderful, you will see silverswords, which grow only on the volcanic slopes of Maui and Hawaii. This plant blooms once, after 5 to 20 years, then dies. It has barely survived the many years of habitat damage from human visitation and cattle ranching.

The road ends at the Puu Ulaula Overlook at the summit, from where you can often see the nearby islands of Molokai, Lanai, and Oahu.

HAWAII VOLCANOES

The Big Island of Hawaii is crowned by two of the world's most active volcanoes—Kilauea and Mauna Loa. Both are within Hawaii Volcanoes National Park. The park's 344 square miles (890 km²) incorporate vast craters, steaming fumaroles, sulfur-belching calderas, and lava fields, including the occasional effusion of red-hot magma at the end of the Chain of Craters Road.

Various trails lead to bizarre and fascinating landscapes created by millennia of powerful eruptions. One of the park's best walks is the Kilauea Iki Trail, a four-hour round trip that descends through rain forest and leads across a crater, past steaming lava flows.

The park's most celebrated bird is the nene, a native goose. It barely escaped being wiped out by predators such as mongooses, and has been rescued by a breeding program. Groups of nene are often seen in the Kilauea area. BD

The ohia lehua, with its bright red blooms, will grow on dry lava.

TRAVELER'S NOTES

Access International flights to Honolulu. Haleakala NP: flight to Kahului, Maui, then rent a car: 1-hour drive to park. Hawaii Volcanoes NP: flight to Kailua-Kona or Hilo, Hawaii, then rent a car. 3-hour drive from Kailua-Kona, 1-hour from Hilo. Some direct flights to Maui and Hawaii from mainland USA

When to visit Nov–Mar

Information Haleakala NP, Box 369, Makawao, Maui, HI 96768, USA;

tel. (808) 572-9306. Hawaii Volcanoes NP, Box 52, HI 96718, USA; tel. (808) 967-7311.

Accommodation Campgrounds in both parks, hotels and guesthouses in nearby towns. Hotel in Hawaii Volcanoes NP

Notes Summit areas parks can be rainy and cold any time of year

Central and South America

ECOTRAVEL *in* CENTRAL *and* SOUTH AMERICA

Central and South America have more species than anywhere else on Earth,
many of them still waiting to be discovered.

When it comes to biodiversity, Central and South America reign supreme. The Amazon Basin supports the world's largest rain forest and 10 percent of the Earth's flora and fauna. In the Andes, you'll find rare quetzals and dazzling hummingbirds, cloud forests clothed in bromeliads and orchids, high plateaus dotted with alpine flowers, and snow-covered volcanic peaks. In the coral-laced waters off Belize, striped angelfish swim among waving sea fans. Great whales gather in the nutrient-rich waters of Baja California, giant tortoises lumber through the highlands of Galápagos, ostrich-like rheas race across Argentina's pampas, and Magellanic penguins nest in huge colonies on the wind-swept shores of Patagonia.

CENTRAL AMERICA

Despite rampant population growth and unsustainable economic practices that have led to the loss of 60 percent of the region's forest cover, the number of parks and preserves in Central America has grown eight-fold since 1970. Ecotravelers can visit more than 350 protected sites from Mexico to Panama.

Tiny Costa Rica is a popular destination because of its extensive system of protected land: 25 percent of the country is within national parks and reserves. If you want to watch sea turtles laying eggs on an Atlantic beach, hike in a cloud forest set among mist-shrouded volcanoes, and look for exotic birds in a forest on the edge of the Pacific, then you should follow the roads that link Tortuguero, Poas Volcano, and Manuel Antonio national parks.

From Costa Rica you can easily travel to other natural areas. To the south, Panama's Darien Gap is a rugged, tropical wilderness between Colombia and the Panama Canal. It is home to hundreds of species of bird and is the last remaining barrier to the Pan American Highway, the legendary route that would otherwise link the Northern and Southern hemispheres.

Another popular Central American ecojourney takes in

BIODIVERSITY *The rain forests of Costa Rica (left) and Belize (above) are home to such colorful species as the scarlet macaw (top) and the red-eyed tree frog (below).*

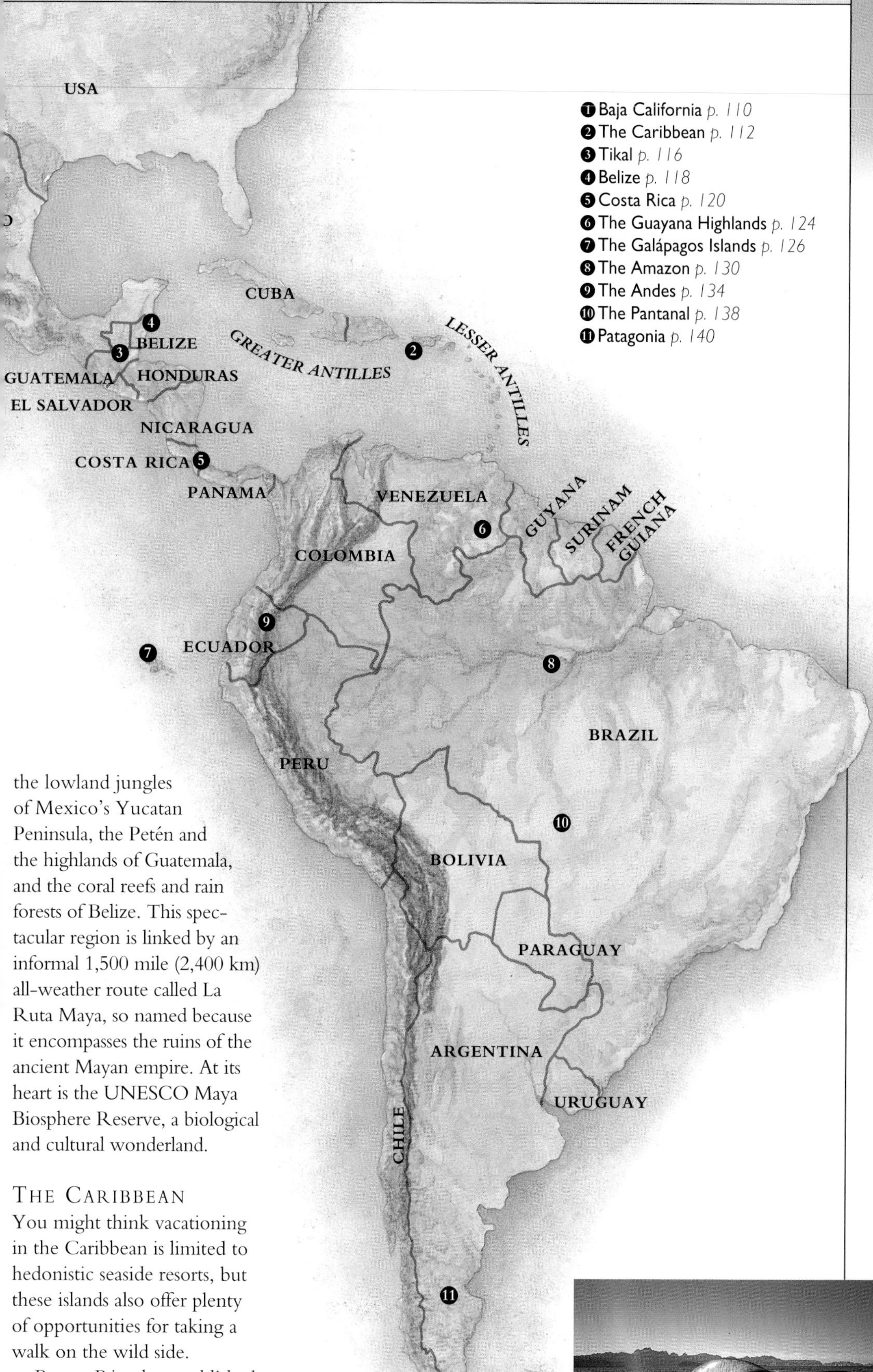

USA

CUBA

BELIZE ❹

❸

GREATER ANTILLES

LESSER ANTILLES

GUATEMALA HONDURAS

EL SALVADOR

NICARAGUA

COSTA RICA ❺

PANAMA

VENEZUELA

❻

GUYANA

SURINAM

FRENCH GUIANA

COLOMBIA

❾ ECUADOR

❼

❽

BRAZIL

PERU

❿

BOLIVIA

PARAGUAY

ARGENTINA

URUGUAY

CHILE

⓫

the lowland jungles of Mexico's Yucatan Peninsula, the Petén and the highlands of Guatemala, and the coral reefs and rain forests of Belize. This spectacular region is linked by an informal 1,500 mile (2,400 km) all-weather route called La Ruta Maya, so named because it encompasses the ruins of the ancient Mayan empire. At its heart is the UNESCO Maya Biosphere Reserve, a biological and cultural wonderland.

THE CARIBBEAN

You might think vacationing in the Caribbean is limited to hedonistic seaside resorts, but these islands also offer plenty of opportunities for taking a walk on the wild side.

Puerto Rico has established a system of forest reserves that covers 4 percent of its territory, and its El Yunque National Forest has become a popular destination for hikers.

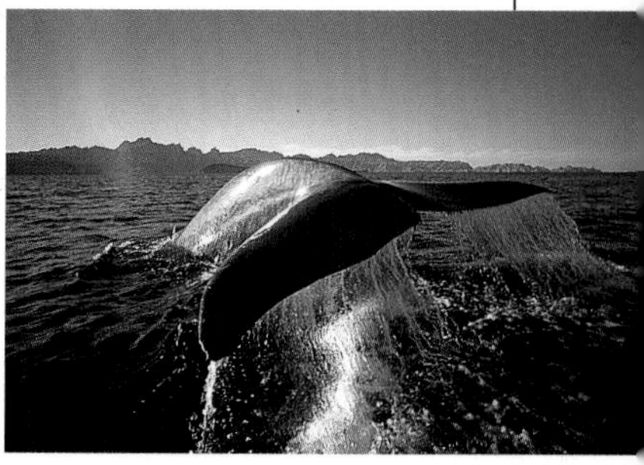

BAJA CALIFORNIA in Mexico is one of the world's top whale-watching spots.

In Grenada, you can follow a government-funded walking trail to 75 foot (25 m) high Royal Mount Carmel Falls.

In addition, many of the island nations have taken steps to protect their beaches and reefs. More than 100 marine reserves have been established throughout the Caribbean and some countries, most notably the Virgin Islands, boast eco-friendly coastal resorts.

AMAZONIA

Although slash-and-burn farming, cattle ranching, and logging have cut huge swathes through the rain forest, more than 390,000 square miles (1 million km²) have been set aside as parks and reserves in the Amazonian areas of Brazil, Bolivia, Colombia, Ecuador, Peru, and Venezuela.

Park management varies from place to place. A lack of funding, planning, and

A WATERY WORLD *A tributary of the Amazon winds through the rain forest (right). A three-toed sloth swimming in a Panamanian river (far right). A greater frigatebird on the Galápagos (below).*

management, combined with pressures from settlers, prospectors, and developers (particularly in the petroleum industry) means that some parks are parks in name only. An increasing number, however, are improving their conservation practices, often aided by revenue from ecotourism.

Peru's Manú National Park is a good example. Cooperation from the local community has been won by allowing economic activities in the buffer zones that encircle a core zone of 5,860 square miles (15,200 km²). The core zone protects an abundance of wildlife while the buffer zones support local residents.

Nature lovers will find a wide range of ecotravel possibilities in Amazonia. On most jungle tours you can learn about the medicinal uses of plants from the native guides. In Brazil, you can combine a cruise on the Amazon with a visit to the wetlands of the Pantanal.

Not all of Amazonia is readily accessible. Obstacles include remoteness, lack of transport, and political instability. Colombia, for example, is a wonderful eco-tourist destination but terrorist activities and crime associated with the illegal drug trade make travel in parts of the country extremely dangerous.

THE INCA TRAIL *in the Peruvian Andes.*

THE ANDES MOUNTAINS AND THE GALÁPAGOS

The Andes run the length of South America and connect scores of parks, reserves, and World Heritage sites. This still-growing range plays a vital role in the continent's biosystem. Lowland tropical and cloud forests cover the lower north-western and eastern slopes, leading up to temperate forests, high grasslands, and icy peaks. Rain shadows created by the Andes along the central-western and southeastern portions of the continent have formed the Atacama Desert and the arid plains of Patagonia.

The Andes support 17 per-cent of the world's bird species, thousands of plant species, and unusual animals such as vicunas and guanacos. The fascinating wildlife, combined with dramatic mountain scenery and a rich cultural heritage, makes the Andes a popular destination. Thousands of people visit the UNESCO Biosphere Reserve of Machu Picchu each year, drawn by the ruins of this Inca city.

You can easily combine a visit to this region with a cruise to the continent's most popular nature destination—the Galápagos Islands.

Ever-expanding human populations mean that large areas of Andean virgin forest are being cleared for agri-culture, and conservationists are racing to preserve what they can. In the Galápagos, laws have been introduced to control poaching.

PATAGONIA

Patagonia covers the southern reaches of Chile and Argentina and contains numerous na-tional parks and extensive wilderness areas. On the Chilean side, you can combine a visit to the glorious lake district with a trip to the icy reaches of Tierra del Fuego. The southernmost city, Punta Arenas, is a jumping-off point for cruises to Antarctica.

Touring in Argentina can take you to thundering Iguazu Falls, to windswept Península Valdés to see whales, dolphins, and seals, and to Los Glaciares National Park where you can hike among the glaciers.

MAKING PROGRESS

Uncontrolled population growth, widespread poverty, corrupt governments, and pressure for development from multinational industries con-tinue to be the major problems in Central and South America. However, significant progress has been made during the last decade, with a number of new preserves being created and conservation organizations working with national gov-ernments to strengthen legislation protecting this region's natural treasures. **DH**

THE DRIEST PLACE ON EARTH
Chile's Atacama desert (above) lies in a rain shadow of the Andes. The guanaco (left) is a close relative of the llama. It inhabits southern Chile and Tierra del Fuego.

Baja California

Mexico

A long the peninsula of Baja California, sea, mountains, and desert meet in grand vistas, gorgeous sunsets, and a rich diversity of species. The waters nurture a fantastic array of marine life, from pods of whales and dolphins, to huge schools of tuna and tropical fish. The Gulf of California (formerly the Sea of Cortez) lies between Baja and the mainland, dotted with islands harboring unusual plant communities, huge seabird breeding colonies, and great rookeries of sea lions, fur seals, and elephant seals.

If you have a few weeks to spare, it is fascinating to drive the 700 mile (1,130 km) long peninsula, taking time to explore the beaches, mountains, and deserts along

The gray whale can weigh up to 40 tons, reach a length of 50 feet (15 m), and eat a ton of crustaceans per day.

the way. However, even a one-week cruise allows you to see the whales and visit some of the islands and the desert. Kayaking is terrific on the gulf's calm bays and inlets.

THE GREAT WHALES

The mangrove-lined lagoons of Baja's Pacific coast are the calving grounds for the world's entire population of gray whales, currently estimated at 21,000. Since the enactment of the Marine Mammal Protection Act in 1972, the species has recovered from near extinction.

Every year, these huge creatures migrate 12,000 miles (19,300 km) from their arctic feeding grounds to these waters—the longest migration of any mammal.

January through March is the peak season for observing gray whales in Baja's three protected whale lagoons: Ojo de Liebre (Scammon's Lagoon), San Ignacio Lagoon, and Magdalena Bay. To protect the whales, the number of boats allowed in each bay per day is limited.

Baja's waters are also wintering grounds for nine other species of whale, including the humpback and the blue whale—the world's largest mammal—while at any

time of year, you will be able to see common dolphins gathering in pods of up to 10,000 animals.

The northernmost coral reef in the world lies off southeastern Baja, and its amazing variety of marine life includes some 3,000 species of fish and invertebrate. Tropical species such as manta ray and whale shark—the world's largest fish—migrate into the gulf in summer, joining great schools of damselfish and surgeonfish. Large colonies of frigatebirds, boobies, gulls, terns, and pelicans breed during winter on the islands. Albatrosses and other ocean-going birds can be seen in the gulf during summer, blown off-course by tropical storms.

Deserts cover two-thirds of the peninsula and are dotted with bizarre plants such as the boojum tree, which looks like an inverted carrot; the elephant tree, with its thick, gnarled trunk; and the cardón, the world's tallest cactus. The

Hikers will come across desert flora such as cardón cactus and elephant tree (above), while divers can swim through curtains of tropical fish (left).

blooms of yuccas, agaves, ocotillos, and annuals brighten the landscape in April in the north, and in July in the south.

Baja faces serious threats. Since the Colorado River was dammed in the United States in 1965, the upper gulf has been drying up. The river once deposited a vast amount of nutrient-rich water in the gulf, but it is now reduced to a trickle, polluted with pesticides and factory waste. Overfishing by Asian trawlers is depleting Baja's huge fisheries at an alarming rate, and there are plans to expand salt mining in the whale lagoons. **SM**

Enormous schools of fish attract both bottle-nosed dolphins (above) and brown pelicans (right) to Baja's waters.

TRAVELER'S NOTES

Access International flights to San Diego, California, and La Paz, Mexico, or drive on Hwy 1 from San Diego. Ferries to La Paz from Mazatlán or Topolobampo in mainland Mexico

When to visit Nov–Mar coolest, best for desert; Jan–Mar for whale-watching; Mar–Apr for wildflowers and shorebird migration; June–Sept for diving, but also hurricane season. May–Oct very hot

Information Servicios y Turismo de Tijuana, Cámara Nacional de Comercio, cnr Avenida Revolución and Calle 1a,

Tijuana, Mexico; tel. (66) 858-4721 881-685. Tijuana Baja Information Center, Mission Center Court, San Diego, CA 92108, USA; tel. (800) 522-1516

Accommodation On board cruise ships. Camping on beaches or in national parks. Hotels and resorts in towns

Notes If driving, carry food plus extra gasoline and water. Book all cruises before arrival

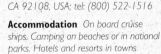

The Caribbean

West Indies

Although the Caribbean is famous for its wonderful beaches, a growing number of ecotourists are visiting the region for its flora and fauna. Most of the 50 or so major islands that encircle this warm, fecund sea are buried in thick jungle and tropical flowers. Others are desert-dry plateaus dotted with cacti and riddled with caves.

CHAINS OF ISLANDS

In the northwest are the Greater Antilles: Cuba, Jamaica, Hispaniola (Haiti and the Dominican Republic), and Puerto Rico. They began to heave from the sea about 150 million years ago and, on Hispaniola, the mountains are as high as 10,000 feet (3,000 m). Curling east and south are the younger, smaller, and mostly volcanic Lesser Antilles. These constitute the Leeward and Windward isles. Virtually all are fringed by coral reefs.

While there are whole islands—Dominica, for example—that are unsullied troves of botanical and zoological treasures, many have been

The coral flower, which grows in the El Yunque region of Puerto Rico.

ravaged since Columbus sailed these waters 500 years ago. Forests were felled and wetlands drained for sugar and, later, bananas. Tourist resorts and teeming populations edge up against much that remains. Many endemic wildlife species have been wiped out. (Almost 90 percent of the world's endangered bird species live on these islands.) Yet there are still wild places remaining, strewn like isles within the isles, as varied as they are numerous, ranging from coastal mangrove swamps to montane cloud forests.

AWASH IN ECOTOURISM

Only a decade ago, visitors to the Caribbean had to look hard for protected areas, but national parks and wildlife reserves are now appearing from Miami to Maracaibo as a result of increased environmental awareness. The islands continue to depend heavily on resort based, sun-seeking tourists, but a growing number of visitors are forsaking sandals for hiking boots and are following mountain trails in search of indigenous culture, showering in waterfalls, and shooting birds through the lens of a camera. Visiting any three or four islands will provide a range of treats.

JAMAICAN DELIGHTS

No other island offers the ecotourist more than Jamaica. In Montego Bay Marine Park you can gambol with polka-dotted and zebra–striped fish. The road south leads to Rocklands Bird Feeding Station, where streamertail hummingbirds will alight on your finger. Farther south, beyond mountainous Cockpit Country, lies the Great Morass, a wetland teeming with crocodiles and waterfowl. Boats make their way into the wetlands from the town of Black River, near the Font Hill Reserve. Here, you can follow trails through the mangroves and thickets of logwood and acacia to see herons, egrets, and crocodiles.

Galley Bay in Antigua (above).
Caribbean manatees (left). Sea horses
are found around the reefs (below).

To really appreciate the island's diverse beauty, visitors should then take the coast road east to the fishing hamlet of Alligator Pond where an area of wetlands provides a refuge for the endangered manatee. Once you have driven through Kingston, the capital, you come to the glorious Blue Mountains, crisscrossed by roads, paths, and trails. Here you can hike the 7 mile (11 km) trail to Blue Mountain Peak (7,402 feet [2,258 m]) up through forests thick with vines, towering tree-ferns, and bamboo; then cloud-swathed thickets festooned with mosses and orchids; to the dwarf trees of elfin woodland close to the summit.

TRAVELER'S NOTES

Access International flights to Montego Bay, Jamaica; San Juan, Puerto Rico; and Vieux Fort, St Lucia. Inter-island travel by regional airlines. Cruises from Miami and San Juan

When to visit Hot and humid year-round. Rainy seasons: May–June, Sep–Oct. Hurricane season: Aug–Oct

Information Jamaica: Jamaican Tourist Board, PO Box 360, Kingston 5, Jamaica; tel. 929-8692. Puerto Rico: Puerto Rico Tourism Co., Calle San Justo 301, Old San Juan, Box 4435, Puerto Rico 00905; tel. 721-2400. Dominica: Dominica Tourist Office, Cork St, Box 73, Roseau, Dominica; tel. 448-2351. St Lucia: Govt Tourist Office, Govt Bldg, Castries, St Lucia; tel. 452-1706

Accommodation Full range

Notes Limited services in national parks and reserves; private guides and specialist tour companies on most islands

Rain forest on the lower slopes of Morne Trois Pitons in Dominica (above). Hot springs in Dominica's Valley of Desolation (right).

PUERTO RICO

A hop over Hispaniola takes you to Puerto Rico. The highlight of this island's numerous wildlife reserves is the Caribbean National Forest, known as El Yunque, a few miles east of San Juan. The park protects 70 percent of the virgin forest on the island. The rugged El Toro Trail (6 miles [10 km] one-way) begins from the Cienaga Alta ranger station on the western boundary and winds steeply over Mount El Toro (3,523 feet [1,075 m]), passing through the park's four tropical-forest ecosystems en route to the El Yunque Recreation Area.

Birders might also head to nearby Las Cabezas de San Juan Nature Reserve, at the island's north-eastern tip, whose boardwalks probe all seven of Puerto Rico's ecological zones, from mangrove swamp to dry forest. The yellow-crowned night-heron, white-crowned pigeon, belted kingfisher, and Puerto Rican parrot are among the scores of species you may see.

Bean-shaped Mona Island, off Puerto Rico's west coast, is a pristine nature reserve that can be reached only by private boat or plane. It has no hotels and no electricity,

The Mona ground iguana.

but you may camp. Harsh cacti and scrubby forest smother this Galápagos-like mesa. Red-footed boobies, three species of marine turtle, giant iguanas, honeycombed caves, and coral reefs top the attractions.

DOMINICA'S TREASURES

No ecotourist should skip nearby Dominica, the largest of the Windward Islands. This 280 square mile (720 km²) jewel of vine-draped volcanoes is a haven for naturalists and hikers tempted by orchids, bromeliads, waterfalls, and clear mountain lakes. Hikes in Morne Trois Pitons National Park range from a 10-minute stroll to

Trafalgar Falls to a strenuous excursion (a round trip that takes about 7 hours), with a guide, to the Valley of Desolation and its colorful hot springs.

You'll find Dominica's underwater topography is just as dramatic if you go scuba diving among the corals and caves of Soufrière Crater, formed by the rim of a sunken volcano. This is in the Pointe Guignard region, less than a mile north of the village of Soufrière. You can dive, snorkel, and swim with humpback whales between January and March, while the timorous can watch from boats.

Dominica is home to the only surviving Carib Indians, who live in six villages on a reserve on the rugged Atlantic coast.

St Lucia—Showing the Way

To the south of Dominica lies St Lucia, whose fledgling National Trust is creating a system of protected areas islandwide. The crowning glory of the island's wildlife is the *Jacquot*, an endemic parrot whose near demise in the 1970s prompted calls to save the forests.

To see some of St Lucia's abundant birdlife you can hike from Mahaut to Fond St Jacques along the 7 mile (11 km) trail through part of the Edmund Forest Reserve. The reserve can also be reached along the west coast by a road that snakes uphill and plunges into gorges behind the twin volcanic spires of the Pitons. Some of the best reefs are off the nearby coast, and the western walls of the Pitons plunge far below sea level, providing a thrilling setting for scuba diving. CB

THE ENDANGERED JACQUOT

An exemplary tale is that of the endangered *Jacquot*, or St Lucia parrot, a multicolored dazzler that is found in the rain-forest canopy. The islanders of St Lucia once considered the parrot a delicacy. Countless numbers were also killed to brighten creations in milliners' shops in Europe. Once numbering tens of thousands, by the 1970s only 150 of these green, red, and blue birds remained.

To save the *Jacquot*, its habitat was declared a sanctuary. Fines for killing parrots were raised to the equivalent of the average yearly income and a "parrot bus" set out to educate locals about the parrot's plight. Thus, the *Jacquot* became a symbol of St Lucia's beauty and the island's fragile environment. As a result, its numbers have doubled.

The volcanic spire of Gros Piton in St Lucia (top). The belted kingfisher (above) can be seen in Puerto Rico's Las Cabezas de San Juan Nature Reserve. The endangered St Lucia parrot (right).

Tikal

Guatemala

In the Petén region of northern Guatemala lies Tikal, the greatest Mayan religious center so far uncovered. Its majestic temple-pyramids are surrounded by forest stretching as far as the eye can see—home to all sorts of mammals and a glorious variety of butterflies and birds. The 230 square mile (600 km²) Tikal National Park is part of the UNESCO Maya Biosphere Reserve and lies at the center of La Ruta Maya, a figure-of-eight route that runs through the region once occupied by the Mayan empire.

The Mayan civilization—the greatest ancient civilization in the New World—lasted an amazing 3,530 years (2000 BC to AD 1530).

The endangered ocellated turkey (below) lives in the rain forests of Mexico, Guatemala, and Belize.

TIKAL NP

●Flores   La Ruta Maya

MILES
0   10   20
0   20   40
KM

GUATEMALA
BELIZE

Tikal was mysteriously abandoned around AD 900, but at its peak the city and associated family compounds may have spread over as much as 50 square miles (130 km²) and had a population of about 70,000.

TIKAL'S TEMPLES

Nowhere is it easier to combine natural history with archeology than at Tikal. The five great temple complexes tower above the rain-forest canopy, providing great perches from which to watch the birds and monkeys. Toucans walk along nearby branches at eye-level, white hawks circle above in courtship flight, and the low bellows of howler monkeys can be heard booming through the rain forest. You may even see the rare orange-breasted falcon dart into one of the temples, taking food to its young.

Six miles (10 km) of trails will take you through deep jungle to Tikal's many structures, ranging from the Great Plaza and the North Acropolis to the Temple of Inscriptions. So far, only a few of the city's 3,000 or so buildings have been restored. Keep an eye out for troops of spider monkeys or white-nosed coatis. You are bound to see some of Tikal's 300 bird

The North Acropolis at the Great Plaza (above). One of the five temple complexes that rise like islands out of the forest (right).

species, which include the violaceous trogon, the royal flycatcher, three species of toucan, and the purple-crowned fairy hummingbird. In the early morning, you may see ocellated turkeys feeding along the edge of the forest. They will dart back into cover if they're disturbed.

The forest, classified as a dry tropical forest, consists of tall hardwoods such as mahoganies and Spanish cedars, and there is little understory. In places, this high forest is replaced by a lower forest of escoba and botan palms, choked with thick underbrush and vines. Spotlighting at night is a great way to see some of the small mammals, such as the kinkajou, a tree-dwelling member of the

raccoon family, and visitors occasionally see jaguars.

If you have time to do some additional exploring, you could follow La Ruta Maya into the highlands of Guatemala. Here there are mountain villages set among a patchwork of terraced slopes, plus spectacular lakes and hot springs. If you take a walk in the cloud forest, you might well come across the resplendent quetzal, Guatemala's national bird. SM

Spider monkeys swing through the trees using their long arms and legs and prehensile tail.

TRAVELER'S NOTES

Access International flights to Guatemala City, Guatemala, and Belize City, Belize. By road or air to Flores. Rental cars available in Flores. Shuttle buses from Flores to Tikal. Most roads unpaved

When to visit Dec–Apr dry season. Steamy and buggy and roads often flooded in wet season (May–Nov)

Information Instituto Guatemalteco de Turismo (INGUAT), 7 Av. 1–17, Zona 4, Guatemala City, Guatemala; tel. (31) 133-3147

Accommodation Hotels in Flores.

Limited lodging and camping at Tikal. Bring water if camping

Notes Book accommodation and transport 6 months ahead. Carry water and gasoline if driving. Travelers have been held up on the Flores–Tikal road by armed bandits: for information on current situation, check US Dept of State travel advisories (see p. 34), or contact your embassy in Guatemala City

117

Belize

Belize

A strip of land south of Mexico's Yucatan Peninsula, Belize (formerly British Honduras) is culturally and spiritually in the Caribbean, and historically Mayan. This little country, the size of Wales or Vermont, borders one of the world's longest barrier reefs. Ten days or so will give you time to see the underwater wonders of the reef and explore the lush rain forests of the interior where waterfalls tumble, monkeys swing through the trees, and colorful birds flash overhead.

Belize is rapidly becoming the ecotourism capital of the Caribbean. Parts of the reef are preserved within a national park, and the temptation to build luxury resorts has been resisted. The Programme for Belize has bought massive areas of rain forest using donations from benefactors throughout the world who then "own" a part of the jungle, saving it from destruction.

REEF TO RAIN FOREST

Most visitors come to Belize for the turquoise waters and the beaches of the reef. The former pirate hideouts along the ribbon of coral islands, known as cayes (pronounced "keys"), are now dotted with glass-bottomed boats ferrying tourists. The more adventurous can swim with barracudas, parrotfish, eagle rays, and moray eels by diving west of Caye Caulker. Also teeming with marine life is Blue Hole, a huge sinkhole off Ambergris Caye, where you can dive to 130 feet (40 m).

Mainland Belize has much to offer the nature traveler. At the Bermudian Landing Community Baboon Sanctuary, an hour's drive from Belize City, local farmers have dedicated 20 square

Since 1986, a reserve in the Cockscomb Basin has protected the habitat of the jaguar, the largest cat in the Americas.

Map labels: MEXICO, Northern Hwy, Ambergris Caye, Caye Caulker, BERMUDIAN LANDING, Belize City, San Ignacio, Western Hwy, Xunantunich, MOUNTAIN PINE RIDGE, Lighthouse Reef, Dangriga, COCKSCOMB, GUATEMALA, BELIZE, Southern Hwy, MILES 0 15 30, 0 20 40 KM

Blue Hole (left) and the islands of Ambergris Caye (above) provide superb snorkeling and diving opportunities. Black howler monkeys (far left) and king vultures (below) inhabit the forests of mainland Belize.

miles (50 km²) to protect 1,600 endangered black howler monkeys (known locally as baboons). A guide will take you through the reserve, where vines twine and black howlers swing among the palms and gumbo-limbos. These large monkeys howl to defend their territories, sustaining their deafening roar for minutes at a time.

In the rain forests of western Belize, you can visit the remains of massive Mayan cities. The best example is at Xunantunich, two hours' drive from Belize City. The ruins are now home to howler monkeys and the venomous fer-de-lance snake.

Not far from Xunantunich is Mountain Pine Ridge Forest Reserve, a 300 square mile (800 km²) forest of tall pines, mahogany, and sapodilla trees, crowded with exotic flora and fauna, ranging from orchids to toucans. A track leads to the Hidden Valley Falls, which plunge in a glorious 980 foot (300 m) silver cascade.

One of the best places to explore the jungle is at Cockscomb Basin Wildlife Sanctuary and Forest Reserve, the world's first jaguar preserve. It is south of Belize City, about two hours' drive past the town of Dangriga. Jaguars are elusive but you may well see tapirs—locally known as "mountain cows" and related to the horse—ocelots, and jaguarundis, and you are bound to spot bird species such as the scarlet macaw, the keel-billed toucan, and the king vulture. JH

TRAVELER'S NOTES

Access International flights to Belize City. Flying is most efficient method of local travel. Roads are poor and driving is for the adventurous. A 4WD is useful for visiting many reserves. Motor launches connect Belize City with Caye Caulker and Ambergris Caye

When to visit Oct–May. Peak season Dec–Apr. June–Nov is the wet season, with the chance of hurricanes

Information Belize Tourist Board, 89 North Front St, Belize City, Belize; tel. (02) 77213/73255.

The Belize Audubon Society, 29 Regent St, Belize City, Belize; tel. (02) 77369 offers the best advice regarding reserves to visit

Accommodation Hotels from budget to luxury in Belize City and on the cayes. Inexpensive lodging available with locals at Bermudian Landing

Notes Never wear jewelry in the sea: it attracts nibbling barracudas

Costa Rica

Costa Rica

Diminutive Costa Rica has an extraordinary range of habitats. This warm, wet region at the junction of North and South America, lies where two pieces of the Earth's crust—the Pacific and the Caribbean plates—converge.

Nature is the prime reason tourists visit Costa Rica and tourism is the nation's chief income earner. Reflecting this, some 27 percent of the nation's 20,000 square miles (50,000 km²) is preserved in national parks, wildlife refuges, and other sanctuaries. New parks are being created and existing reserves amalgamated to form eight Regional Conservation Units.

ALONG THE COASTS

Costa Rica boasts remarkably diverse terrain, with 12 distinct ecological zones and climatic variation to match. Favored lowland destinations are Tortuguero and Manuel Antonio national parks, on the Caribbean and Pacific coasts respectively. Both encompass rain forests, mangroves, and other wet, lowland habitats.

Viewing wildlife is easy at Manuel Antonio, a 2½ square mile (6.5 km²) emerald jewel where a rare swatch of humid tropical forest sweeps down to stunning pocket-sized beaches. Capuchin (white-faced) monkeys often greet visitors. After snorkeling above the coral reef, you can explore the network of trails and look in the branches for howler monkeys, sloths, toucans, and endangered squirrel monkeys and scarlet macaws.

At Tortuguero, a watery world with fewer visitors, most wildlife watching is done from canoes. The park is a haven for green sea turtles, which can be seen laying their eggs on the beach.

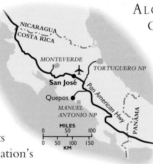

Bromeliads (far left) collect rainwater in their reservoirs, providing water supplies for arboreal animals such as the red-eyed tree frog (left).

The lush growth of Costa Rica's rain forests (above) provides habitat for myriad species, including the capuchin monkey (right).

A NOAH'S ARK ON THE MOUNTAIN

About 5 percent of all known species on Earth hop, skip, crawl, burrow, flit, and fly in Costa Rica, and a good portion inhabits the montane cloud forest that swathes the slopes of the Cordillera de Tilaran. The Monteverde Biological Cloud Forest Preserve straddles this volcanic backbone separating the Caribbean Sea and the Pacific Ocean.

In many ways, Monteverde (Green Mountain) is a microcosm of Costa Rica. The 46 square mile (120 km²) reserve encompasses eight ecological zones, from 2,500 feet (760 m) above sea level on the Caribbean slopes to 5,636 feet (1,719 m) at the summit. Trails lace the reserve, where moisture-laden winds shroud stunted woodland in near-constant mist. On lower slopes, clouds float through forests of cedar and giant cotton trees festooned with bromeliads, orchids, and other epiphytes ("air plants") that gain nourishment from the detritus on branches and the sodden air.

The lush milieu of Monteverde Preserve harbors over 100 species of mammal, more than 400 species of bird, and some 120 species of amphibian and reptile. Thousands of insects add their lisps and croaks to the spectral gloom.

TRAVELER'S NOTES

Access International flights to San José. Most internal travel by car or bus: 3½ hours to Manuel Antonio; 5 hours to Tortuguero; 4 hours to Monteverde. Also flights from San José to Quepos (near Manuel Antonio) and Tortuguero

When to visit Mists and rain year-round. Dec–May driest, but busy. July–Sept for turtles at Tortuguero

Information Costa Rica Tourist Board, Plaza de la Cultura, Calle 5 and Avenida Central, San Jose, Costa Rica; tel. 222-1090. Monteverde Visitor Center open 7.30 am–4.30 pm daily; tel. 661-1255

Accommodation Lodges and hotels from budget to expensive in towns of Manuel Antonio, Tortuguero, Monteverde, and Santa Elena

Notes Bring warm clothing and rain gear

Tropical birds include the keel-billed toucan, which lives in the canopy of the rain forest.

With patience, you will usually see capuchin monkeys and howler monkeys, whose stentorian roars will make your hair stand on end. Sloths can also be spotted, moving at a pace comparable to rigor mortis. Electric-blue morpho butterflies float by, flashing their neon-bright wings, and poison-dart frogs hop boldly about the forest floor, secure by day in brightly colored coats that scare predators away. Visitors are not likely to see pumas, jaguars, ocelots, tapirs, and other retiring creatures, but should beware the venomous fer-de-lance snake, curled up in burnished coils.

BIRDS! BIRDS! BIRDS!

If you remain silent and hidden, you'll be able to see some of the numerous birds that contribute to the chorus of calls: bright-billed toucans and toucanets, tanagers, jacamars, oropendolas, violaceous trogons, scarlet-thighed dacnis, and a host of other brilliantly colored species. The three-wattled bellbird is difficult to spot, though the male's eerie, metallic call haunts the mist-shrouded forest.

Thirty hummingbird species also inhabit the cloud forest. These beautiful birds, shimmering purple, cerulean, and green, hover at feeders near the trailhead outside the visitor center. The Holy Grail of the cloud forest is the resplendent quetzal, whose mournful two-note whistle is the

QUAKERS AND THE GOLDEN TOAD

A group of Quakers from Alabama established the village of Monteverde in 1951 on land that had already been cleared. Then, in 1964, scientists discovered *Bufo periglenes*, a poisonous, deaf and dumb, tree-dwelling toad, known by the locals as *sapo dorado*, golden toad. The Quakers, who recognized the importance of the forest as a "sponge" for rainfall, teamed up with the scientists in 1972 to purchase 1⅓ square miles (3.3 km²) of cloud forest, the initial tract of Monteverde Preserve.

Mysteriously, golden toad numbers declined during the 1980s and there have been no sightings at all since 1989. The gilded amphibian that helped spawn Costa Rica's first private reserve may now exist only on the covers of tourist brochures.

The cloud that cloaks the slopes of the Monteverde Preserve (top) is an important source of moisture for the diverse flora and fauna. The snowcap (below) is one of the 30 delightful hummingbird species found in the reserve.

A three-toed sloth grooming itself (above). The endangered resplendent quetzal (right) nests at Monteverde Preserve.

most alluring of calls. Birders flock to Monteverde simply to catch sight of this pigeon-sized bird, with its iridescent green plumage, fiery chest, audacious punk hairdo, and 24 inch (60 cm) long, sweeping, forked tail. The resplendent quetzal is endangered throughout its 1,000 mile (1,600 km) range—from southern Mexico to Panama—because of the destruction of cloud forest. More than 100 pairs nest at Monteverde. March to June is the best time to see them, when they descend to lower levels and the males put on dramatic mating displays.

FOLLOW THE TRAIL

Moderately easy hikes follow raised walkways. Other trails ooze with mud and are not for the faint-hearted. Sendero Chomogo (3 to 4 hours) leads to a lookout from where, at rare moments when the clouds part, you can see both the Pacific and the Caribbean. Sendero Bosque Nuboso (3 to 4 hours) has educational stops corresponding to a self-guide booklet. Several private trails exist outside the reserve, offering more arduous hikes (1 to 3 days) down the Caribbean slopes to waterfalls where you can be alone. You overnight at an Audubon Center.

AROUND MONTEVERDE

Many animal and bird species migrate between the reserve and adjacent land threatened by deforestation. The community-based Monteverde Conservation League purchases and reforests additional land for incorporation into the reserve.

It also educates local farmers about species preservation and about ecotourism as an alternative source of income. The reserve is joined in the east to the 80 square mile (200 km²) Children's Eternal Rainforest on land purchased by donations from children worldwide. To the west is the 2¼ square mile (6 km²) Santa Elena Cloud Forest Reserve, owned by the local community. Santa Elena has virtually all the species of its more famous neighbor, plus endangered spider monkeys.

Other pockets of cloud forest exist throughout Costa Rica at elevations above 4,000 feet (1,200 m), including areas within the Tapantí Wildlife Refuge, and Chirripó and La Amistad national parks. Elsewhere, nature lodges, such as the tiny Los Angeles Cloud Forest Reserve, tout their own private patches. CB

123

The Guayana Highlands

Venezuela

In the southeastern corner of Venezuela, about 100 flat-topped mountains rise like islands out of a rain-forest sea. Called *tepuis* by the local Pemon people, these sandstone mesas were formed by millions of years of uplift and erosion. In this wondrous country, you'll find the country's tallest mountain and the world's highest waterfall.

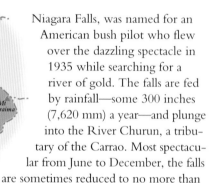

ANGEL FALLS

Angel Falls—known locally as Salto Angel—drops 3,218 feet (981 m) over the sheer face of Auyan Tepui (Devil's Mountain). The cascade, which is nearly 18 times higher than Niagara Falls, was named for an American bush pilot who flew over the dazzling spectacle in 1935 while searching for a river of gold. The falls are fed by rainfall—some 300 inches (7,620 mm) a year—and plunge into the River Churun, a tributary of the Carrao. Most spectacular from June to December, the falls are sometimes reduced to no more than a fine mist during the rest of the year.

Though Jimmy Angel never found his El Dorado, he did discover a land brimming with biological riches. Of the 10,000 plant species found growing here, half are considered unique. Nine hundred species of orchid bloom here, some no bigger than a pin. Other unusual plants include several kinds of carnivorous pitcher plant, and fungi that kill their insect and plant prey with poison. Huge rodents called capybara live along the creeks and rivers, and the rain forest is filled with the chirps and squawks of hundreds of bird species. These include scarlet macaws roosting on the ledges of the *tepuis* and colorful trogons, tanagers, and parrots at lower elevations.

Mount Roraima in Canaima National Park (above). Sundews (left) lure and trap small insects with their sticky leaves.

THE LOST WORLD

The wealth of flora and fauna has intrigued scientists and explorers ever since British botanist Everard Im Thurn scaled the area's tallest peak, 9,094 foot (2,774 m) Mount Roraima, in 1884. The tales he told of this rugged, remote place fueled the imagination of author Sir Arthur Conan Doyle, who used it as the setting for his novel, *The Lost World*. Indeed, much of the land remains "lost", and its inaccessibility has helped to protect it from the human activities that have ravaged so many other parts of South America.

Further protection has come from the creation of Canaima National Park, which includes Mount Roraima and Angel Falls within its boundaries. It covers nearly 11,582 square miles (30,000 km²) and encompasses a sprawling region of savanna known as La Gran Sabana.

Mount Roraima and Angel Falls are 125 miles (200 km) apart as the macaw flies. Allow 7 to 10 days to see them both. It's best to take in Angel Falls on a scenic flight from Ciudad Bolivar, then fly to the town of Santa Elena de Uairen near the Brazilian border. There you'll find operators offering one- or two-day tours of La Gran Sabana and treks to Mount Roraima.

A spectacular road leads from Santa Elena to La Gran Sabana, with waterfalls and *tepuis* lining the way. If you want to climb Mount Roraima, you can hire a guide in the village of Paraitepui. The weather in La Gran Sabana is tropical, but it can be cold and rainy on the mountaintop. The hike to the summit takes about two days and in addition to the glorious views you will see rare plants and geological wonders such as black rocks, pink beaches, and plunging gorges. DH

Angel Falls (above right). White-plumed antbird (right).

TRAVELER'S NOTES

Access International flights to Caracas. Domestic flights to Ciudad Bolivar and Santa Elena de Uairen

When to visit June–Dec best for hiking; Dec–May best for dramatic views of the waterfalls

Information Inparques, Edificio de la CVG, Avenida Germania, Ciudad Bolivar, Venezuela; tel. 285-4106

Accommodation Simple lodgings in most villages; undeveloped campsites throughout park

Notes Obtain permits for Canaima National Park and camping from Inparques

The Galápagos Islands
Ecuador

Galápagos provides a wildlife experience unlike any other. The animals here have developed no fear of people: you can swim with playful sea lions and walk among dancing blue-footed boobies. Situated on the equator, 600 miles (1,000 km) west of Ecuador, these volcanic islands are a land of contrasts—stark lava formations, turquoise waters, pristine beaches, cactus-covered lowlands, and lush green highlands. Galápagos is a living laboratory, home not only to teeming seabird colonies, sea lion rookeries, and pods of whales and dolphins,

but also to giant tortoises, marine iguanas, and equatorial penguins. The ancestors of Galápagos's extraordinary animals arrived via the ocean and the air from all directions. Isolated from the mainland and its predatory mammals, new species gradually evolved and flourished.

VOLCANIC FEATURES
Situated over a hot spot in the Earth's crust where three tectonic plates meet, the islands are only five million years old and are still being created by volcanic eruptions. The oldest one, Española (also known as Hood), is in the southeast, and the volcanically active island, Fernandina, is in the northwest. In all, there are 13 major islands and many islets, covering 3,100 square miles (8,000 km²) of land scattered over 17,400 square miles (45,100 km²) of ocean.

Galápagos is a wonderful example of volcanic geology. You can see shield volcanoes and pahoehoe (rope-like) and aa (jagged) lava flows, and snorkel in submerged calderas.

The giant tortoise enjoys a symbiotic relationship with the small ground finch: the bird feeds on the tortoise's ticks.

Great frigatebirds can be seen in their nesting colonies (above) from February to May. Golden rays (right) live in the open ocean. Their wing-like disks make them powerful swimmers.

The islands were discovered by the Bishop of Panama in 1535. They soon became known for their giant tortoises—a source of fresh meat for mariners—and were called Galápagos (Spanish for saddle) because of the tortoises' saddle-shaped shells. They became famous as a result of Charles Darwin's visit in 1835 and his subsequent development of the theory of evolution. In 1959, Ecuador declared the archipelago its first national park, although the human settlements that had already been established on Santa Cruz, Isabela, San Cristóbal, and Floreana were exempt.

Because of the long distances between islands, Galápagos is best visited on a cruise of at least one week. You'll visit about 10 islands, traveling between the major islands at night, and have the chance to snorkel almost every day. A two-week cruise will allow you to explore most of the visitor sites. A wide variety of Ecuadorian vessels are permitted to operate tours in Galápagos, offering a range of itineraries and amenities.

PENGUINS AND TORTOISES

The national park headquarters is located on Santa Cruz, in the center of the archipelago. A day on this island will allow you to look for giant tortoises and woodpecker finches in the fern-laden highlands and to visit the Charles Darwin Research Station in Puerto Ayora, where baby tortoises are reared.

TRAVELER'S NOTES

Access International flights to Quito or Guayaquil; domestic flights to Baltra or San Cristóbal. Book organized tour on yacht or cruise ship before arrival; a few boats offer day trips from Puerto Ayora on Santa Cruz to nearby islands

When to visit Year-round. Nov–Mar (warm season) for snorkeling and diving; Feb–Mar for flowers and breeding land iguanas and finches; Apr–Oct (cool season) for breeding seabirds; Dec–Jan peak season

Information Servicio Parque Nacional Galápagos, Puerto Ayora, Isla Santa Cruz,

Galápagos, Ecuador; tel. (05) 526-189, fax (05) 526-190. Visitor Center at Charles Darwin Research Station, Santa Cruz

Accommodation Limited number of small hotels on Santa Cruz and San Cristobal

Notes Book at least 6 months ahead. Visitors must be accompanied by licensed naturalist guide at all visitor sites

The mating routine of the male blue-footed booby includes this sky-pointing display.

127

To the east, on the tiny uplifted island of Plaza Sur (South Plaza), you can see land iguanas, lava lizards, and swallow-tailed gulls, all endemic to Galápagos. In the southeast, on Española, you can walk among thousands of blue-footed and masked boobies and magnificent waved albatrosses in their breeding colonies. In the southwest, on Floreana, greater flamingos and green sea turtles make their nests, and at nearby Corona del Diablo (Devil's Crown) there is spectacular snorkeling among curtains of fish, with the occasional hammerhead shark appearing from the depths.

On Genovesa (Tower), in the northeast, you will find millions of seabirds: great frigate-birds, red-billed tropicbirds, red-footed and masked boobies, and a constant

Marine iguanas with a Sally Lightfoot crab.

On Bartolomé, you can enjoy striking views of Pinnacle Rock (above) and go snorkeling with Galápagos penguins (left).

cloud of storm petrels. On your walks through the sea-bird colonies you'll also see Darwin's finches, Galápagos doves, and, perhaps, a short-eared owl. To the west, the colder waters of Fernandina and Isabela nurture flightless cormorants, Galápagos penguins, three kinds of dolphin, sperm whales, and large colonies of marine iguanas. Hundreds of tortoises breed in the misty highlands of Alcedo on Isabela, reached via a backpacking trip that is only for the hardy. East of Isabela, Santiago offers terrific tidepooling, where color-ful Sally Lightfoot crabs scuttle and shorebirds search out edible tidbits. Bartolomé affords excellent snorkeling and spectacular views of lava flows on neighboring Santiago.

The marine environment of Galápagos is exceptional. Not only are there huge schools of fish, but of the more than 300 species, 17 percent are endemic. On a typical snorkeling trip, you'll see a wide variety of tropical fish, including rainbow wrasse, the endemic yellowtail damselfish, moorish idol, king angel, and four kinds of parrotfish. Added to the abundant fishlife are the delights of swimming with flightless cormorants, marine iguanas, Galápagos penguins, California sea lions, spotted

eagle rays, and the occasional green sea turtle. For the diver, there are immense schools of jacks, grunts, snappers, and hammerheads, and the occasional whale shark. Because of the cool waters, there are few coral formations except for slow-growing black coral at great depths. Galápagos is a dive destination only for the experienced open-water diver, because of the strong ocean currents.

Much of Galápagos has not changed since Darwin visited the islands over 100 years ago, but serious conservation issues threaten this pristine reserve. Unchecked population growth, the introduction of non-native species, and unlimited fishing of sea cucumbers and sharks for Asian markets are serious problems. The Charles Darwin Research Station is the center for ongoing research and conservation projects. Its major programs include the eradication of introduced species such as goats, pigs, cats, dogs, and rats, and the rearing and reintroduction of giant tortoises and land iguanas. SM

CHARLES DARWIN

At the age of 22, Charles Darwin (1809–82) boarded the HMS *Beagle* as naturalist for a five-year journey around the world. During his five-week stay in Galápagos, his observations of the various rather drab-looking finches (now collectively known as Darwin's finches) formed the basis of his theory of evolution. He speculated that the 13 species he saw had evolved from one mainland finch.

Some of the finches are seed-eaters, like their mainland ancestor, but others have evolved to take advantage of various niches that were available to them in the absence of other land birds. The woodpecker finch, for instance, has a long, sturdy bill to probe for insects in bark, while the large ground finch (below) has a bill for eating large seeds.

In 1859, Darwin published his book *The Origin of Species by Means of Natural Selection*, arguing that only those species best suited to their environment will survive, passing on the characteristics that enabled them to do so to the next generation. His work dramatically changed the way people view the natural world.

Greater flamingos (above) can be seen feeding in salty lakes.
Land iguanas (top) dig their nesting burrows in fine soil.

129

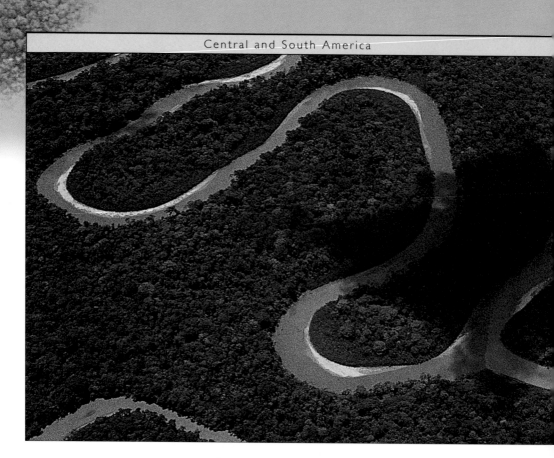

The Amazon

Brazil, Ecuador, and Peru

From the air, the Amazon Basin is a green ocean—the world's largest tract of tropical rain forest. Bounded by the Atlantic Ocean in the east and the Andes in the west, it covers 3 million square miles (8 million km²) in equatorial South America. The mighty Amazon River flows eastward 4,018 miles (6,470 km) from its source high in the Peruvian Andes to the Atlantic.

Warm temperatures and constant moisture nurture the region. The main rains in the Andes fall from November to May. In the Amazon, showers can occur any time and high humidity is constant. Nowhere is there greater biodiversity. Over 1,000 bird species live in these forests and about 3,000 species of fish swim in the rivers. Scientists have estimated that there are as many as 500 species of tree in any area of about an acre, and over 400 kinds of animal in each species of tree. A chorus of calls from frogs, insects, birds, and mammals will awaken you and squeaks, sputters, howls, and whistles emanate from the greenery all day.

FOREST HABITATS

The best way to visit the Amazon is to stay at a lodge that has a birding tower or canopy walkway for viewing the animals and that offers daily outings on foot and by canoe. Live-aboard boats offer another way to explore. Stay at least a week, if you can, as there is much to see. Habitats include *terra firme* (forest that does not flood); black-water rivers (silt-free ones that are black from vegetation); white-water rivers (silty ones);

The poison-dart frog is brightly colored to warn off predators (left). A Majoruna woman from the Peruvian Amazon (right).

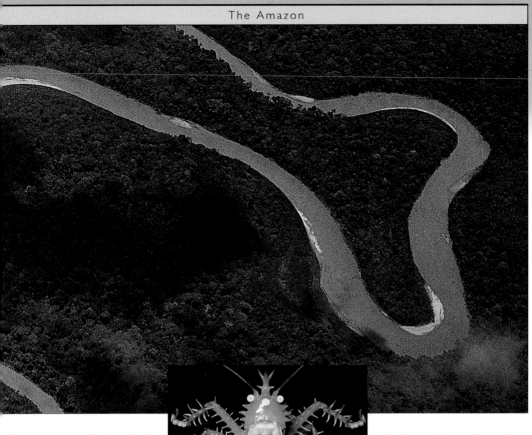

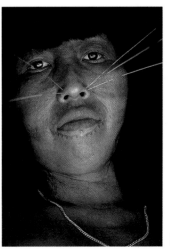

The silt-laden Pinquina River snaking through Manú National Park (above). A spiny-headed katydid (left).

igapó and *várzea* (the lowland forest flooded by black water and white water respectively); oxbow lagoons (former river channels that have been cut off by the river changing course); and islands.

Visitors seldom see tribespeople as they tend to avoid contact with outsiders. Three million Amerindians were living in Amazonia when the Spanish arrived in the sixteenth century. Now only 50,000 or so remain, living in settlements that dot the forests. These people are mainly nomadic, hunting and practicing slash-and-burn farming. They clear small plots to farm crops such as manioc and plantains, moving on after a few years. So far, they have been able to retain aspects of their culture, but deforestation and development threaten their survival.

Amazonia can be divided in two. The Lower Basin embraces the region from Brazil's western border to the Atlantic. This area receives a little less rain than the Upper Basin and has more distinct wet and dry seasons. The Amazon and its largest tributary, the Negro, converge near the town of Manaus, making it a good location from which to explore the Lower Basin. There is a range of jungle lodges in the vicinity, from which you can visit the white-water Solimões (the western part of the Amazon), the black-water Negro, and the Archipelago das Anavilhanas, the world's largest river archipelago.

An amazing 102 inches (2,600 mm) of rain per year falls in the Upper Basin, which lies to the west, at the base of the Andes.

TRAVELER'S NOTES

Access Brazil: international flights to Manaus then by boat. Ecuador: international flights to Quito, domestic flight to Coca then 3-hour canoe ride to Yasuni. Peru: international flight to Cuzco then domestic flight or 2-day drive and 6-hour canoe trip to lodge near Manú

When to visit Manaus: Mar–Aug for flooded forest. Yasuni: year-round. Manú: June–Aug, as this is drier season

Information Emantur, Avenida Taruma 379, Manaus, Brazil; tel. (092) 243-5983. Cetur, Ministerio de Turismo, Avenida Eloy Alfaro 1214 y Carlos Tobar, Quito, Ecuador; tel. (02) 224-970, fax (02) 229-330. Tourist Office, Portal Belen, Cuzco, Peru; tel. (084) 237-364

Accommodation All-inclusive lodges or riverboats, ranging from rustic to luxurious

Notes Rain gear and insect repellent essential. Best to visit on a pre-booked tour. Heed political advisories for Peru

This region contains hot spots where the greatest diversity of species has developed. Prime jungle lodges are located near Yasuni National Park along the Napo River in eastern Ecuador and in Manú National Park in southeastern Peru.

MANÚ NATIONAL PARK

The gem of the entire Amazon Basin is Manú National Park. It protects a massive forest covering 7,300 square miles (18,900 km²)— almost the entire watershed of the Manú River. This is the largest tract of protected rain forest in the world and is designated a UNESCO Biosphere Reserve and World Heritage Site. Because it's so remote, Manú is not easy to reach, but getting there is part of the adventure.

Within the rain forest there is surprisingly little under-growth because of the tall trees' dense canopy. Vines with huge leaves entwine enormous buttress and stilt roots; palms of every sort grow among the seedlings of mature trees; bromeliads cover limbs, their brilliant flowers blooming year-round; tiny orchids are sprinkled across the forest floor; and all sorts of spikes cover tree trunks to protect them from being eaten.

You'll see amazing insects, such as lines of leafcutting ants toting leaves they've cut to mulch in their underground dwellings. (The ants feed on a fungus that grows on the chewed-up leaves.) Other wildlife is harder to see. Colorful frogs, lizards, and birds merge with the shadows, and you'll seldom spot mammals unless they drop fruit from above or make a slight movement on the forest floor.

It's easier to see the wildlife from a canoe, traveling on day trips up the Manú River. In the early morning, you'll see scores of scarlet macaws feeding at mineral licks on the river banks and you may see a jaguar. You're certain to see many species of monkey, including the tiny pygmy marmoset. Huge lagoons lined with water-hyacinth branch off the river, where giant otters play and the *bouto*, a pink, freshwater dolphin, swims. Sunsets at Manú are unforgettable, with the sun and stately palms reflected in the water and hundreds of parrots and macaws flying home to roost. At night, you'll hear the hooting of the black-banded owl as you spotlight for black caimans (alligators) in the lagoons.

Local people use canoes to travel the waterways (above). A southern taman-dua anteater on a termites' nest (left).

WHAT IS BEING LOST

A rich store of pharmaceuticals lies within the Amazon Basin and botanists are working with indigenous peoples and pharmaceutical companies to identify the medicinal properties of numerous plants. Many medicines contain extracts from tropical flora, but so far only 1 percent of rain-forest plants has been analyzed for medicinal value.

The lushness of the Amazonian rain forest suggests that it must be growing on rich soil. In fact, the incessant rains leach most of the nutrients from it: the nutrients within the ecosystem are fixed in the living plants and animals. When an organism dies, it breaks down and rots quickly and the minerals are immediately taken up by the surrounding forest. When rain forest is cleared, the soil is depleted within three or four years. If the cleared area is more than a few acres, the forest cannot fully regenerate.

While more than 80 percent of the rain forest in this vast region remains intact, deforestation is occurring at the rate of about 6,250 square miles (16,200 km²) a year. Along with grave concern regarding the loss of plant and animal species, scientists fear that forest destruction is contributing to global warming. Debt cancellation in return for setting up parks, ecotourism, and changes to farming practices are initiatives aimed at helping to preserve this unique region. SM

THE FLOODED FOREST

In the rainy season, the waters of some rivers rise up to 50 feet (15 m)—as in the case of the Rio Solimões at Manaus—flooding areas of forest for up to eight months of the year. Many saplings become completely submerged. In the nutrient-poor, black-water areas this forest is called *igapó*; in the silt-rich, white-water areas it is known as *varzéa*. Many trees fruit during the floods, providing food for fish that migrate from the rivers into the flooded forest. Fish feast on the fruit, assisting in seed dispersal.

The principal predator here is the *bouto*. This dolphin's eyesight is poor and it uses echolocation to navigate in search of fish.

Floating meadows are widespread in *várzea*—carpets of aquatic plants teeming with insects, frogs, and freshwater shrimp. These provide shelter for caimans and fish, and food for the endangered manatee—a large herbivorous mammal that lives solely in fresh water.

Piranhas in the Amazon River (top). A yellow-fronted parrot, preening (top right). The bouto, a freshwater dolphin (above right).

The Andes

Ecuador and Peru

Clothed in cloud forests and studded with snow-covered volcanic peaks, the Andes are the longest continuous mountain chain in the world, extending down western South America from the Caribbean Sea to Cape Horn. There are 13 stunning peaks above 20,000 feet (6,000 m) and the range is still in the making, with earthquakes and volcanic activity occurring regularly. In the rain shadow of the Andes lie the Atacama Desert along the Peruvian and Chilean coasts and the dry, windswept steppes of Patagonia (see p. 140).

Two of the most interesting areas to visit are the species-rich ranges of Ecuador and the area surrounding the incomparable archeological ruins of Machu Picchu in Peru. These regions offer the naturalist opportunities to visit tropical cloud forests, temperate coniferous forests at higher elevations, and the paramo—

During its courtship display, the male cock-of-the-rock extends its crest farther forward to totally cover its bill.

a high-altitude habitat of grasses, shrubs, and wildflowers just below the snowline. Allow at least a fortnight to explore the various mountain habitats and to visit Machu Picchu. You will need to stay another week if you would like to visit part of Upper Amazonia (see p. 130) as well.

ECUADOR

Quito, the capital of Ecuador, is an excellent base from which to explore this fascinating country. The city lies at 9,500 feet (2,900 m) in a long, narrow valley between the two Andean ranges along what is known as the Avenue of Volcanoes. On a clear day, you can see the snow-covered peaks that surround the city, and the sunrises and sunsets can be glorious. To the west are the humid lowlands and the Pacific, and eastward lie the jungles of Amazonia. You can take day trips from Quito to visit different habitats at varying altitudes.

About two hours' drive east of Quito you come to spectacular Papallacta Pass, home to high-altitude species. Near the pass, you'll find patches of polylepis, a tree that is a member of the rose family. Farther on, above the town of

The snow-capped cone of Cotopaxi (above). An Uro Indian poling his reed boat on Lake Titicaca (right).

Papallacta, orchids and flowering shrubs line the road. This is hummingbird territory, where three of the larger hummingbirds—the sword-billed, the great sapphirewing, and the shining sunbeam—hover with smaller hummers at their favorite feeding sites. As the road winds its way down the steep slopes of the lush eastern Andes, waterfalls stream down the mountainsides and vast, forest-covered ridges extend far into the distance. You may see the white-capped dipper busy in one of the many rushing rivers. This is an amazing bird that walks and even swims underwater to catch insect larvae and crustaceans.

To the west, the old cobblestone Nono Mindo Road winds through steep cloud-forested slopes to Mindo-Nambillo National Forest Reserve at 4,000 feet (1,200 m), an area famous for its butterflies, colorful tropical birds, and orchids. Here you can walk through emerald-green meadows where toucans perch in the trees. Keep an eye out for the Jesus or basilisk lizard along the Mindo River. This 2 foot (60 cm) lizard runs on the surface of the water.

The fleet and fluffy vicuña (right) inhabits high-altitude grassland in Peru.

TRAVELER'S NOTES

Access International flights to Quito, Ecuador, and Lima, Peru

When to visit Year-round. Sept–May rainy season; June–Sept dry season, best for trekking; Jan–July wildflowers

Information Cetur, Ministerio de Turismo, Avenida Eloy Alfaro 1214 y Carlos Tobar, Quito, Ecuador, tel. (02) 224-970, fax (02) 229-330. Tourist Office, Portal Belen 115, Cuzco, Peru; tel. (084) 237-364

Accommodation Wide variety of hotels in major cities, and small haciendas in countryside

Notes Mountain weather is highly changeable: pack cold-weather clothes. Rain gear and rubber boots imperative. Beware of symptoms of altitude sickness (see p. 48). Heed political advisories and do not travel alone in Peru

Steep, muddy trails lead upward to where the brilliantly colored male cock-of-the-rock displays high in the forest. Bromeliads and ferns cover the limbs of trees, nourished by daily fog, and silver-leafed cecropia trees tower above the canopy.

LLAMAS AND THEIR RELATIVES

Four relatives of camels are native to the high Andes—llamas, alpacas, vicuñas, and guanacos. Like camels, they have long necks and short tempers, but they're smaller and they don't have humps.

Llamas, the largest, were domesticated by the Incas. You often see them in Peru, wearing decorated packsaddles. The Spanish eradicated them from Ecuador in the course of wiping out the Inca civilization, but today there are llama farms throughout Ecuador's Andes.

The smaller alpaca was also used by the Incas as a pack animal. Alpacas are prized for their thick, soft wool, and Peruvians still make alpaca sweaters, hats, and blankets in traditional Inca patterns.

The vicuña, the smallest of the family, once ranged from Ecuador to northern Argentina but was hunted almost to extinction for its wool and pelts. In the 1960s, a reserve was set up near Nazca, where over 30,000 now roam. The southern relative, the guanaco, lives in Chile's beech forests and on the plains of Tierra del Fuego.

To the south stands Cotopaxi, the world's highest active volcano (19,344 feet [5,900 m]), its snow-capped cone sharp against the bright blue sky. In Cotopaxi National Park, about three hours' drive from Quito, the road snakes up to the windswept paramo at 14,000 feet (4,300 m), where tiny alpine flowers dot the slopes and wild horses roam. On a clear day, this is a photographer's dream, for you can see as many as 30 mountain peaks within 100 miles (160 km). The air here is thin, so you must walk slowly and be alert for symptoms of altitude sickness (see p. 48). Cotopaxi also offers challenging ice and glacier climbing for experts.

PERU

In Peru, the Andes become more rugged and there are few roads. The mountains branch into three broad ranges. The western slopes are arid whereas the eastern slopes receive more than 40 inches (1,000 mm) of rain a year. The source of the Amazon River is high among the slopes in southeastern Peru, as is Lake Titicaca, the world's highest navigable lake. Northeast of the lake is the mysterious, abandoned Inca city of Machu Picchu,

A waterfall in the foothills of the Andes (above). Llamas (left) are used widely throughout Peru as pack animals, and their owners often attach colorful tassels to their ears.

The spectacular ruins of the Inca city of Machu Picchu, in the mountains of southern Peru (above), where Andean condors (left) dip and soar.

which is now classified as a UNESCO Biosphere Reserve.

Reaching Machu Picchu is an adventure in itself, for you must first fly into Lima on the coast and then up to Cuzco at 12,000 feet (3,700 m), once the center of the Inca civilization. Allow two days to explore Cuzco and the nearby Urubamba Valley where you can see many archeological ruins. At the far end of the valley lies Ollantaytambo, the only surviving Inca village that carries on the ancient traditions. From here, you take the train to Agua Calientes and then a bus up a steep zigzag road to Machu Picchu.

If you prefer, you can take the train to km 88 and then hike the 20 mile (32 km) Inca Trail to Machu Picchu. This three- to five-day strenuous and rather muddy trek passes remote ruins with views of snow-covered peaks and crosses three 12,000 foot (3,700 m) passes. You'll hike up to cold, arid plateau country, known as *puna*, and then descend to the cloud forest, at times making your way along narrow cliff ledges. The wildflowers are lovely, you'll see hummingbirds feedings on blossoms and hawks high above, and, at dusk, night monkeys emerge from their roosts in hollow trees.

Machu Picchu is often shrouded in the mists of the surrounding cloud forest. With its mortarless stone temples and terraces, the city seems to almost grow out of the mountaintop on which it stands. The Urubamba River tumbles in the gorge below, on its way to join the mighty Amazon. Behind the ruins, a steep, winding trail climbs up the mountain of Huayna Picchu, from where you can look down on Machu Picchu and the surrounding mountains and gorges. You may even see the magnificent Andean condor, with a wingspan of up to 10 feet (3 m), cruise by on the updrafts.

For more high Andean scenery, the train ride from Cuzco to Puna, which takes 14 hours, is unsurpassed. It will take you to sacred Lake Titicaca at 12,524 feet (3,820 m). Since long before the beginning of Inca civilization, the Uro Indians have lived in huts on floating islands of reeds on the ice-cold waters of the lake. SM

A Peruvian Indian woman in traditional costume. Native people make up about 50 percent of Peru's population.

The Pantanal

Brazil

Most people think of Amazonia when they imagine Brazilian flora and fauna, yet the Pantanal, which sprawls across the states of Mato Grosso and Mato Grosso do Sul and southeast into Bolivia and Paraguay, is a watery haven for one of South America's greatest concentrations of wildlife.

About half the size of France, the Pantanal is a vast, grassy plain dotted with palms and stands of trees and woody shrubs, crossed by the Paraguay River. During the rainy season the river's network of tributaries floods and the region becomes the largest freshwater wetland in the world. The rains begin in October and water levels peak around February. By July, much of the region has dried out and the water that remains is in ponds and creeks.

The gateway to the Pantanal is the city of Cuiabá. From here, it's about 60 miles (100 km) south to Pocone where the Transpantaneira Highway, a two-lane dirt road, begins.

Along the Transpantaneira Highway, you may see the capybara, the world's largest rodent (left). Caimans (right) can be spotted near creeks.

This 90 mile (150 km) highway takes you into the heart of the Pantanal, crossing creeks teeming with frogs and caimans (a type of alligator). The highway and a strip of land about 20 feet (6 m) on either side are protected, but much of the land is privately owned and used for ranching. Cattle sharing a field with storks and dozing caimans is a common sight.

WET AND DRY

The Pantanal offers one of the most superb birding experiences in South America. More than 600 species of bird are found here, from

Wading birds such as woodstorks (above) search the sodden savannas for fish. Various species of macaw, including the scarlet (left) and the hyacinth (far left), perch in the trees.

ibises, herons, snowy egrets, and roseate spoonbills, to the towering tuiuiu, a 5 foot (1.5 m) tall stork. Cara caras are but one of 25 species of hawk in the region and you will also see rheas and brilliantly colored tropical birds such as toucans and macaws.

During the dry season, a short walk from the road takes you close to the wildlife, and most travelers see a staggering array simply by spending several days along the highway, based at a local inn. But should you be sufficiently intrepid to come during the rains, you'll see rarer creatures clustered on the islands that form as the waters rise. These include marsh deer, giant anteaters, giant river otters, pumas, and sometimes even a jaguar. At this time of year, however, guides are a necessity and you will need to explore by boat.

At the end of the Transpantaneira, in Porto Joffre, you can take a boat trip along the Cuiabá River to Cara Cara Reserve, which is now part of Pantanal National Park. Anacondas, up to 25 feet (7 m) long, lurk in the shallows waiting for prey, such as capybara and wading birds. Howler monkeys race through the trees, and fishermen can be seen hauling in catfish, dorado, and piranha.

Poaching is rife in the Pantanal. Macaws and parrots are smuggled overseas, and caimans are shot to be made into handbags and shoes. Brush-cutting by ranchers has eroded riverbanks, and the use of mercury to mine for gold has polluted the water. But the greatest threat is a plan to build a dam on the Paraguay River, which would destroy the unique ecology of the region. **EP**

TRAVELER'S NOTES

Access International flights to Rio de Janeiro. Domestic flight to Cuiabá (2½ hours), then drive south on the Transpantaneira Highway to Porto Joffre

When to visit July–Sept ideal for birding; Oct–Mar is rainy season and brings spectacular floods, sometimes making visits impossible

Information Embratur, SCN Quadra 2, Bloco G, CEP 70710, Brasilia DF, Brazil; tel. (061) 225-9666; fax (061) 225-6241

Accommodation About a dozen inns of varying quality along the highway; reservations essential in July and Aug

Patagonia

Argentina and Chile

Patagonia is a vast, 300,000 square mile (800,000 km²) area that takes in parts of Argentina and Chile. It extends south from the Rio Colorado and east from the Andes down to Tierra del Fuego. This windswept, semi-arid region has few human inhabitants, but dedicated travelers are drawn by its dramatic land-scapes and fascinating wildlife.

Patagonia's size makes touring difficult, so it's best to focus on one of the parks. Take Argentina's Península Valdés, for instance. This scrub-covered land

meets the Atlantic in steep cliffs and gravel beaches. Although much of the peninsula is privately owned, the area is managed as a provincial park and is home to rheas (similar to ostriches), tinamous (forest fowl), maras (a hare), and guanacos (related to llamas). Whales and dolphins are abundant in the waters, and the shore at Punta Norte is often thick with sea lions and elephant seals. In the peninsula's south, you'll find dense concentrations of Magellanic penguins, as well as giant petrels, cormorants, and flightless steamer ducks.

LAND OF GLACIERS

The most spectacular national park in Argentina is Los Glaciares, near the foot of the Andes—a region of mountains, lakes, and vast glaciers.

Most visitors fly to the town of Calafate on Lake Argentino, a huge lake covering some 600 square miles (1,600 km²). About 40 miles (65 km) southeast of Calafate, a road winds through forest to the Brazo Rico arm of the lake where you can walk to the face of Glacier

An orca whale approaches a group of sea lions on Península Valdés (left), where you can also find the Patagonian armadillo (opposite).

In Los Glaciares National Park, you can walk up to the face of Glacier Moreno (above). The Paine Horns, twin peaks of granite tipped with black slate (right), are found in Torres del Paine.

Moreno, a 200 foot (60 m) wall of ice. The glacier extends down the mountain opposite and across the water to the nearside forested bank, damming the arm. Every few years, rising water causes the dam to explode and a torrent of water rages past the ice into Lake Argentino.

To visit the mountainous northern half of Los Glaciares—a great attraction for hikers and climbers—you'll need to buy supplies in Calafate and then take a bus along the northern shore of Lake Viedma to the tiny town of El Chaltén. For much of the trip, you will be surrounded by dry, dusty steppe, then suddenly snowcapped Mount FitzRoy and its neighbors will rise before you.

In the foothills, hiking trails lead through beech forests where woodpeckers tap, and follow rivers to alpine lakes surrounded by superb scenery.

About 200 miles (320 km) south of Los Glaciares lies Torres del Paine, the jewel of Chile's national park system. Its lakes and colorful, mossy bogs are fed by melting glaciers and fringed by forests and meadows. Guanacos and ñandús (small rheas) abound, and you might see a mountain lion. Eagles and condors soar over the jagged mountains in search of prey. The park is named for the three spectacular glacier-carved columns of pink granite near the Andes' southern tip—*torres* is Spanish for tower.

EP

TRAVELER'S NOTES

Access International flights to Buenos Aires, Argentina, or Punta Arenas, Chile. Península Valdés: 2-hour flight from Buenos Aires to Trelew, then 60 mile (95 km) road trip to Puerto Madryn. Los Glaciares: 3-hour flight from Buenos Aires to Calafate. Torres del Paine: gravel road from Calafate or 160 mile (260 km) bus trip from Punta Arenas to Puerto Natales

When to visit Península Valdés: Oct–Apr best for wildlife. Los Glaciares/Torres del Paine: Dec–Mar best weather; avoid rainy season Apr–May

Information Servicio Nacional de Parques Nacionales, Avenida Santa Fé 690, Buenos Aires, Argentina; Dirección Nacional de Turismo, Avenida Santa Fé 883, Buenos Aires, Argentina; tel. (01) 312-2232

Accommodation Península Valdés: hotels in Trelew and Puerto Madryn. Los Glaciares: hotels and camping in Calafate and El Chaltén. Torres del Paine: hotels in Puerto Natales; hotels and camping in park

141

Europe

ECOTRAVEL *in* EUROPE

Europe's densely populated landscape has been modified by thousands of years of human activities. Yet surprisingly large areas of this diverse continent remain unspoiled.

Along with glorious cultural legacies, Europeans have inherited a richly varied landscape that has been radically altered by human activities. Over the centuries, forests that once covered much of the continent have been cleared for planting and grazing, shipbuilding and construction; wetlands have been drained; and rivers straightened to facilitate transportation.

Despite this, parts of Europe remain relatively unspoiled. In remote regions, exploitation proved uneconomical, so large areas of pristine land can be found in the icy tundra of Scandinavia, the mountains of central Europe, and along rugged coastlines. Other areas, such as the forests of northeastern Poland, were left untouched because they were royal hunting grounds.

THE NATIONAL PARKS

Although a few national parks were established early this century—the first were Sarek and Stora Sjöfallet in Sweden in 1909—it wasn't until after the Second World War that the preservation of wildlife and natural areas became a priority. Vanoise, France's first national park, wasn't established until 1963 and former East Germany had no national parks until 1990.

The level of protection that European preserves offer varies considerably. In many countries, national parks include private land, towns, and villages, making it difficult for park authorities to control activities that may be detrimental to the environment.

Many animal species are now extinct in Europe. Wolves, wolverines, brown bears, polar bears, lynx, elk, moose, and bison once roamed the continent in great numbers, but all are now threatened species. In some cases their numbers are dangerously low, but protection and breeding and reintroduction programs are ensuring their continued existence. Even in Germany,

NATURE AND CULTURE *can easily be combined on a visit to Europe. Areas such as the Tatras Mountains in Slovakia (below) and Spain's Estremadura (right) are rich in both history and wildlife. Alpine gentians in bloom (above left).*

one of Europe's most densely populated and industrialized countries, wolf and lynx numbers are growing.

Europe's large human population means that you will seldom find yourself entirely alone with nature, especially in July and August, but the other side of the coin is that even remote travel destinations are easy to reach by public transport. Furthermore, it's easy to combine visits to cultural sites with trips to wild places.

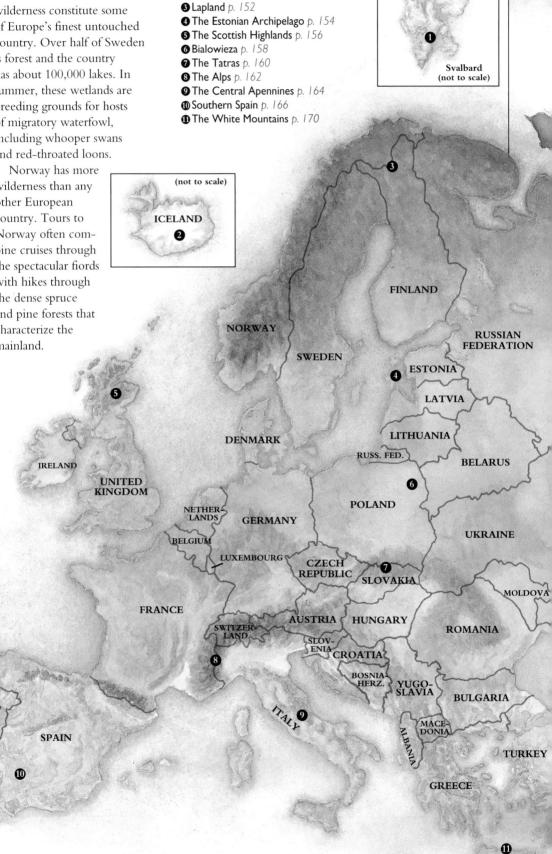

NORTHERN EUROPE

Scandinavia's vast stretches of wilderness constitute some of Europe's finest untouched country. Over half of Sweden is forest and the country has about 100,000 lakes. In summer, these wetlands are breeding grounds for hosts of migratory waterfowl, including whooper swans and red-throated loons.

Norway has more wilderness than any other European country. Tours to Norway often combine cruises through the spectacular fiords with hikes through the dense spruce and pine forests that characterize the mainland.

Svalbard
(not to scale)

(not to scale)

ICELAND

THE FAR NORTH *offers the largest areas of wilderness in Europe and fascinating wildlife. A bearded seal on the remote island of Spitsbergen (below). Reindeer with a Saami herder (right) in northern Finland.*

Above the Arctic Circle, a plethora of parks in Norway, Sweden, and Finland balance the protection of nature with the needs of the Saami, the indigenous people.

In the United Kingdom and Ireland, several thousand nature reserves have been set aside, ranging from large tracts of land, such as the Cairngorm Nature Reserve in Scotland and Brecon Beacons National Park in south Wales, to small areas administered by local authorities or private conservation organizations such as the Royal Society for the Protection of Birds.

Two weeks' touring will enable you to sample much of the region, as distances are short. You can travel to the southwest of England to visit the varied habitats of Exmoor, where wild ponies and red deer roam; climb the rugged fells in the Lake District, in the northwest; and then perhaps tour the wild, beautiful islands of the Outer Hebrides in Scotland.

WESTERN CENTRAL EUROPE

Despite extensive human settlement, western central Europe is still rich in wild places. In the Alps, national parks protect a variety of rare fauna, ranging from chamois to golden eagles. However, ski resorts, heavy tourism, and hunting are all taking a toll on the environment.

Germany's forests draw many ecotravelers. The Bavarian Forest National Park became Germany's first national park in 1970. It now adjoins Sumava National Park across the border in the Czech Republic. Together, these parks constitute the largest single wooded area in central Europe. Acid rain is by far the most serious threat to this environment, having already destroyed over 50 percent of German forests.

France offers remarkable habitat diversity. The wetlands of the Camargue, in the south, are a valuable stopover for millions of migrating waterfowl and breeding grounds for the greater flamingo. On the Spanish border, the Pyrenees National Park safeguards a 60 mile (100 km) stretch of mountains that incorporates superb hiking trails.

EASTERN CENTRAL EUROPE

Many areas of the former communist bloc were heavily exploited following the Second World War and environmental safeguards were nonexistent. Air pollution in Poland, for instance, has almost destroyed the forests in the country's southern mountains and most Hungarian lakes are so polluted that swimming in them

REMOTE AREAS *of the British Isles, such as the Scottish Highlands (left), offer a wealth of flora and fauna. Badgers (above) are found throughout the British Isles, normally in deciduous woodlands.*

is forbidden. In Romania, agricultural development and plans to dam the river continue to threaten the Danube Delta. (This region is one of Europe's most valuable wetlands and the breeding ground for pink pelicans.)

On the other hand, eastern Europe is a haven for many animal species that face extinction elsewhere in Europe. There are hundreds of brown bears in Russia, Poland, and Romania, but only isolated populations in the west. The European otter is almost extinct in western Europe, but relatively large populations can be found in Hungary, Poland, the Czech Republic, and Slovenia. There are only about 2,000 white storks in western Europe, but there are tens of thousands of them in the east.

The real jewels of this area are to be found in remote regions, such as the Carpathian Mountains, northeastern Poland, and Estonia. Some ecotours to Romania combine a visit to the Danube Delta with a journey through the Carpathian Mountains. In Hungary, where travel is easier than in many other Eastern European countries, Hortobagy National Park— a vast area of grasslands and wetlands—is not to be missed.

THE MEDITERRANEAN

Spain boasts of some of the least developed landscapes in Europe. In the south, the wetlands of Coto Doñana National Park provide sanctuary for rare mammals such as the lynx and countless thousands of migratory birds. In the north, the national parks of Aigües Tortes and Ordesa–Monte Perdido protect areas of the beautiful, rugged Pyrenees Mountains. A trip to either of these regions could easily be combined with a visit to the plains of Estremadura, in central Spain, where you will find the greatest number of bird-of-prey species in Europe.

In Italy and Greece, tourist developments and poaching

are still serious threats to wildlife and habitats. In 1991, in an effort to protect its remaining wilderness areas, the Italian government created 13 new national parks. The expansion of the park system means that you are now never far from a national park in Italy. You can thus combine a tour of Rome with a visit to Abruzzo National Park, or a stay in Venice with a trip to the majestic, pink-hued peaks of the Dolomites in the Dolomiti Bellunesi National Park.

Mount Olympus National Park is Greece's most important preserve. The forests that cloak the mountain—the home of the gods in Greek mythology—provide habitat for wolves, eagles, and vultures.

Though some of the beautiful Greek Islands are overrun by tourists, others, most notably Crete, are a paradise for birders and botanists. TW

THE HIGH COUNTRY

Much of Europe's wildlife is concentrated in mountainous areas, such as Abruzzo National Park in Italy (far left). Ibex in the Alps (left). A European brown bear (top).

147

Svalbard

Norway

Head across the Barents Sea from Norway toward the North Pole and, almost at the edge of the pack ice, you will come across a small, isolated group of islands called Svalbard. Their total land area is about 24,000 square miles (63,000 km²), two-thirds of which is covered with the most spectacular glaciers.

The largest of the islands is Spitsbergen, Dutch for "pointed mountains", which was discovered by William Barents in 1596. Norwegian Longyearbyen is the main settlement, while a short distance along the coast is Barentsburg, a Russian town. Both were established to house miners and most of the island's 3,400 people rely on coal mining for a living.

Svalbard is so far north that, for the six months of the polar night (October to March), it is locked in the

Svalbard poppies.

same ice that surrounds the pole itself. In summer, when the sun never sets, this ice melts, leaving the sea ice-free from June to September.

During this brief summer, the islands teem with life. Small, yellow Svalbard poppies, purple mountain saxifrage, and mountain avens are among the 165 plant species found here. The cliffs throng with nesting birds—kittiwakes, black and Brunnich's guillemots, and puffins— while eider ducks, barnacle geese, and Arctic and great skuas inhabit low-lying areas. In all, 108 migratory bird species have been recorded.

More than half of Svalbard is protected. There are three national parks, three nature reserves, fifteen bird sanctuaries, and three plant reserves.

ON THE ICE FLOES

About 20 percent of the world's polar bears are found around Svalbard. Even so, only the fortunate see these animals as they tend to remain out on the pack ice east and north of the islands in summer. The warmer months are the hungry time of year for these animals. The bears can be safely watched from a ship, but they can pose a threat to people on shore. Ringed and bearded

The Monaco Glacier in the Liefdefjord, Spitsbergen (above). A colony of Brunnich's guillemots (right). A walrus (below).

seals may be seen along the coast, but even more spectacular are the walruses that haul out on the ice floes or rest on Moffen, an island walrus sanctuary to the north of Spitsbergen.

From Longyearbyen you can explore Spitsbergen on foot or travel around its coasts by ship. The latter is faster, you see more of the island, and there are plenty of opportunities to go ashore in inflatable boats. The later in summer you go, the more the ice will have melted and the farther you can travel around Spitsbergen. Most cruises last one or two weeks and the longer ones travel to extremely remote areas where sightings of polar bears, for instance, are more frequent. Some tours offer a cruise around the coast by ship and then guided backpacking through the national parks.

Cruise ships generally travel north to Danskoya and sidle right up to the soaring blue cliffs of the 14 July Glacier, which calves from time to time. Many cruises also travel to Reindyrflya, the largest area of tundra on Spitsbergen. This fragile habitat is an excellent place for birding. Most boats land at Ny Alesund on Kong Fjord as well, which is one of the most beautiful parts of the island. Here, at the base for Norwegian Arctic research, scientists from various countries continue the quest for knowledge about this remarkable polar region. MW

TRAVELER'S NOTES

Access International flights to Oslo. Then by air to Longyearbyen via Tromso

When to visit Islands most accessible and days longest mid-June to end Aug

Information Norwegian Tourist Board, PO Box 499, Sentrum 0105, Oslo 1, Norway; tel. (2) 427-044; fax (2) 336-998

Accommodation Hotels and campsites in Longyearbyen. Cruise ships have accommodation on board

Notes Independent travel is difficult; tours are the best way to see these islands. Unwise to venture outside Longyearbyen without an armed guide because of polar bears

Iceland

Iceland

Situated in the Atlantic Ocean, with its north coast just nudging the Arctic Circle, Iceland is a geologist's paradise: a land molded, and still being shaped, by the immense natural forces of earthquakes, volcanoes, and glaciers. The island is a center of volcanic and geothermal activity: lava flows, craters, and thermal springs abound. Iceland's Geysir area, with its spouts of superheated water, gave the world the term "geyser". In a little over 1,000 years, there have been over 30 major volcanic eruptions here.

Iceland was originally covered in birch and willow forests, but these were gradually cleared by settlers. Today, less than 1 percent of the island supports trees and only a quarter will support plant cover. This is not to say that the island is without color. The rocks themselves display a whole palette of oranges, reds, terra cottas, grays, and pale greens, while the lakes and pools add vivid blues. Furthermore, from May onward, wildflowers bloom in patches of bright color and 70 or so species of nesting bird add their own shades and sounds to the landscape.

About 9 percent of Iceland is protected by national parks. The best of these areas can be taken in on a two-week visit by flying to Akureyri, collecting a rental car, and driving to Rekjavik down the eastern side of the island, along Route 1, the Ring Road.

MYVATN LAKE

From Akureyri, it's 60 miles (100 km) to Myvatn Lake, considered by many to be Iceland's most beautiful area. The lake is not large—it takes less than an hour to drive round it— but there is enough in the way of scenery and wildlife to occupy you for four days. Numerous short trails lead to extraordinary examples of past volcanic activity, such as the lava pillars at Kalfastrond and the craters of Skutustadir, as well

Map labels: MILES, 0 35 70, 0 50 100 KM, JOKULSA CANYON NP, Akureyri, Myvatn Lake, Skutustadir, Vatnajökull Icecap, Geysir, Reykjavik, SKAFTAFELL NP

The arctic fox is Iceland's only indigenous mammal.

Myvatn Lake (above). Svartifoss in Skaftafell National Park (right). An eider duck (below) on the Laxá River, north of Myvatn Lake.

as bubbling mud pools and steam vents. Myvatn's shallow waters attract an abundance of water-fowl; indeed, the lake has more species of nesting duck than any other place in Europe. At any one time, there are likely to be around 20,000 ducks of 16 different species, including scaup, tufted duck, Barrow's goldeneye, mallard, pochard, wigeon, teal, pintail, and harlequin.

About 60 miles (100 km) north of Myvatn lies the rocky, barren landscape of Jokulsa Canyon National Park. Here, a glacial river has eroded the soft rock creating a canyon that extends 19 miles (30 km). At Asbyrgi, a forested plain is hemmed in by a horeshoe-shaped gorge. From here you can drive, or take a two-day hike southward along the canyon, to Dettifoss. On the way, you'll see hot springs, basalt pillars, caves, and pockets of lush vegetation. Dettifoss is Europe's most powerful waterfall. Here, the Jokulsa River falls 144 feet (44 m). On a hot day, snowmelt can treble its volume.

South of Jokulsa, the road runs inland, skirting the barren interior and providing superb views of the distant mountains of Vatnajökull. It then returns to the coast, winding along inlets and bays before reaching Skaftafell National Park.

This area is greener and lusher than the north and vascular plants and several tree species grow here. Hiking in the park is excellent: trails lead into the woods and across the glacial outwash plains, and there are guided tours of the glaciers. A one-and-a-half hour walk leads from the campground to Svartifoss Waterfall, where you can scramble along a trail that runs behind the cascade.

South of Vatnajökull, on Breidamerkur Sands, there is the largest arctic skua colony in the northern hemisphere. MW

TRAVELER'S NOTES

Access International flights to Keflavik, near Reykjavik. Domestic flights to 12 airports. Car rental in main towns. Most roads unsealed; 4WD required for interior. Excellent bus services.

When to visit Late May to early Sept. 24-hour daylight during much of that period. Weather is changeable

Information Icelandic Tourist Information Center, Bankastraeti 2, 101 Reykjavik, Iceland; tel. (91) 623-045, fax (91) 624-749

Accommodation Hotels, guesthouses, youth hostels, and campsites in towns. Campsites in some parks. Elsewhere you can camp anywhere (with permission from landowner where relevant)

Lapland

Finland

The region known as Lapland falls almost entirely within the Arctic Circle, where it is light for most of the summer and dark for most of the winter. Lapland covers parts of Norway, Sweden, Finland, and Russia. The indigenous people are the Saami, commonly known as Lapps, and they number about 70,000.

Traditionally, the Saami were nomadic reindeer herders. Now, instead of living in tents and moving with their herds, most Saami live in villages and travel out to their herds on snowmobiles. In some places, this has led to environmental abuse from the use of snowmobiles and from overstocking. In addition, much of their herding range has been lost as a result of mining, logging, the construction of power stations, and pollution from factories and the nuclear power station at Chernobyl. It is only in national parks that portions of the traditional Saami lands remain intact.

The thick fur of the wolverine protects it from the arctic cold.

Lemmenjoki, Finland's largest national park, lies on the country's northern border, where it adjoins Norway's Ovre Anarjokka National Park. Together, these parks form a protected area of 1,544 square miles (4,000 km²)—one of the largest wilderness areas in Europe. Lemmenjoki is one of the main Saami settlement centers and is an excellent place to experience the arctic environment.

EXPLORING LEMMENJOKI

Most visitors enter the park at the village of Njurkulahti, which lies on the Lemmenjoki River. Before there were any roads in the region, rivers were the highways and the Lemmenjoki remains the quickest and easiest way into the park. You can travel the 12 miles (20 km) from Njurkulahti to Kultasatama by boat–taxi, stopping on the way to admire the Ravadaskongas Falls. The rocky river valley runs through open moorland dotted with

Large herds of reindeer (left) roam the moorland around the Lemmenjoki River (above).

Scots pines in which you may spot Siberian tits, pine grosbeaks, waxwings, and Siberian jays, among many other bird species.

You can spend a day exploring the river or head off into the backcountry. Challenging hikes can be made in remote parts of the park, particularly northward toward the Vaskojoki River, where only low-growing mountain birches thrive. By venturing farther afield, you will experience the true flavor of this northern wilderness and have a greater chance of seeing its rarer mammal species, such as brown bear, wolf, and wolverine. You may also see golden eagles and ospreys. Many birds fly south in winter, before snow blankets the ground, but hardy cross-country skiers may see Tengmalm's and great gray owls.

The great gray owl is among the few birds that winter in Lemmenjoki.

Lemmenjoki's national park status means that the environment is strictly protected, but certain human activities continue within its boundaries. Trekkers will come across a number of gold panners' huts. There was a minor gold boom here in the 1940s and a few hardy prospectors persevere.

Lemmenjoki is surrounded by a number of Saami villages and there is one, Lisma, within the park. Herds of Saami reindeer live in the area and not far from Lisma, at Sallivaara, there is a reindeer roundup site that is also an important Saami cultural center. Just 8 miles (14 km) southwest of Inari, there is a reindeer farm where visitors can participate in activities that provide an insight into traditional Saami life. MW

TRAVELER'S NOTES

Access International flights to Helsinki, then flights to Ivalo. From Ivalo, coach to Njurkulahti and Lisma. 750 miles (1,200 km) from Helsinki to Njurkulahti

When to visit May–Sept

Information Finnish Tourist Board, Toolonkatu 11, 00100 Helsinki, Finland;

tel. (0) 403-0011, fax (0) 448-841

Accommodation Campgrounds, huts on trails, and backcountry camping. Accommodation in cabins and private houses in Njurkulahti

Notes Can be cold at night in summer. Masquitoes in July and Aug

The Estonian Archipelago

Estonia

Like a highway rest stop, the Estonian Archipelago provides a place for weary birds to relax and refuel after flying across Europe and before heading north across the Baltic Sea. Here they can rest easy, for the islands of Hiiumaa, Saaremaa, Muhu, and Vormsi, along with numerous islets, are protected by the West Estonian Archipelago Biosphere Reserve. The islands cover 1,560 square miles (4,040 km²) and there are a further 4,300 square miles (11,150 km²) of sea within the reserve.

A Eurasian bittern.

Although the reserve was created after Estonia regained its independence, it owes its pristine character to the policies of the former Soviet Union. The regime prohibited access to much of Estonia's coastline and islands for fear of Western invasion and to discourage Estonian emigration. This has resulted in undeveloped wetlands and lagoons; uncut forests of pine, spruce, and deciduous trees; untrampled dunes and meadows; and undiked peat moors and bogs.

BIRD SANCTUARY

Hiiumaa, which is less than 14 miles (22 km) from the mainland, is the most visited of the islands. Some 1,000 species of plant grow here, many of them at the edge of their range of occurrence. Entomologists have identified more than 1,300 types of beetle.

Hiiumaa is also renowned for its birdlife. The island's Kaina Bay Bird Sanctuary attracts more than 230 species, 70 of them nesting. Because its opening to the sea is so narrow, Kaina Bay is more like a coastal lake than a bay. It covers 3½ square miles (9 km²) and

Mute swans on the waters of the Estonian Archipelago (above). Juniper berries (right). A greylag goose (below).

is dotted with 20 islets that are covered by low herbaceous plants such as juniper, rowan, buckthorn, and wild rose. Thick reed beds crowd the shore.

In spring, migrating birds leave their winter homes on both sides of the Mediterranean and stop off in Kaina Bay before heading north to Scandinavia and the Arctic. Nearly 10,000 water-fowl touch down here, including large flocks of greylag goose, mute swan, crane, and avocet. Whooper swans provide a melodious sound whenever they are present. Many species are unusual for this part of the world, including gadwall and bearded titmouse. Along the coast, you'll come across redshanks, lapwings, and meadow pipits. Sedge warblers, reed warblers, and bitterns live among the reed thickets.

The Orjaku Nature Path provides access to the reserve. It crosses meadows and winds between juniper clumps and reeds beside the water. At points along the route, wildlife observation towers have been built to provide elevated views.

ECOTOURISTS NEEDED

Estonia has done much to preserve these islands but years of economic hardship have left the government hard-pressed to finance additional conservation measures. More protection will be needed as industrial development grows through-out the Baltic region. Major threats to fragile coastal areas like Kaina Bay include increasing amounts of oil being transported over Baltic waters and the construction of marine terminals and oil refineries in neighboring countries.

Ecotourism can be used to raise awareness among Estonians of their natural resources and can play an important role in promoting and financing environmental programs to safeguard the islands. **DH**

TRAVELER'S NOTES

Access *International flights to Tallinn. Bus leaves Tallinn bus station 3 times a day for Kardla on Hiiumma. Trip includes ferry ride*

When to visit *Apr–May for spring bird migration. Snow from Nov through Feb. May–Aug warmer, but be prepared for cold, wet spells*

Information *The Hiiumaa Center for the Biosphere Reserve, Vabrikuvaljak I, Kardla, EE3200, Estonia; tel. 469-6276*

Accommodation *Hotels and inns on island*

Notes *Obtain trail map for Orjaku Nature Path*

The Scottish Highlands

United Kingdom

The Scottish Highlands are one of the last wild places in Europe. Within a relatively small area you can visit expanses of moor, dark lochs, towering mountains, and great stretches of rocky shore.

Much of the Highlands was once covered in forests of broad-leafed trees and pine. Most of the trees have disappeared, cleared by people, grazing animals, and fire, but in the Cairngorm Mountains, in the heart of the Highlands, small areas of pine forest remain. This granite range covers some 400 square miles (1,000 km²). The rounded peaks of Cairn Gorm, Cairn Toul, Braeriach, and Ben MacDui (Scotland's second highest peak at 4,296 feet [1,310 m]) dominate the area, their summits streaked with snow even in early summer.

About 100 square miles (260 km²) of the range have been designated a National Nature Reserve—the largest in the United Kingdom.

The reserve has a number of trails and small visitor centers. South of Aviemore, near Inverdruie, a nature trail runs through the forest of pines and junipers around Loch an Eilean. Here you may encounter roe deer, red squirrels, and blue and mountain hare, which are all native. Capercaillie and black grouse, two of the most distinctive Highland bird species, are also found in the forest, and you may see otters near the water.

A few miles farther south, beyond Balnespick, at Achlean, a track zigzags up Càrn Ban Mór to moors covered in heather and deergrass. Here there are fewer animals, but you might see a mountain hare. Higher up, on the slopes of Sgòran Dubh and Sgor Gaoith, conditions are similar to those in the arctic. Moss campion and wood rush are among the few plants that can

The name capercaillie derives from the Gaelic for "horse of the woods".

156

Loch an Eilean in the Cairngorms (above). A mountain stream on Rhum (right). A young sea eagle (below).

withstand the wind and cold but you will also find mountain rockcress and alpine speedwell. Golden eagles and peregrine falcons soar above the slopes, as do osprey, although these birds are best seen at the famous osprey sanctuary at Boat of Garten, which can be reached by steam train from Aviemore.

OVER THE SEA TO RHUM

To view Scotland's coastal wildlife, head west (via Fort William) to Mallaig, where boats leave for the Hebrides. All the Hebridean islands are fascinating, but none more so than Rhum, which has been designated a UNESCO Biosphere Reserve. All journeys on Rhum, which belongs to the Nature Conservancy Council, must be made on foot. Here you can walk across heather-clad moors, where red deer roam, to storm-tossed beaches where gray and common seals haul out.

In the south, the Cuillin Mountains provide terrific ridge walking. Alpine flowers are plentiful and in the valleys stunted birch, holly, hazel, rowan, and wild hyacinth grow. Golden eagles are found here, as are sea eagles, reintroduced from Norway in 1981 (the species became extinct on Rhum early this century). Along the sea cliffs, there are large colonies of Manx shearwaters, guillemots, razorbills, fulmars, and kittiwakes. You will also see puffins, arctic terns, and shags.

Limiting the number of overnight visitors on Rhum has helped preserve its wild environment. In the Cairngorms, however, the situation is different. Aviemore is Britain's largest winter-sports center and proposals to expand the ski fields have resulted in considerable conflict between developers and environmentalists. EP

TRAVELER'S NOTES

Access International flights to Glasgow and Edinburgh. By car, it's about 3 hours to Aviemore from Edinburgh and 4 hours from Glasgow. From Aviemore to Mallaig it's about 3 hours. Trains from Glasgow and Edinburgh to Aviemore; trains from Glasgow to Mallaig. Ferry to Rhum

When to visit May–Sept. Rain, wind, and snow the rest of the year

Information Aviemore Tourist Information, Grampian Road, Aviemore, Scotland; tel. (01479) 810-363; Mallaig Tourist Information,

Mallaig, Scotland; tel. (01687) 2170

Accommodation Hotels and camping in towns in Cairngorm; huts and camping in Cairngorm Reserve. Luxury and hostel accommodation at Kinloch Hotel on Rhum. Camping on Rhum requires permit

Notes Weather is very fickle, so rain gear, waterproof hiking boots, and topographic maps are essential for all hikes

Bialowieza

Poland

Visiting Bialowieza Forest is like stepping back in time. It is the sole remaining patch of low-land virgin forest in central Europe, an area that was once largely covered with trees. This forest of evergreens and giant deciduous trees spreads across 585 square miles (1,515 km²) of almost entirely flat countryside in northeastern Poland and western Belarus. About 21 square miles (54 km²) in Poland is protected by Bialowieza National Park, which was set up in 1821. In Belarus, the Belovezhskaja Pushha National Park protects another 340 square miles (880 km²).

A wild boar and its young.

Bialowieza's preservation results from its having been a favored hunting ground of Polish kings, Lithuanian princes, and Russian tsars, who insisted that it remain in its pristine state. Today, most of Bialowieza National Park is still under strict control, and you can only visit the central part of the forest on a guided tour. Visitors can, however, roam freely on roads and trails around the perimeter of the park.

INTO THE WOODS

Starting at the entrance to the park in the town of Bialowieza, tours take visitors into the heart of the forest, along a 4 mile (7 km) track. Since the forest has never been logged, the ground is covered with fallen trees and rotting vegetation. Some of the giant oaks, spruce, limes, and hornbeams stretch as much as 160 feet (50 m) into the sky. Here and there, marshes and peat bogs have formed clearings.

Spring is when the forest really comes alive. In the drier areas, among fallen trees and carpets of mosses, you will come upon rare flowers, including lesser and greater butterfly orchids, bird's-nest orchids, wood anemones, and stars of Bethlehem. In marshy

A herd of European bison in Bialowieza forest in winter (above). The Biebrza River Basin (right) is one of Europe's largest untouched areas of marshland. The Clark's nutcracker (below).

areas, bog rosemary, cranberry bushes, and carnivorous sundews bloom among the peatmoss.

The forest is rich in fauna, including red deer, wild boar, and moose. Wolves and lynx also dwell here but are seldom seen. Nutcrackers, eagle owls, and black storks are among the many bird species.

The park's main attraction is the European bison. These animals once inhabited much of this region, but habitat destruction and hunting almost led to their extinction. By the early 1920s, the only existing specimens were in captivity. In 1923, an international rescue effort was set up, which has been successful in breeding and reintroducing the bison to the wild.

Today, there are about 3,000 European bison worldwide, of which 250 live in Bialowieza National Park. They can be viewed in the park's Bison Reserve, but also roam free in the forest and adjacent fields.

There is much else to see in this corner of Poland. About 90 miles (145 km) to the northwest lies Biebrzanski National Park. The park is best known for the beaver colonies that give the Biebrza River its name, but elk, deer, and wild boar may be spotted around the pockets of forest. These wetlands are also famous for their birds, including white and black storks and rare waterbirds such as water rail and double snipe.

The main threat to these unique environments is pollution. Acid rain is poisoning parts of the forest, and the lack of efficient sewers and the dumping of waste in rivers is having a detrimental effect on local waterways. TW

TRAVELER'S NOTES

Access International flights to Warsaw, then either rent a car or take a train or bus for 125 mile (200 km) trip to Bialowieza. All main towns connected by train; buses connect villages.

When to visit May–Sept vegetation lushest. Oct–April cold and snowy. Dec–Feb for sleigh rides

Information Polish Tourist Association (PTTK), ul Senatorska 11, 00 075

Warsaw, Poland; tel. (22) 265-753. For tours of Bialowieza NP, contact Bialowieski Park Narodowy, Park Palacowy 5, 17-230 Bialowieza, Poland; tel. (835) 12306, fax (835) 12323

Accommodation Hotels and campgrounds in and around Bialowieza, Bialystok. Rooms for rent in private homes. No camping in parks

The Tatras

Slovakia and Poland

The Tatras are a part of the great crescent of the Carpathian Mountains that stretches over 750 miles (1,200 km) from Poland south to Romania. These majestic, jagged peaks were uplifted about a million years ago and then shaped by glacial forces.

For decades, the highest peaks in the Tatras have been protected by the High Tatras National Park, which lies on the Slovakian–Polish border and is managed by both countries. There are about 200 miles (300 km) of well-maintained hiking paths in the park. These trails will show

you the best of this dramatic landscape, taking you past waterfalls and clear mountain lakes and through narrow passes between dark granite peaks.

Deep, green forests, made up mostly of spruce but sprinkled with beech and mountain maple, surround the mountains to about 5,000 feet (1,500 m) and cover a large part of the park. At higher levels, the forests give way to twisted dwarf pines. Still higher, there are alpine meadows, which extend up to 7,500 feet (2,300 m) above sea level.

AMONG THE PEAKS

One of the best ways to explore the region is to take the Magistrale, a 28 mile (46 km) hike that runs the length of the park, from Podbanské in the West Tatras to Lake Zelené in the eastern White Tatras. It's one of the oldest trails in the region and offers the hiker fantastic panoramas of mountain lakes, craggy summits, and the forests surrounding the mountains. The trail is well signposted, and there are comfortable mountain huts along the way.

Looking down on Lake Popradské from the Magistrale Trail.

At Lake Popradské, a rewarding detour leads to the summit of Mount Rysi (8,194 feet [2,499 m]), Poland's highest mountain. From the peak you look out over the entire range. It's a strenuous seven-hour round trip, but it's well worth the effort.

Along the higher-altitude paths you will pass through alpine meadows carpeted with wildflowers. You'll see plants such as glacial carnations, glacial androsace, edelweiss, and glacial gentian. There are over 1,200 types of vascular plant in the High Tatras and hundreds of kinds of moss, lichen, and fungus.

A number of rare animals live in the park. You may spot a Tatra chamois, a type of mountain goat found only in this area. Bears, lynx, wildcats, and wolves, long extinct in most areas of Europe, also live here, but they are shy. In the forests,

you're sure to see roe deer. With a little luck, you will also come across rare grouse, such as the hazel grouse, black grouse, and capercaillie.

There are other national parks in the Tatras that are well worth a visit. In the Low Tatras National Park, bears are more common than in the higher mountains and you can see rare birds of prey such as the eagle owl and the peregrine falcon. The Low Tatras is a paradise for spelunkers, boasting one of the largest cave systems in Europe.

The most serious threat to this region is, unfortunately, the growing number of tourists. In order to prevent further damage to its fragile habitat, the White Tatras area of the High Tatras National Park is now closed to visitors. TW

The Tatras from Lake Strbské (top). Edelweiss (above). A lynx (right).

TRAVELER'S NOTES

Access *International flights to Brno in Slovakia, or Katowice and Kraków in Poland. Train and bus to park entrances at Zakopane in Poland and Stary Smokovec, Tatranske Lomnica, and Strbské Pleso in Slovakia*

When to visit *May–Sept for wildflowers. Late Aug to Oct best for hiking. Dec–Mar for snowshoeing and cross-country skiing*

Information *Satur, Mileticova 1, SK-84272 Bratislava, Slovakia; tel. (7) 53816*

Accommodation *Hotels in towns. Numerous campgrounds, but backcountry camping not permitted in parks*

Notes *Weather very changeable; always carry warm clothing and check local conditions before you set out*

The Alps

Italy and France

Few regions need as little introduction as the Alps. Their
stony heights extend from
Slovenia to France and their
name has become synonymous
with high, mountainous regions.

Gran Paradiso National Park
in northwestern Italy, and Vanoise
National Park in France, which adjoins it, lie
only a few miles south of the Alps' highest
peaks—Mont Blanc and Monte Rosa—and
constitute one of the largest protected landscapes in Europe. They are an
enchanting world of forested
valleys, alpine meadows, scree,
glaciers, snow, and craggy peaks.

The two parks include similar
habitats. Though large areas of
forest have been logged over the
years, in the valleys there are
still beech, oak, and larch trees
scattered among the Swiss pine
and spruce communities. These
woodlands are home to wild boars, and
foxes, ermines, and badgers prowl at night.

The high-country is characterized by lush
alpine meadows which in spring are decorated by
lady's-slipper orchids, paradise lilies, Turk's-cap
lilies, and blue monk's hood. You may catch
sight of marmots, but you are more likely to hear
their shrill whistles—alarm calls to other marmots.

The highest areas are the domain of the ibex
(a mountain goat), the chamois, and a number
of bird species including the golden eagle,
Cornish chough, and rock ptarmigan. You will
also find rare alpine plants such as edelweiss and
Swiss androsace.

Either park provides an excellent introduction to this environment. In Vanoise,
you can make short hikes from the
villages of Termignon and Pralognan.
Bonneval, a traditional village

*Gran Paradiso National Park was
established as a sanctuary for the ibex.*

The peaks of Gran Paradiso in winter (above). In summer, the alpine meadows glow with wildflowers (right).

on the eastern edge of the park, serves as a convenient base. On the Italian side of the border, the villages of Champorcher and Cogne are both delightful places to stay.

GRAN PARADISO

Gran Paradiso National Park lies in Italy's north-western corner. Its chain of peaks culminates in the summit of Gran Paradiso itself, which towers 13,315 feet (4,061 m) above sea level.

The reason for the park's existence is the ibex. This species was once common throughout the Alps. By the mid-nineteenth century, however, as a result of hunting and poaching, the only ibex that remained were in the Gran Paradiso region. In 1856, King Victor Emmanuel II made the area his private hunting grounds. Under the care of his gamekeepers, the ibex thrived. In 1922, the reserve became a national park.

There are now 3,000 of these elegant animals in the park. They spend summer high in the

Marmots are found in the high country.

mountains, descending to the lower slopes in winter. Unfortunately, many of these slopes lie outside the park and the ibex are there-fore still vulnerable to hunting and poaching.

There are many trails in Gran Paradiso. One of the most popular is the Alta Via 2 which takes you from Courmayeur, down through the park, to Champorcher. It takes at least seven days to complete, but you can walk sections of it, such as from Eaux-Rousses to Cogne, which is about a nine-hour round trip. An easier and somewhat shorter trek goes from Pont up to Terre, through forests and across meadows.

Much of the land within Gran Paradiso is in private hands and remains vulnerable to logging and hunting. In both parks, hordes of summer visitors threaten the fragile habitat. TW

TRAVELER'S NOTES

Access International flights to Paris, Geneva, Turin; domestic flights to Chambéry and Aix-les-Bains. Car or bus to smaller towns

When to visit Sept–Oct best for hiking. July–Aug peak season and best avoided

Information Parc National de la Vanoise, 135 rue du Docteur Julliand, BP 705, F-73008 Chambéry Cedex, France; tel. 7962-3054, fax 7996-3718. Parco Nazionale Gran Paradiso,

Via della Rocca 47, 101.23 Turin, Italy; tel. (011) 817-1187

Accommodation Hotels and guesthouses in villages throughout region. Huts and campgrounds in parks

Notes In Vanoise, the Friends of the National Park offer guided walks in summer: contact the park or local tourist offices for information

The Central Apennines

Italy

The Apennines form the back-bone of Italy, extending 870 miles (1,400 km) from Genoa, near the French border, to the southern tip of the peninsula in Calabria. At the heart of this range, in the Central Apennines, a number of reserves protect an extraordinary and unique ecosystem that was once widespread throughout central Italy. Here, only a few hours' drive from the historic centers of Florence, Rome, and Naples, significant populations of bear and wolf roam over alpine terrain and through ancient beech forests.

The Abruzzo chamois is now being reintroduced to other parts of the Apennine range.

Jewel of the Apennines and the Italian parks system is Abruzzo National Park. Set up in 1922 to protect dwindling populations of brown bear and Abruzzo chamois, the park has successfully combined conservation with economic development. Local communities have benefited from ecotourism, to the extent that some villages have requested that the park be expanded to include them.

Abruzzo National Park currently encompasses 170 square miles (440 km²) of forests and limestone mountains that rise steeply from 2,000 feet (600 m) to over 6,500 feet (2,000 m). At lower levels, you'll find mixed broadleaf forests of downy oak, turkey oak, field maple, and hop-hornbeam. However, the habitat that best characterizes Abruzzo is the ancient beech forest that covers 60 percent of the park. Parts of this forest are many hundreds of years old.

On walks through the beech woods, along trails such as the Val Fondillo and the Valle Iannanghera (both easy day walks), you'll find songbirds; woodpeckers such as the white-backed woodpecker; red deer; and rare plants such as the beautiful lady's-slipper orchid. The park's bears, wolves, and wildcats are elusive, but

164

Abruzzo National Park (above). The Camosciara Trail begins in the beech forest (right). A European wolf (below).

there are healthy populations of all three species. The wolf, in particular, has thrived in recent years. Pulled back from the brink of extinction in the 1970s, it has dramatically extended its range northward along the Apennines toward the French Alps. With continued protection, this population could spread into central Europe.

IN THE HIGH COUNTRY

By the time the park was founded, most of the forest above 5,900 feet (1,800 m) had been cleared for grazing, but amid the alpine meadows you can still find occasional thickets of mountain pine, a species now rare in the rest of the Apennines. On the Camosciara and Passo dei Monaci trails in the high country, you're likely to see the Abruzzo chamois. This relative of the alpine chamois once roamed throughout the region. Look, too, for rock partridges, choughs, and golden eagles. In spring, columbines, irises, lilies, and gentians bloom in profusion.

Many of the animals and birds found at the highest levels, such as the snow vole and the snow bunting, arrived during the last ice age and are now found only on the highest peaks in Italy.

The success of Abruzzo National Park has inspired the creation of other reserves, most notably three nearby national parks: Maiella, which protects the wildest backcountry in the Apennines; Gran Sasso–Laga, site of the highest peaks in the range; and Sibillini, an area rich in myths that is home to important populations of golden eagle and peregrine falcon. Together, these reserves constitute one of Europe's most important conservation networks. This was recognized in 1995, with the formation of the APE (Apennine Park of Europe)—a national body set up to coordinate conservation throughout the region. PP

TRAVELER'S NOTES

Access International flights to Rome. 2-hour drive to Pescasseroli, or train to Avezzano then bus to Pescasseroli. Summer bus service from Rome

When to visit Year-round, though snow is likely any time Nov–Apr

Information Information Office, Viale Tito Livio 12, 00136 Rome, Italy; tel. (06) 3540-3331, fax (06) 3540-3253. Information Office, Vico Consultore 1-67032, Pescasseroli, AQ, Italy; tel. (0863) 91955

Accommodation Hotels and guesthouses in towns and villages, camping in parks

Notes Quotas in force on some trails in summer—book in advance

Southern Spain

Spain

For wildlife enthusiasts, the sun-scorched landscapes of southern Spain are among the most rewarding regions in Europe. Driving west and then south from Madrid, you see range upon range of sierras, underlining the fact that, after Switzerland, Spain is Europe's most mountainous country. The landscape gradually becomes more distinctively Mediterranean. The air is laced with the scent of pine trees, wild lavender, thyme, and lentisk, and the fields are full of cistus, asphodel, and oleander.

In the province of Estremadura, two wild areas stand out—the Sierra de Gredos and Monfragüe Natural Park. Farther south, in Andalusia, lie the great unspoiled wetlands of Coto Doñana, Spain's most famous national park. All three areas can be seen on a short tour—allow at least a week. For birders in particular, they are a delight.

Eagle owls are resident at Monfragüe.

ESTREMADURA

Of all the provinces of Spain, Estremadura—the "land beyond"—remains the one least touched by the late twentieth century. Austere and slow to change, it is the wildest and the most intensely Spanish.

As in most other parts of Europe, the native forests here were cleared over the centuries to make way for grazing animals and to supply wood for shipbuilding. The pattern of forest clearance that occurred in Estremadura created two main types of habitat: wide, arid plains that resemble steppe or savanna, and fields dotted with clumps of oak trees—a landscape known as *dehesa*.

The oak species in the *dehesa* include the evergreen oak, whose branches are lopped to make charcoal, and the cork oak whose wrinkly bark is regularly stripped, leaving the bare trunks a rich terra-cotta red. Free-ranging pigs, sheep, and black bulls graze under the oaks. The most fertile land is ploughed once every three years to grow grains. For the rest of the time, it lies fallow, producing wildflowers and grasses. This is a type of agriculture that has survived since the Middle Ages, and the *dehesa* is now strictly protected,

El Salto del Gitano and the River Tajo in Monfragüe Natural Park (above). Storks nesting on Herguijuelas Castle (right).

with heavy fines levied against anyone who clears trees.

The *dehesa* is a paradise for birds. Birds of prey, in particular, thrive here because they can use the trees for nesting and as perches from which they can easily spot prey in the open fields. The savanna offers them further scope for hunting. This ideal raptor habitat has resulted in Estremadura having the highest concentration of birds of prey in Europe. Among the many species are goshawks; black-winged kites; and booted, short-toed, Bonelli's, and Spanish imperial eagles. Perhaps most notable are the cinereous and Egyptian vultures, whose constantly circling presence underscores southern Spain's closeness to Africa.

On the arid plains, shrikes, hawks, and buzzards perch on fence posts and telephone wires. You'll also find a number of birds here that are rare else-where in Europe, including the great bustard, little bustard, pin-tailed sandgrouse, and black-billed sandgrouse.

In March, white storks build their huge, stick nests on almost every village church tower, and vast numbers of migrant birds arrive from Africa, including cuckoos, nightingales, bee-eaters, hoopoes, and woodchat shrikes.

THE SIERRA DE GREDOS

The most spectacular approach to Estremadura is from Avila, following the road to Plasencia over Puerto de Tornavecas Pass.

A cinereous vulture and chick on the nest.

TRAVELER'S NOTES

Access International flights to Madrid; car to Plasencia (5 hours via Avila); Plasencia to Monfragüe (15 mins); Monfragüe to Coto Doñana (7 hours). Trains and buses from Madrid to Plasencia. International flights to Seville, close to Coto Doñana.

When to visit March–May for birds and wildflowers; June–Aug very hot

Information Spanish National Tourist Office, Barajas Airport, Madrid, Spain; tel. (01) 305-8656

Accommodation Hotels and para-dores (excellent state-run hotels in historic buildings) in towns. Campsites at Navaconsejo and elsewhere in Jerte Valley

Notes Local guides recommended for extended hikes in the Gredos Mtns: Sociedad de Guias del Valle de Jerte, tel. (927) 472-015. Coto Doñana cruises, tel. (956) 363-813; 4WD tours tel. (959) 430-432

Once you are over the pass, the road drops steeply into the Jerte Valley, where cherries grow in terraced orchards on the hillsides.

From the village of Navaconcejo, midway down the valley, the 15 mile (24 km) Carlos Quinto hiking trail runs up into the Sierra de Gredos to Jarandilla de la Vera in the neighboring valley. A wonderful variety of alpine flowers grows on these slopes, including drifts of dwarf narcissi in March, and you will have a good chance of seeing eagles and vultures. This is also the home of one of the largest populations of Spanish ibex.

Although lacking the grandeur of the Pyrenees, the bald, granite summits of the Sierra de Gredos reach a height of 8,504 feet (2,594 m) at Pico de Almanzor, and are covered with snow from November to March. Between the summits, rushing streams have formed deep gorges, sometimes crossed by medieval stone packhorse bridges. There are wild boar and red deer in the woods; eagles haunt the high tops; and the lower reaches are rich in butterflies, including the unusual Spanish festoon.

A red deer stag at rest.

Common cranes flying over the oak trees of the dehesa (above). Portugal and southern Spain are the only places in Europe where the azure-winged magpie is resident (left). It is also found in Asia.

MONFRAGÜE NATURAL PARK

For close-up views of Estremadura wildlife and a taste of what the landscape was like before the trees were cleared, head for Monfragüe Natural Park, southwest of Plasencia. The park takes its name from the twelfth-century castle ruins, perched on a crag above the River Tajo. In the middle of this century, parts of the park were cleared and planted with eucalyptus trees. But, in 1979, thanks to the tireless campaigning of Jesus Garzon, a visionary Spanish conservationist, Monfragüe's remaining 69 square miles (178 km²) of Mediterranean forest were saved for the nation.

Monfragüe is a haven for Mediterranean flora and fauna. Lynx and wild boar roam woods and glades where wildflowers such as peonies and snake's-head fritillary grow. The park is a stronghold for two of Europe's rarest birds: the black stork and the cinereous vulture. Both species breed here, as do Spanish imperial eagles and eagle owls. It's worth spending at least a day here, if only to watch the griffon vultures soar around the twin pinnacles of El Salto del Gitano—the Gypsy's Leap. An hour's walk from the information center will bring you to Monfragüe Castle— another great viewpoint for vulture-watching.

COTO DOÑANA NATIONAL PARK

As you head south into Andalusia, Spain's deep south, the country becomes even drier. The focus for wildlife enthusiasts here is Coto Doñana National Park, which covers 298 square miles (772 km²) of the celebrated freshwater marshes at the mouth of the Guadalquivir River.

Named after Doña Ana, wife of the seventh Duke of Medina Sidonia 400 years ago, this former hunting reserve is now Spain's largest wildlife stronghold. In a unique position midway beween Europe and Africa, its wetlands are a vital stopover for migrating ducks and geese. More than 250,000 wildfowl pass through the Coto Doñana every year, together with large numbers of flamingos, marsh harriers, waders, shrikes, and rare birds of prey such as the Spanish imperial eagle. The main migration periods occur in February and April and between September and November.

Here, too, among the mosaic of dunes, marshes, pines, and cork oak forests, roam red deer and the elusive lynx.

In order to ensure protection for this wealth of wildlife, access to the park is strictly controlled. Visits are for the most part confined to four-hour guided four-wheel-drive tours along the sandy shores and a few regularly used tracks. You can also take a four-hour cruise from Sanlucar de Barrameda, which includes two short guided hikes and the opportunity to spot red deer and wild boar. Otherwise, birders should head for the marshland village of El Rocio that lies at the edge of the park. This is the closest spot from which you can freely observe Doñana's bird species.   BJ

EUROPE'S LAST GREAT WETLAND

Most Mediterranean river basins have been robbed of much of their water for agriculture, and the Guadalquivir is no exception, with grandiose rice-growing schemes around the delta threatening to drain the famous Coto Doñana marshlands dry. A few years ago, there was even a plan to turn the area into a holiday playground. Fortunately, after an international outcry, the scheme was dropped.

In 1993, conservationists, farmers, planners, and politicians agreed on a plan of sustainable development for those areas of the delta outside the park. In 1995, funding for the plan was forthcoming. Some of the money is being used to help local farmers to farm in more environmentally friendly ways. Remaining natural woodlands will be preserved and alien eucalyptus plantations replaced by native trees.

Money will also be spent on protecting the region's natural water sources, particularly its aquifers. It is also hoped that controlling farming and development will increase the amount of fresh water reaching wildlife in the wetlands.

Flamingos in Coto Doñana (above). A black stork (right).

The White Mountains

Greece

The Greek islands shine like pearls cast upon the sea by gods. Of the hundreds of islands that dot the Aegean Sea, Crete is the largest and offers the greatest range of habitats. The island's outstanding natural area is the aptly named White Mountains.

These peaks rise out of the sea, shining bright with snow in winter and treeless, shrubless karstic rock in summer. This rugged wilderness has changed little since the days of the Minoans. Trails lead to deep gorges, including spectacular Samariá Gorge, and climbers can tackle a dozen summits that are over 6,500 feet (2,000 m). At the foot of the mountains, coves and beaches lie waiting to be discovered by ecotravelers escaping the tourist hordes that have overrun so many of the Greek islands.

Peonies are among the many native wildflowers.

The only way to discover the White Mountains is on foot, via a series of hiking trails that lead deep into the range. So beautiful and rich in natural heritage is the area around Samariá Gorge that it was made a national park in 1962.

The most popular trail follows the gorge for 10 miles (16 km) from its mouth at Ayía Roúmeli on the south coast to its head at Ksilóskala. Steep walls of limestone that soar as high as 1,000 feet (300 m) line a twisting river that is a raging torrent half the year and the other half a quiet trickle. Cypress trees and oleander sprout impossibly from the faces of sheer cliffs like tropical epiphytes. Golden eagles and Egyptian vultures soar on thermals overhead. Wild goats scamper along rocky ledges. And everywhere there is an air of mystery.

You will find an incredible collection of unusual plants and wildflowers growing in this rocky world. Crete, as a whole, is a botanist's dream. The island has

Map labels: Haniá, Omalós, Ksilóskala, Samariá Gorge, SAMARIÁ GORGE NP, Pákhnes, Ayía Roúmeli, MILES, KM

The peaks of the White Mountains (above). The trail through Samariá Gorge (right). A golden eagle (below).

been isolated from the mainland for at least 10 million years, resulting in a large number of plants evolving into separate species. Approximately 10 percent of the 2,000 or so flowering plants found on the island are endemic.

The endemics found in Samariá Gorge include the Cretan wall lettuce. Not a lettuce at all but a member of the bellflower family, this plant features long spikes bearing blue flowers. Another colorful endemic is *Ebenus cretica*, a silver-gray, low shrub with masses of spikes bearing pink, pea-shaped flowers.

The gorge is also home to plenty of birds and mammals. Bonelli's eagles and griffon vultures live in aeries built atop the cliffs. Crag martins career crazily down the rock faces, while choughs swarm like insects and common crossbills and yellow and green citril finches feed among the trees.

Resident mammals include stone martens, foxes, badgers, wildcats, weasels, and dormice. The Cretan wild goat, called *kri-kri* by the locals, is a rare beast whose existence was one of the main reasons for making the region a national park. Males sport huge horns that curve backwards.

From the gorge's end at Ksilóskala, hikers can take another trail for a high-level traverse of the mountain range. The trail provides access to the highest summits, including 8,043 foot (2,413 m) Pákhnes. Climbers' huts are strategically placed along the route, offering shelter and food. The trip promises spectacular views and a challenge for all who are willing to tackle it.

DH

TRAVELER'S NOTES

Access *International flights to Athens, domestic flights to Haniá. 1½-hour bus trip from there to head of gorge, or ferry to mouth of gorge*

When to visit *May–Oct. Samariá Gorge open these months, sunrise to sunset*

Information *Ministry of Agriculture and Forestry, National Parks Section, 3–5 Ippocratous St, Athens, Greece. The Ellinikós Orivatikós Síndhesmos (The Greek Alpine Club), Kentrikí*

Platía 16, 136 71, Akhamés, Greece; tel. (01) 246-1528

Accommodation *Hotels and guesthouses at Ayía Roúmeli and Omalós. Camping outside Ayía Roúmeli. Climbers' huts in mountains*

Notes *No camping permitted in Samariá Gorge*

Africa

ECOTRAVEL *in* AFRICA

In Africa, wildlife is present on a massive scale. Nowhere else boasts such a panoply of mammals—more than 60 species of ungulate alone—and the birdlife is equally extraordinary.

A great, rolling plateau scalloped by massive depressions, Africa stretches from the Sahara and the Nile Basin in the north, through belts of woodland and equatorial rain forest spanning West and Central Africa, to swamps, deserts, and high veld in southern Africa. East Africa offers spectacular scenery, most of the continent's lakes, a series of volcanic peaks, and wildlife-filled savannas.

NORTH AFRICA

North Africa is dominated by the Sahara Desert, a vast expanse of rock and shifting sands where the heat is fierce and wildlife is rare. Oases, however, offer pockets of delight. Merzouga, in southern Morocco, and Lake Ichkeul, in Tunisia, are two of many havens for flamingos and migratory waterfowl; and mountainous Tassili N'Ajjer National Park in southern Algeria (currently off-limits to tourists for political reasons), is remarkable for its permanent flowing water that sustains 20 species of large mammal.

In Morocco, the Atlas Mountains—a stark landscape of multicolored gorges slicing between snow-capped peaks—offer rewarding hiking. To the east, in Egypt, the lakes of the Nile Delta are a great draw for birders, and the coral reefs of the Red Sea offer superlative diving.

THE NATURE TRAIL *Lammergeiers (left) are found in parts of Africa, southern Europe, and central Asia. A school of lyre-tailed goldfish in the Red Sea (below). A hiker on Mount Toubkal in the Atlas Mountains (below right).*

CENTRAL AND WEST AFRICA

Overgrazing fosters the spread of the Sahara along the northern Sahel, but farther south there are belts of savanna, semi-humid woodlands, and dense forests culminating in equatorial rain forest, with mangrove swamps along the coasts of countries such as Senegal, Ivory Coast, and Cameroon. At the heart of the region lies the vast Congo Basin, swathed in rain forest that is second only to that of the Amazon in extent and diversity.

Among the many parks in this region, Comroe National Park in Ivory Coast boasts good tourist facilities, all three species of African crocodile, eleven species of monkey, and many other mammal species.

Long, wet summers make it difficult to move around the dense jungles of Zaire

MO

WESTERN SAHARA

MAURITANIA

SENEGAL

THE GAMBIA

GUINEA-BISSAU   GUINEA

SIERRA LEONE   IVO CO

LIBERIA

and Congo. Some areas, such as Congo's Noubale-Ndoki National Park, can only be reached via muddy logging tracks or by river steamers resembling the *African Queen*.

Logging and hunting threaten even the remotest regions of the Congo Basin. Congo may have lost as much as three-quarters of its woodlands to foreign logging companies in recent decades. War and political instability in several countries in the region have devastated wildlife and kept tourists away. Manovo-Gounda-St Floris National Park in the Central African Republic, for

example, has been severely affected by strife in Chad and Sudan. Heavily armed poachers sell ivory and horn to buy firearms for warfare.

East Africa

East Africa's vast savannas and semi-arid lands, where the animals are usually in full view, offer ideal conditions for wildlife watching.

Kenya and Tanzania are Africa's top tourist attractions. They have numerous national parks and the facilities to cater to those wishing to watch wildlife in comfort.

For example, you can combine a classic "tented" safari—camping in the bush—with stays at some of the finest lodges, many of which are located at prime wildlife-viewing spots.

The central plateau of Kenya is bisected by the Great Rift Valley, dotted with bird-filled lakes. Volcanic mountains rise from the edge of the Rift, such as Mount Kenya, clothed in montane forest and capped with alpine moorland. To the north, the plains drop away to semi-arid lands where wildlife is plentiful, such as in Meru and Samburu national parks. To the east lie coastal forests, mangroves, and coral reefs in the Indian Ocean, such as in Malindi Marine National Park. Along the western border there is great birding in the Kakamega rain forest and around Lake Victoria, and the renowned Masai Mara lies in the south.

Pressures on the wildlife are extreme, however. These include poaching for ivory and horn, which has reduced elephant and rhino populations; stress caused by tourist hordes in places such as Masai Mari and Amboseli; and competition for land from the country's rapidly increasing human population. The Kenyan

ON HIGH *A trekker in the Great Rift Valley (above). Viewing mountain gorillas in Uganda (right) normally involves a long hike through dense jungle. An elephant on the plains, backed by cloud-shrouded Mount Kilimanjaro (below).*

government has recently initiated policies to protect wildlife, including an aggressive anti-poaching campaign.

Tanzania boasts some of the world's best-known eco-tours: a hike for the fit up Mount Kilimanjaro, Africa's highest mountain (19,340 feet [5,899 m]); a safari to the Serengeti; and a visit to the Ngorongoro Crater, a vast caldera packed with wildlife. In remote Selous Game Reserve, in the south, you can explore on foot or by boat.

To the west, gorilla-tracking safaris once led into Rwanda and Burundi, where mountain gorillas live on the slopes of volcanoes. As a result of war, these countries are currently off-limits to tourists.

In neighboring Uganda, however, you can find gorillas in Bwindi Impenetrable Forest National Park and Mgahinga Gorilla National Park. Uganda also boasts plains animals in profusion and great concentrations of crocodiles at Kabalega National Park.

SOUTHERN AFRICA

Until recently, political instability prevented many southern African nations from focusing on tourism, but the situation is gradually improving. The region has larger concentrations of wildlife and fewer tourists than East Africa, and its parks are well managed. High temperatures in the interior can make wildlife viewing uncomfortable, so the dry season—from April to October—is the best time to visit.

Most of Botswana and Namibia is desert, yet these countries are rich in wildlife. Between January and April, rains in Namibia's Etosha Pan draw astonishing concentrations of elephants, giraffes, zebras, and lions; and the awesome solitude of Botswana's vast Kalahari is broken by herds that gather to drink at water holes. Coastal fogs nourish the animals in Namibia's Skeleton Coast National Park, where elephants and giraffes roam and lions prowl the desert shore.

In lush contrast, Botswana's Okavango, the world's largest inland delta, supports a dizzying variety of animals and birds. Proposals to drain the delta

OUT ON A LIMB *Lionesses relax in a tree in Ngorongoro Crater, Tanzania.*

cays draw snorkelers and divers and provide visitors with the chance to see the giant Aldabra tortoise and millions of nesting seabirds. Introduced species and habitat destruction are problems, but the islands still constitute an idyllic retreat.

to supply the growing cities, however, threaten the eco-system. Furthermore, fences erected to protect grazing rights prevent zebra and wildebeest populations from making their annual migrations.

Thirteen percent of Zimbabwe is protected by parks and preserves. Three national parks, Mosi-oa-Tunya in Zambia, and Victoria Falls and Zambezi in Zimbabwe, protect the forest around Victoria Falls—a thundering curtain of water that attracts thousands of tourists each year. The country's largest park, Hwange, safeguards approximately 100 species of mammal and about 400 species of bird.

In South Africa, ecotourism is boom-ing. You can select from reserves in habi-tats ranging from desert dunelands such as Umlalazi Nature Reserve, to sub-tropical mountain forest, as in Mountain Zebra National Park. The biggest draw is Kruger National Park, in the Eastern Transvaal, home to more mammals than any other park on the continent.

MADAGASCAR AND THE SEYCHELLES

Off the coast of Mozambique lies the island of Madagascar. Habitat destruction has led to the loss of many species and erosion is a major problem, but this large island is still a remarkable destination for naturalists. A huge number of plant and animal species are unique to the country, includ-ing 28 species of lemur—dainty, large-eyed primates. Tourist facilities are limited and distances are considerable.

The Seychelles are a popular addition to many Kenyan safaris. These forested granite islands and jewel-like coral

CHALLENGES

Much of Africa's wildlife has been hunted and poached to the edge of extinction. Its elephant population is 500,000, down from 3.5 million in 1960; black rhinos have been reduced from 75,000 to fewer than 4,000 in the same period. Parks and reserves throughout the continent protect much that remains but poaching continues. Logging in Central and West Africa is increasing.

Increasingly, initiatives are focusing on ecotourism as a way of financing conservation and providing a better stan-dard of living for Africa's rural people, thereby giving them a vested interest in wild-life protection.

CB

BY LAKE AND SEASHORE *The coast-line of La Digue Island in the Seychelles (above). A Parson's chameleon in Madagascar (above right). Lechwe in the wetlands of Okavango (right).*

The High Atlas

Morocco

Morocco commands the northwestern corner of Africa. Rugged, purple-hued mountains rise gradually from the scrubby Atlantic and Mediterranean littorals, reaching snow-tipped heights of over 13,000 feet (4,000 m) before falling away to sun-glazed sand and rock desert to the south. The three ranges of the Atlas—the Rif, the High Atlas, and the Anti-Atlas—cut across the country east to west for 1,000 miles (1,600 km). The most beautiful and accessible of the ranges is the High Atlas, whose stack upon stack of pink and mauve peaks culminate in the spectacular crown of Jebel Toubkal (13,660 feet [4,200 m]). Few roads penetrate these mountains that are home to the hardy Berber people, but the many trails around Mount Toubkal National Park, 45 miles (70 km) south of Marrakesh, and the stunning scenery lure adventurous hikers.

TO JEBEL TOUBKAL

It is a straightforward journey to the town of Asni, 17 miles (28 km) southeast of Marrakesh, and thence, snaking above the fertile valley of the Oued Rhirhaia, to Imlil, a mountain village where you lace up your boots and, perhaps accompanied by Berber muleteers, set out on the two-day hike to Toubkal. En route to Imlil, palm groves give way to cork, cedar, and Kermes oak, and shrubs such as tamarisk, broom, and argan nipped by goats.

The trail out of Imlil follows the Mizane River to Aremd, on a spur above its fertile valley. Marked rocks show the zigzag way uphill to the pilgrimage site of Chamharouch and Nelter, beneath the gaze of Jebel Toubkal. Nelter marks the spring snowline, and the hike up here will take you about a day. Vegetation is sparse, but

Pack horses on the well-used track that crosses the pass from the Imlil Valley, on the way to Mount Toubkal.

the dazzling high–desert landscapes are sublime.

To climb Jebel Toubkal, you should set out at first light and follow the vaguely defined scree-covered South Corrie Trail. It will take you about three hours to reach the summit and it's tough going in parts, but the views across the stark peaks are staggering.

Once you have spent another night at Nelter, you can ascend the Tizi Ouanoums Pass in the cool morning air to arrive at Lac d'Ifni. This is one of the largest African mountain lakes and is popular seasonally with waterfowl and other birds migrating between Europe and Africa. Barren slopes give way to groves of walnut and apple trees as you descend eastward through the beautiful Tifnout Valley to Amsouzerte. From here you can loop north, making your way back to Asni.

Animals exist in abundance in the Atlas Mountains,

The High Atlas behind the village of Tinerhir (above). The death's-head hawkmoth (left) is named for the skull-like pattern on its back.

albeit hidden in cool crannies during the heat of the day. Rodents, for example, remain underground when it's hot. Vipers and scorpions are common, as are chameleons and spiny-tailed lizards. In summer, the low-mountain forests attract rare butterflies and spectacular hawkmoths, some of which resemble hummingbirds in form and in hovering flight.

Birds of prey, such as kites, shrikes, and falcons, soar alongside vultures. You may even glimpse a gennet, a jackal, or a wildcat among the tree-heathers and aromatic myrtles. The Atlas are also rich in fossils, for the land was a seabed before tectonic forces raised it skyward. CB

TRAVELER'S NOTES

Access International flights to Agadir and Tangier. Bus or rail to Marrakesh. Bus every two hours to Asmed and Imlil (90 minutes).

When to visit July–Oct. Mountains under snow Nov–June

Information Morocco Tourist Information Office, 31 rue Al-Abtal Angle Oued Fes, Agdal Rabat, Morocco, BP19; tel. (7) 23272

Accommodation Luxury hotel at Asni. Rustic huts and Berber homes while trekking

Notes Even in midsummer, weather can change abruptly and snow is not unusual. Warm clothing essential

An ammonite fossil.

The Red Sea

Egypt and Israel

The turquoise and sapphire-blue waters of the Red Sea, rimmed by white beaches and surrounded by rust-red mountains and desert, are blessed with a fascinating marine environment. The sea's unique ecosystem has fostered the development of hundreds of varieties of coral and more than 1,000 species of fish. Its transparent waters make it possible for divers and even snorkelers to observe a torrent of colors created by striped emperor, angelfish, parrotfish, and walls of undulating coral. The great fans of pink and red gorgonians, or soft corals, that line its shores are what give the Red Sea its name.

The sea was formed more than 20 million years ago by seismic forces that split the Arabian Peninsula, creating a basin that runs from the Gulf of Suez to the Straits of Bab al Mandeb, where Africa meets the Indian Ocean. Most of its fish and coral species entered the sea from this bottleneck around 5 million years ago. They evolved into unique species because of several unusual environmental factors. First, no permanent rivers flow into the sea's deep waters. Second, there are almost no tides, so little silt settles on the reefs. And, above all, sunlight, which is so necessary for building reefs, easily penetrates to great depths because of the clarity of the water.

The Red Sea has thousands of miles of unspoiled coastline and the reefs in Sudan and Eritrea are particularly notable, but they are not easy to reach. The northern end of the sea is much more accessible and Israel, Jordan, and Egypt have all embarked on major tourist developments. Reefs in the region have already been harmed by divers taking coral and the endless flow of tankers and freighters. Environmentalists are concerned that

A peacock grouper emerging from a cave in the Red Sea. Groupers are widespread in tropical waters, especially on coral reefs.

A diver among soft coral in Ras Muhammad National Park (above). Western honey buzzards (right).

a heavy influx of tourists could do further damage. There are, however, areas in Egypt and Israel where the coral is protected.

SHARM EL SHEIKH AND EILAT

In Egypt, Sharm el Sheikh and nearby Na'ama Bay are the main centers for exploring the Red Sea's underwater world. Just south of Sharm el Sheikh is Ras Muhammad National Park. This 80 square mile (200 km²) park at the southern tip of the Sinai Peninsula is a maze of turquoise bays, sand dunes, and beaches. A mere 20 feet (6 m) from the water's edge, the reefs sport soft coral cloaks and anemones in limitless colors.

The Israeli town of Eilat, at the top of the Gulf of Aqaba, is another busy dive center. It's also the site of Coral World, a huge underwater observatory and aquarium housing all the main species of fish found in the Red Sea.

Eilat is on the migratory flyway of tens of millions of birds of several hundred species, including gulls, terns, plovers, and raptors, which touch down to rest and feed at the beaches, ponds, salt pans, and fields. From March to May, it is a great place to see these birds as they fly north from Africa to nesting areas in Europe and Asia. The Eilat Bird Sanctuary is a haven for birds and birders.

Tour companies in Sharm el Sheikh and Eilat organize excursions to the Sinai Desert. These trips include visits to palm-fringed oases and the sixth-century Monastery of Saint Catherine on Mount Sinai. BL

TRAVELER'S NOTES

Access International flights to Cairo, Jerusalem, and Eilat. Daily domestic flights from Cairo and weekly flights from Jerusalem to Sharm el Sheikh. Eilat is a 1-hour flight from Jerusalem and about a 3-hour drive from Sharm el Sheik

When to visit Year-round. Nov–Feb is cool season, around 70°F (21°C). July–Sept best for diving, water about 70°F (21°C), air above 100°F (38°C)

Information Eilat Tourist Information Center, Arava Yotam Junction, Eilat

88111, Israel; tel. (07) 372-111, fax (07) 376-763. Ras Muhammad NP, Sharm el Sheikh, Egypt; tel. (62) 600-668. Egypt Tourist Authority, Misr Travel Tower, Abbassia Square, Cairo, Egypt; tel. (02) 823-510, fax (02) 830-844

Accommodation A wide range available, from campgrounds to apartments and luxury hotels

An orangefin anemonefish.

Uganda

Uganda

Sir Winston Churchill once wrote, "For magnificence, for variety of form and colour, for profusion of brilliant life ... for the vast scale ... Uganda is truly the pearl of Africa." This beautiful country is still all that and more. Situated between the eastern and western forks of the Great Rift Valley, Uganda is where East African savanna merges with West African rain forest. In the north, there is a band of the arid Sahel semi-desert. Africa's tallest mountain range, the Ruwenzoris (the Mountains of the Moon), towers over a portion of the western border, the highest peaks rising nearly 17,500 feet (5,250 m). Almost 25 percent of the country is covered by lakes, swamps, and rivers, including the source of the River Nile. The variety of ecosystems makes Uganda one of the most biologically diverse nations in Africa.

HIPPO TERRITORY

Exceptional ecological variety is to be found in Queen Elizabeth National Park, in the southwest. For many travelers, the highlight of a visit here is a launch trip along the Kazinga Channel, linking Lakes Edward and George. This puts you in the midst of the world's largest concentration of hippos—a population of about 35,000. Packs of these behemoths wallow in the channel, sometimes bumping the boat. Other large mammals, such as elephants and buffaloes, come to the water to drink. It is not unusual to see up to 60 of the park's 550 bird species here, among them saddlebill storks; goliath herons; tiny, jewel-like malachite kingfishers; pelicans; and cormorants.

Much of the park is a blend of open woodlands and savanna. On the plains, you will see

Hippos wallow in the waters of Queen Elizabeth National Park.

A young mountain gorilla (above) in the Bwindi Impenetrable Forest National Park. A male chimpanzee (right).

warthogs, elephants, lions, leopards, spotted hyenas, buffaloes, and antelope such as bushbucks and topi. There are thousands of Uganda kob—a russet-colored antelope. The males display on breeding areas, posturing to attract females, while defending these circular territories from each other.

To the south lies Bwindi Impenetrable Forest National Park where more than 300 mountain gorillas live. Some have been habituated to tourists, who can observe them from about 20 feet (6 m) away. A muscular

Uganda kob males display on breeding areas, posturing with their corrugated horns.

male, the troop ruler, may plop down to munch bamboo. Youngsters chase each other and try to engage him in fun. He tolerates them, then cuffs them away. Other adults loll about, feeding and grooming one another.

To reach this scene, you will hike for from one to six hours (depending on where the gorillas are), at an altitude of about 7,500 feet (2,250 m), with vines clutching at you and mud sucking at your boots. You may be tired, but the one hour allowed will be one of the best of your life. You may see other primates, such as chimpanzees and colobus monkeys, too, and the forest is inhabited by dazzling birds such as the touraco.

For those who seek further ecoadventures, Kibale Forest and Murchison Falls national parks, to the north, are also immensely rewarding. EW

TRAVELER'S NOTES

Access International flights to Entebbe, near Kampala. Tours and car rental in Kampala. 4WD best for parks

When to visit June–July best but good year-round except during wet seasons in Apr–May, Oct–Nov

Information Ministry of Tourism, Wildlife, and Antiquities, PO Box 4241, Kampala, Uganda; tel. (41) 232-971. Uganda National Parks, PO Box 3530, Kampala, Uganda; tel. (41) 530-158, fax (41) 530-159

Accommodation Tented camps, cabins, and campgrounds in parks. Lodges in national parks. Hotels in towns near parks

Notes Independent travel difficult. Uganda generally safe, but bandits north of the Nile. Permit required for Bwindi—book 3 months in advance through National Parks office in Kampala

The Great Rift Valley

Kenya and Tanzania

The Great Rift Valley provides some of Africa's most dramatic scenery—steep escarpments; a valley floor covered at times with lush vegetation, at others with desert; and freshwater and soda lakes that are a birder's paradise. Here you will find parks such as Hell's Gate and Serengeti (see p. 186), and archeological sites, such as Olduvai Gorge, that show that *Homo sapiens* and his predecessors originated here.

Running north–south through Kenya and Tanzania, the rift is the largest crack in the Earth, extending from the Dead Sea in the Middle East down to Mozambique. This geological wonder was created 12 million years ago by deep crustal movements. Varying from 30 to 50 miles (50 to 80 km) wide, it is characterized by trough-like lakes and step-like blocks along its walls. Volcanic activity is still evident in boiling pools and geysers at Lake Bogoria and volcanoes such as Mounts Kenya and Kilimanjaro, Africa's highest peaks.

Most of Africa's lakes lie in the rift. The shallow soda lakes—Nakuru, Bogoria, and Manyara—have no outlets and their floors are covered with volcanic alkaline deposits. Quantities of blue-green algae and crustaceans grow in these lakes, attracting vast numbers of flamingos.

The marsh-lined, freshwater lakes—Baringo and Naivasha—are renowned for kingfishers, Goliath herons, and lily-trotters. Baringo is a delightful spot to spend a few days. You can take a boat trip in the marshes and walk

184

Greater flamingos.

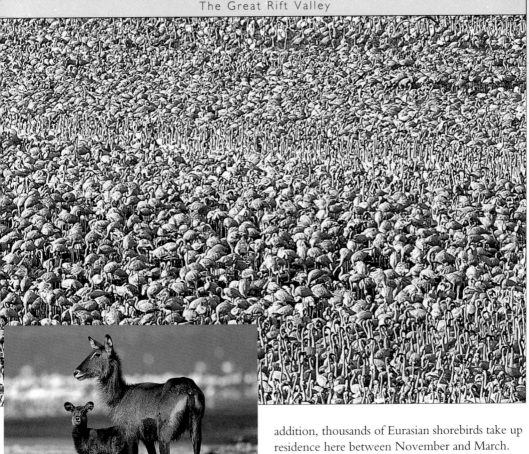

along the rift wall where hornbills and bee-eaters live. Naivasha is a good base for visiting Hell's Gate National Park where zebras, giraffes, and elands roam and Verreaux's eagles nest on cliffs.

LAKE NAKURU NATIONAL PARK

Lake Nakuru lies about three hours' drive north of Nairobi. Most years it is rimmed in pink during the day, as two to three million deep-pink lesser flamingos and smaller numbers of the taller, pale-pink greater flamingos feed along its shores. At night, they move to the center of the lake for protection from leopards. During times of drought, when the water is too salty to produce blue-green algae, the flamingos fly to Bogoria or Manyara.

From the road around the lake, you can see waterbucks, hippos, and waterbirds in the marshes and along the mudflats; giraffes in the acacia woodlands; and olive baboons and rock hyraxes at Baboon Point.

Lake Nakuru's rich birdlife includes pelicans, cormorants, grebes, herons, ibises, storks, spoonbills, and geese. In

addition, thousands of Eurasian shorebirds take up residence here between November and March.

A black rhino sanctuary was established at Lake Nakuru in 1986 as part of Rhino Rescue, which is proving successful. Less happily, Lake Naivasha has suffered from the introduction of salvinia, a plant that blocks out the sun for species below water, and from the introduction of fish such as tilapia and Nile perch. Furthermore, Kenya's rapid population growth is threatening native forests with encroaching settlement and agriculture. SM

Flamingos on Lake Bogoria (top).
Waterbucks at Lake Nakuru (above left).
A yellow-billed stork (right).

TRAVELER'S NOTES

Access International flights to Nairobi or Kilimanjaro, Tanzania. Then book a safari or hire a 4WD

When to visit June–Feb dry season; Mar–May monsoon and difficult to get around; June breeding season on lakes; Nov huge migrations of wintering storks, birds of prey and shorebirds

Information No tourist office in Nairobi, but 2 tourist publications available at travel agencies and larger hotels: Kenya Tourist Guide and

What's On. Tanzania Tourist Corporation, Maktaba St, PO Box 2485, Dar es Salaam, Tanzania; tel. (051) 276114

Accommodation Lodges and camping in parks and nearby towns

Notes Hiking and cycling at Hell's Gate, Naivasha, and Baringo, but not at Nakuru because of dangerous animals

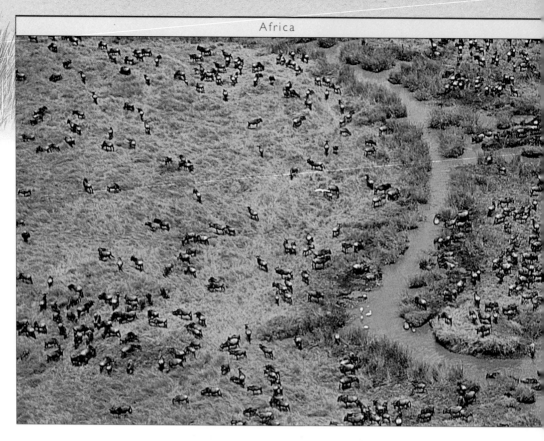

The Masai Mara and the Serengeti

Kenya and Tanzania

The vast plains of East Africa present the most wonderful wildlife spectacle. Here, under a brilliant blue sky, you will see vast numbers of animals—wildebeest, gazelles, zebras, giraffes, elands—moving across the grasslands and clustered around water holes, and at night you will hear the roar of lions and the barking and laughter of hyenas. These enormous stretches of grassland, which are known as the Serengeti ecosystem, span the border of Kenya and Tanzania. About half the region is protected by two great preserves: Masai Mara National Reserve (700 square miles [1,800 km²]) and Serengeti National Park (5,600 square miles [14,500 km²]).

The plains lie just south of the equator at an altitude of 3,000 to 6,000 feet (900 to 1,800 m). The climate is mild and dry for most of the year, with two rainy seasons. The heavy monsoon occurs in April and May and light rains fall in October and November, bringing a second spring.

THE MARA

The Masai Mara is Kenya's most popular reserve. Making your way to the Mara, which is to the west of Nairobi, is an adventure in itself. You can either drive for a full day, almost entirely on dirt roads, or you can take a short flight, which gives you spectacular views of the Great Rift Valley en route. The most dramatic entry is along the Esoit Oloololo Escarpment on the western border of the reserve

The Nile crocodile (right) is one of Africa's most ferocious predators.

where the plains drop away before you in a breathtaking vista. Flat-topped acacia trees and wooded thickets dot the savanna below, which teems with animals. You will need to spend a minimum of three days here in order to see as many species as possible. The highest concentration of wildlife is found along the western edge of the reserve, where animals are attracted to the marshes and the tree-lined Mara River. Look for large pods of hippos in the river and crocodiles stretched out on its banks.

When grazing becomes scarce on the Serengeti in the dry season, more than a million wildebeest migrate north to the grasslands of the Masai Mara (above). Many are injured or drowned as they cross the Mara River (left).

MIGRATING WILDEBEEST

The wildebeest migration is one of the highlights of the Mara. The lives of these large creatures are dominated by an endless search for food and water. In late June, as the Serengeti water holes start drying out and grass becomes scarce, columns of wildebeest, with considerable numbers of zebras and Thompson's gazelles among them, start moving west and then north toward their dry-season refuge in the Mara. Around July–August, more than a million of these great animals pour north across the the Mara River into Kenya, sometimes crossing at suicidal locations. Many are killed by plunging over the high riverbanks, are swept away and drowned, or become hopelessly mired in the mud. But the migration is relentless, the animals continuing to stream into the pastures among the acacia woodlands in the west.

In October, as the rains come again to the Serengeti, the wildebeest start drifting southward, back to the vast shortgrass plains of the southeast. This is where the calving takes place. In all, the wildebeest's year-long, clockwise circuit covers about 500 miles (800 km).

TRAVELER'S NOTES

Access International flights to Nairobi, Kenya, and Kilimanjaro, Tanzania. Fly or drive to Mara from Nairobi; drive to Serengeti from Mara, Nairobi, or Kilimanjaro. Shuttle buses daily between Nairobi and Arusha (5 hours one-way). Possible to drive from Mara to Serengeti but not vice versa because of border regulations. 4WDs recommended

When to visit June–Mar (dry season). Mara peak July–Aug. Serengeti peak Jan–Mar. Difficult to get around during monsoons (Apr–May)

Information No tourist office in Nairobi. 2 tourist publications available at travel agencies and hotels: Kenya Tourist Guide and What's On. Tanzania Tourist Corporation, Maktaba St, PO Box 2485, Dar es Salaam, Tanzania; tel. (051) 276-114

Accommodation Lodges, permanent tented camps, and campgrounds

Notes No hiking permitted in reserves. Book tours and hotels 6 to 12 months ahead

THE SERENGETI

The Serengeti is Tanzania's largest and oldest national park. It is contiguous with the Mara, lying to its south across the Tanzanian border—a sea of grass crisscrossed by tree-lined rivers. Because of its immense size, it's best to stay in two different parts of the park, allowing at least a week for your visit.

The major route into the park is through the southeastern entrance, via Ngorongoro Crater and Olduvai Gorge (see p. 190). This road heads north to the park headquarters at Seronera, a good base for exploring. From here, you can head north toward the Mara or west toward Lake Victoria. Leopards can be found during the day resting in trees along the Seronera River and vervet monkeys are a common sight in among the branches.

Each day that you spend on safari will generally feature two outings in the park to look for and photograph wildlife, since hiking is not allowed because of the abundance of predators. You'll travel in vehicles with pop-up roofs, which act as blinds for aproaching the animals closely. Such outings yield close-up views of elephant families and olive

baboons in wooded thickets, crowned cranes and saddlebill storks in the marshes, and hippos and crocodiles in the rivers.

An astounding assemblage of hoofed animals grazes the plains, including wildebeest, giraffes, zebras, Thompson's and Grant's gazelles, impala, buffaloes, topi antelopes, and kongoni (also known as Coke's hartebeest). You'll see prides of lions relaxing during the day, lying in the tall grass or on rocky outcrops, and preparing to hunt at dusk. In the morning, it's quite common to see hyenas, vultures, and marabou storks cleaning up the remains of a kill from the night before. You never know what you may see —bat-eared foxes at their den, the occasional silver-backed jackal, or the unfolding drama of a speeding cheetah and its unsuspecting prey. Hunting dogs and black rhinos are uncommon, but you may be lucky enough to come across them.

Vultures at a kill (top). Secretary birds (above right). Giraffes use a form of fighting known as necking (right) to assert dominance.

Between late January and mid-March is a fascinating time to visit as this is when most of the female wildebeest calve, resulting in up to 400,000 births. This mass calving results in such a huge volume of prey that predators are sated, providing a good chance of survival for the bulk of the young. Another aid to survival is the fact that the calves can run as fast as their mothers within half an hour of being born.

Many people become ardent birders on safari, entranced by the abundance of large, showy species. These include the ostrich and the secretary bird on the plains, the colorful Schalow's turaco in trees along the riverbanks, and the malachite kingfisher in the marshes.

Be sure to join a night drive, as many animals are nocturnal. You may spotlight a bushbaby (a nocturnal mammal about the size of a rabbit) or a springhare (a rodent that hops).

CONSERVATION ISSUES

Excessive numbers of tourists are putting a severe strain on the Serengeti and the Masai Mara. Tire tracks crisscross the sensitive soils and large numbers of viewers disrupt animals' feeding and mating habits. Other strains on the ecosystem stem from ever-increasing numbers of people living on lands adjacent to the preserves, and the resultant spread of cultivation and of grazing domestic animals. A conservation battle is currently being fought to save the black rhino and the elephant. Rhinos are being poached for their horns and elephants for their ivory, both of which are sold in the Middle East and Asia. SM

THE MASAI

For 500 years before the British arrived in the late 1800s, the Masai had been living on the interior plateaus and in the Rift Valley of Kenya, grazing their cattle on the grasslands. Proud warriors, they resisted the white invasion, but weakened by civil war and disease they eventually capitulated. Forced from most of their tribal land, they now live in the region around Masai Mara and farther south into Tanzania.

Most Masai continue to live in the traditional way. Their villages are groups of mud huts, surrounded by thorn-bush fences. At night, the cattle are herded inside the fence for protection. The Masai rarely slaughter them for meat, instead feeding on milk which they mix with the cattle's blood for additional nourishment.

While the Masai are allowed to graze their cattle in the Masai Mara, they can have no villages there. They have no concept of land ownership, and because they need additional land they are in constant conflict with the authorities.

A cheetah in pursuit of its prey (above). Red clothing and intricate beading are part of a Masai warrior's traditional costume (right).

Ngorongoro Crater

Tanzania

The Ngorongoro Crater is the world's largest intact, unflooded caldera—a crater produced when a volcano collapses. It was formed around 2½ million years ago when, after its final eruption, the cone fell inward. Minor volcanic activity continued for a time, with lava erupting to create small cones and hills on the caldera floor. Eventually the region became covered with grasses, spring-fed lakes, and marshes.

Ngorongoro's walls are spectacularly steep and rocky and the rough roads that lead in and out are negotiable only by four-wheel-drive vehicles. From the forested rim, the view of the 102 square mile (264 km²) crater spread out below is magical. The animals appear as tiny specks on a shimmering sea of grass. There are outcrops of rock and scattered clumps of acacia trees here and there, and Lake Magadi, a shallow soda lake, glints in the sun.

The crater is part of the Ngorongoro Conservation Area, a 32,400 square mile (83,900 km²) reserve that includes the Crater Highlands, Empakaai Crater, part of the Serengeti Plains, and Olduvai Gorge. Unlike the contiguous Serengeti National Park (see p. 186), where domestic animals are not allowed to graze, this huge eco-system is managed in such a way that the wildlife and the tribal Masai can coexist.

Almost all of the crater's elephants are male as the females tend to remain with their young on the forested rim.

190

From the 1,800 foot (550 m) crater walls (above), the view across the grasslands is spectacular. A crowned crane (right).

While they cannot have settlements in the crater, the Masai can graze their cattle here.

Some 30,000 large mammals live in the crater—buffaloes, wildebeest, hippos, lions, elephants, and about 15 rhinos. (Rhino poaching is so widespread in East Africa that this is one of the few remaining populations.) Most of the animals are used to the presence of vehicles, which means that they are easily observed.

TOURING THE CRATER

The road into the crater winds down through a forest of euphorbia trees to the first of many water holes, where you may see lions. Then, traveling clockwise, you drive through shortgrass plains where wildebeest, Thompson's gazelles, and zebras graze. The road continues to Lake Magadi, home to thousands of magnificent pink flamingos.

They periodically leave the safety of the lake's interior to wash the soda from their feathers in the freshwater springs at its edge, where jackals and hyenas wait to attack.

At Munge Swamp, saddle-billed storks can be seen near the pools. About 350 species of bird, including crowned cranes, black-headed herons, and wintering ruffs are found at Ngorongoro.

At Koikoktok Springs, which is spring-fed and green all year, hippos wallow, half-hidden in the mud. Farther on, the road runs through an expanse of high grasses where you may see rhinos.

Despite conservation efforts, Ngorongoro's wildlife remains at risk. Drought, poaching, increased tourism, and agricultural developments that disrupt migratory patterns all threaten this fragile eco-system. BL

Black rhino and calf.

TRAVELER'S NOTES

Access International flights to Kilimanjaro, then a 4-hour drive to the crater. Only 4WD vehicles accompanied by a park ranger are allowed to enter the crater

When to visit July–Sept and Dec–Mar best for viewing wildlife. Heavy downpours in Apr–May can make many roads impassable

Information Ngorongoro Conservation Area Authority, PO Box 776, Arusha, Tanzania; tel. (057) 3339

Accommodation Campgrounds and hotels on crater rim

The Zambezi River

Zimbabwe

At almost 1,700 miles (2,700 km), the Zambezi is Africa's fourth longest river. From its source in northwestern Zambia, it flows south to the magnificent Victoria Falls in Zimbabwe. From here, it flows northeast to form Lake Kariba, a reservoir that marks the Zambia–Zimbabwe border, then makes its way southeast into Mozambique and the Indian Ocean. The Zambezi River and Victoria Falls are at their most striking between February and May, when water levels peak.

Above the falls, the Zambezi is characterized by wide stretches of calm water and islands, best explored in boats on "sundown" trips. Next to the falls is Zambezi National Park, a 221 square mile (573 km²) wilderness where herds of elephants, buffaloes, impala, and kudu roam.

Victoria Falls (above).
Hippos (left) are found
along the lower Zambezi.

The Zambezi's most dramatic feature is undoubtedly Victoria Falls, located within the national park of the same name. Here the river cascades over a series of five 300 foot (90 m) high basalt cataracts, spewing clouds of spray 1,000 feet (300 m) into the air. Before you even see the falls, or what the locals call "the smoke that thunders", the roar of rushing water deadens all other sounds. Tourists can be glimpsed in the mist as they follow a slippery trail along a cliff opposite the falls. The path winds through rain forest to lookouts where the tumultuous curtains of water leave glistening rainbows in their wake. The forest thrives on the constant spray and attracts many birds, including blue waxbills, paradise flycatchers, and scarlet-breasted plovers.

BELOW THE FALLS

Directly below the falls, the current is so fierce that rafting or kayaking is a daredevil proposition, but the intense rapids alternate with half-mile stretches of calm water. Further downriver is Lake Kariba, studded with islands and surrounded by mountains. At its downstream end is a dam and from there the river meanders across flood plains.

Over thousands of years, the river's course across these plains has shifted from time to time, creating ribbons of fertile alluvial soil along its banks. As you approach the river from the interior grasslands, the low jessebush and mopane forest give way to lush woodlands growing in this rich soil. Acacia, mahogany, and other large trees thrive, including the sausage tree, whose huge fruits locals use to treat cancer. The river is home to large pods of hulking hippos and to sleepy crocodiles, and along its banks the wildlife is spectacular. Here you will see elephants, buffaloes, zebras, bushbucks, impala, and even bashful Nyasa antelopes.

Mana Pools National Park, a flood plain that covers about 1,200 square miles (3,000 km²) along the banks of the Zambezi, and Chikwenya Safari Lodge, just beyond the eastern border of the park, are two idyllic places where you can observe

Among Zimbabwe's 600 bird species is the carmine bee-eater, which nests in colonies along the banks of the Zambezi.

the abundant wildlife. The remarkable profusion of animals and birds that can be seen here, combined with the peace and beauty of this stretch of the river, make it some of the most magical country in all Africa.

While the flood plains remain unspoiled, human activities are seriously threatening the Zambezi around Victoria Falls. Vegetation along the banks is being cut for river access. Directly below the falls, in the narrow, turbulent gorges, rafting and kayak operators are creating litter and disrupting the herds of animals that migrate daily to the river. One hotel has even put up an electric fence around its golf course, cutting wildlife off from its migration corridors. BL

TRAVELER'S NOTES

Access International flights to Harare, domestic flights to Victoria Falls and Lake Kariba. Charter flights from Lake Kariba and Harare to Mana Pools and Chikwenya

When to visit July–Sept dry season and best time for viewing animals. Victoria Falls is at its best Feb–May. Chikwenya only open Apr to mid-Nov

Information Zimbabwe Tourist Board, Jason Moyo Ave, Harare, Zimbabwe; tel. (04) 793-666. Chikwenya, Mana

Pools, P Bag 2081, Kariba, Zimbabwe; tel. (61) 2253, fax (61) 2240

Accommodation Victoria Falls: hotels and campsites. Mana Pools: best to visit on camping tour. Chikwenya: 16 lodges

Notes Rain wear can be rented at Victoria Falls parking lot. Chikwenya visit usually includes guided walks, safaris, and boat trips

Etosha

Namibia

In the bushveld of Namibia, there is an 8,598 square mile (22,268 km²) national park to which "all the menageries in the world turned loose would not compare", according to a tourist in 1876. One of the largest African parks, Etosha, 250 miles (400 km) northwest of Windhoek, is still rich in wildlife. Most of the large plains animals are here in astonishing numbers. Etosha is a last refuge of endangered black rhinos, as well as Kirk's dik–dik and black-faced impala, animals no longer found elsewhere in Africa. Huge herds of elephants are a common sight, as are phalanxes of gemsbok (oryx). The park has the densest proportion of lions to prey in Africa and over 325 species of bird, including the largest known breeding population of greater flamingos.

AROUND ETOSHA PAN

At the heart of the park is the 1,800 square mile (4,700 km²) salt plain known as Etosha Pan. In the dry season it is a dusty furnace, but waters trapped beneath the depression seep out and form water holes along its southern edge and here and there on its surface. Animals of every kind make their way to these water holes, running the gauntlet of lions and other predators.

When the rains come, between January and April, the grasslands around the pan turn green once more and the grazing animals fan out across the park.

A black rhinoceros and a pair of yellow-billed oxpeckers. The birds feed on skin parasites.

Ostriches running across Etosha Pan
(above). Greater and lesser flamingos
coming in to land at Etosha (right).

Occasionally, when the rains are heavy, seasonal rivers flood the basin, drawing pelicans, flamingos, marabou storks, and other birds to its mineral-rich waters. Throughout the year, the temperature hovers above 100°F (38°C).

A common first stop for visitors is Namutoni, in the park's east. From the lodge, safari vehicles roam the plains to enable visitors to see a lion kill. A flight or drive westward will take you to Halali Camp, on the edge of the pan. Nearby is the Olifantsbad water hole, a gathering spot for scores of elephants, especially in August and September.

At Okaukuejo, in the far west, you can stay at a camp by a water hole. The water hole is flood-lit at night and you may watch beasts of every stripe and strength make their entrances and exits. By day, wildebeest, gemsbok, springbok, and zebras migrate past, moving east or west with the seasonal rains.

Etosha was proclaimed a Game Reserve in 1907 by the German Government of South West Africa (as Namibia was then known). Declared a national park in 1958, it has since been enclosed by a 500 mile (800 km) fence. This vast corral is estimated to hold over 80,000 mammals.

In the west, there is a breeding farm for rare species, including black rhinos, which number about 400. The breeding program has been so successful that many young animals have been shipped to parks elsewhere in Africa.

Other species have not fared so well. Human intervention has caused the lion population to swell to the point where cheetahs and other predators cannot compete and are dwindling in numbers. Wildebeest herds have also declined, because of increased predation by lions and restrictions on their migration routes. CB

TRAVELER'S NOTES

Access International flights to Johannesburg, South Africa; domestic flights to Grootfontein; charter flights to camps

When to visit May–Sept cooler. Oct–Feb hot. Jan–Apr rainy season

Information Directorate of Nature Conservation and Recreation Resorts, Windhoek, Namibia; tel. (61) 36975

Accommodation Tented camps and lodges. Namutoni open year-round; Okaukuejo and Halali camps open mid-March to Nov. Bookings essential

A Kirk's dik-dik.

195

The Okavango Delta

Botswana

I n the parched northern regions of the Kalahari Desert there is a great oasis, the Okavango Delta—an emerald jewel set in a stark, arid landscape. Eons ago, tectonic movements created a great trough here, into which the Okavango River annually pours billion of gallons of water during the October to May wet season. During this period, the maze of papyrus-lined channels, bordered by small villages, brims with water, creating islands of green. Dry water holes are refilled, and, in good years, water spills southward onto the sands.

The river is fed by rain from Angola's distant highlands. The water flows into a region known as the Panhandle, and then into channels that flow southward, like fingers reaching into the desert, where it spreads to form a vast inland delta.

A MOSAIC OF MIGRATIONS

This diverse, 6,000 square mile (16,000 km²) fan of woodland, savanna, and wetland provides food for a mesmerizing miscellany of wildlife. Some of Africa's largest herds of zebra, elephant, and buffalo come and go with the waters in a shifting mosaic of migrations, rubbing shoulders with aquatic fauna. Hippos honk in ephemeral swamps and permanent lagoons shared with otters and Nile crocodiles. Here you will find the semi-aquatic lechwe deer and the elusive sitatunga antelope, whose splayed hooves are an adaptation to the soggy ecosystem. Birding is spectacular, too: some 550 species add their colors to the sea of green.

For your first look at the Okavango Delta, it's best to fly into the Pom Pom airstrip in the southwest.

Wallowing hippos (left). A sitatunga antelope (opposite).

An elephant safari (above). By using its wings as a shade, the black egret obtains a clearer view of underwater prey (right).

From the air, you'll gain an idea of the scale of the area and will be able to see the animals spread out below. Near the airstrip is Abu's Camp, the only camp in this part of the delta. From here, you can experience the ultimate African eco-adventure: riding an elephant trained to carry you into the wetlands along animal trails.

The next step is to fly to one of the dozen or so camps among the delta islands, to be poled through the oasis in a dugout canoe. Encounters with crocodiles and hippos will leave a lasting impression, as will the sight of elephants and giraffes browsing the waterside forest. Punting also gives you an opportunity to see the wonderful birdlife. Goliath heron, spur-winged goose, African fish eagle, and Pel's fishing owl are among the species that may take wing as you drift by.

A visit to the Moremi Wildlife Reserve is a must. The 3,200 square mile (8,250 km²) reserve covers one-fifth of the delta, in the northeast. It embraces rivers, lagoons, and papyrus and reed swamps, plus mopane forests and dry savanna that support large herds of elephant, buffalo, and a variety of other mammals. You can see these animals on drives from one of the safari lodges. Hippos are common but can be hard to see in the reed beds. Muffled screams and hyena laughter haunt the night.

Over 17 percent of Botswana is set aside in national parks and reserves. The key to the country's success in protecting wildlife is its "game utilization" program. In 1967, farmers were granted part-ownership of the wild animals that roam the nation's extensive cattle- and sheep-grazing lands. Game is treated as a renewable resource and harvesting is permitted. Thus, culling prevents overpopulation and farmers have an incentive to prevent poaching. CB

TRAVELER'S NOTES

Access *International flights to Harare, Zimbabwe, or Johannesburg, South Africa. Connecting flights to Victoria Falls or Maun, then by 4WD or air charter*

When to visit *May–Oct best for viewing animals. Nov–April (wet season) best for birding but certain areas inaccessible*

Information *Tourism Development Unit, Private Bag 0047, Gaborone, Botswana; tel. 53024*

Accommodation *Selection of tented camps and lodges. Reservations essential*

Notes *Do not enter the delta unaccompanied*

The Kalahari Desert

Botswana

The Kalahari Desert, known as "the Great Thirstland" to its people, covers more than 80 percent of Botswana, which lies landlocked deep within southern Africa. This virtually uninhabited, burning-hot flatland of mirages and salt-pans is unyieldingly harsh, yet rich in wildlife. Leopards and lions, for example, are abundant; local populations have adapted to the lack of water by surviving on the body fluids of their prey—animals such as gemsbok (oryx), eland, giraffe, wildebeest, and springbok. These ungulates, too, can exist through lengthy periods of drought. When seasonal rains fall, flamingos and migratory waterfowl wing in by the million, and vast herds of wildebeest and zebra make their way across the dusty plains, drawn by the scent of moist earth. Predators follow, on the fringes of the herds, accompanied by hyenas and vultures.

MAKGADIKGADI PANS AND THE CENTRAL KALAHARI

From Maun, you can fly to Jack's Camp, a traditional safari camp. It adjoins the Makgadikgadi Pans Game Reserve and is the only permanent camp in the Kalahari. The huge salt pans of the Makgadikgadi are relics of a superlake that dried up eons ago as a result of tectonic movements. In the rainy season, the pans fill with water and the region becomes a major wetland.

Large groups of lions prey on wandering herds of wildebeest, hartebeest, gemsbok, and other mammals.

A herd of springbok (above). A hyena (right). A Bushman carrying his traditional hunting gear (below right).

Migrating herds make their way across the neighboring grasslands toward the gleam of water. At Makgadikgadi, Bushmen trackers are available to take you exploring on foot.

The tourist hordes that swamp other parks have made no impression on the 20,000 square mile (50,000 km²) Central Kalahari Game Reserve. Indeed, few visitors have entered this bone-white land in the heart of Botswana. Scores of dead lake beds attest to an erstwhile wetter climate, but the region is now totally without surface water. Nor is there any accommodation within this, the world's second largest reserve, created in 1961 to enable Bushmen to pursue their traditional way of life. Safari operators based in Maun, however, may take you in by four-wheel-drive or plane to take a look. Herds of wildebeest, hartebeest, eland, gemsbok, and springbok roam here, supporting lions, cheetahs, leopards, hyenas, and wild dogs.

KALAHARI BUSHMEN

The Bushmen (also known as the San) arrived in Botswana 25,000 years ago, from the north. Until recently, they eked out a living hunting in the Kalahari with traps, spears, and poison-tipped arrows, but few, if any, live as hunter-gatherers these days. Most live in nomadic bands that reckon their wealth in terms of livestock. In recent years, the meager grasses of the Kalahari have become increasingly threatened by overgrazing.

The 185 mile (300 km) Kuke Fence, erected in the 1950s across the northern Kalahari to separate domestic cattle from disease-ridden wild animals, has restricted the migration of wildebeest moving from the central Kalahari to the waters farther north. As a result, 90 percent of the region's wildebeest have since died of thirst. CB

TRAVELER'S NOTES

Access *International flights to Harare, Zimbabwe, and Johannesburg, South Africa. Connecting flights to Maun. Charter flights to Gweta then drive to Jack's Camp*

When to visit *Wet season, Dec–May, is hot and humid, but this is the time for the annual migration and superb birding. Dry season can be extremely hot*

Information *Tourism Development Unit, Private Bag 0047, Gaborone,*

Botswana; tel. 53024. Jack's Camp, PO Box 173, Francistown, Botswana; tel 212-277, fax 213-458

Accommodation *Jack's Camp, Makgadikgadi. Hotels in Maun*

The Eastern Transvaal

South Africa

South Africa's eastern Transvaal is characterized by seemingly endless scrub grassland known as "lowvelt" or "bushvelt". To the east, the lowvelt is broken by the basaltic outcrops of the Lebombo Mountains, which form a natural boundary with Mozambique.

The eastern lowvelt is dominated by Kruger National Park, on the border with Mozambique, and a series of adjacent private reserves along the park's western border. Kruger is about 220 miles (350 km) long, with an average width of 40 miles (60 km), and provides visitors with excellent opportunities to see Africa's "big five": lions, elephants, black rhinos, buffaloes, and leopards. People generally come in the dry season, from December to March, when the weather is mild and the animals gather around the water holes.

Greater kudus live in dense bushland.

Five major rivers flow across the park, from west to east, fringed by woodland. Hippos and crocodiles loll about in their waters and on the banks. Impala, wildebeest, buffaloes, zebras, cheetahs, baboons, and vervet monkeys can be seen virtually everywhere. Leopards are also common, but you're unlikely to see them as they are largely nocturnal.

VARIED HABITATS

The park consists, broadly, of three zones. Along the western boundary, toward the south, rainfall exceeds 27 inches (700 mm) annually. The wet, dense bushwillow and acacia forests that grow here are home to a large white rhino population.

The central and southeastern region, south of the Olifants River, is drier. Grassy plains, dotted with knobthorn and leadwood trees, spread southward to the Crocodile River, on the park's southern boundary. Impala, zebras, and wildebeest graze the plains, preyed upon by lions and African hunting dogs. Giraffes, black rhinos, cheetahs, and jackals also roam the grasslands. Much of the animal viewing takes place in this area.

North of the Olifants, the park is remote and arid, characterized by mopane woodland and

Burchell's zebras in the southern sector of Kruger (above). Zebra means "striped donkey" in Swahili. Giraffes (left) feed mainly on the foliage of acacia trees.

baobabs. Elephants gather here, as do roan and sable antelopes.

Many of the larger animals are so used to vehicles that they barely acknowledge their presence. You can go on two- and three-day treks in the park, providing you are accompanied by an armed guide. Trekking is the best way to see the park's 500 bird species, about 100 of which are endemic. They include a variety of raptors and waterbirds, as well as weaver birds and the charming white-fronted bee-eater.

A New Approach

Two reserves in the region are particularly notable, in that they combine high-quality wildlife viewing with a commitment to sustainable development and rural economic growth. (Relatively few local people have benefited from Kruger's tourist earnings.) Londolozi Reserve, adjacent to Kruger, and Ngala Reserve, within the park (the land is leased from the National Parks Board), both provide luxury accommodation and highly informative safaris. They also involve local people in all aspects of the projects.

The South African government is now committed to conservation and throughout the country there exists a widespread understanding that wildlife earns tourist dollars. In growing numbers, unprofitable farms are being turned into profitable private reserves and wildlife is on the increase.

TRAVELER'S NOTES

Access *International flights to Johannesburg, domestic flights to Skukuza and Phalaborwa, adjacent to park entrances. Cars and 4WD can be rented in Johannesburg, Pretoria, and at Skukuza. Some lodges organize tours*

When to visit *July–Sept best for seeing the larger animals. Oct–Nov is when many animals give birth. Jan–Feb hot and humid but best for birding*

Information *National Parks Board, Box 787, Pretoria, 0001, South Africa;* tel. (012) 343-1991, fax (012) 343-0905. Londolozi and Ngala: ConsCorp, 4 Naivasha Rd, Sunninghill, Sandton, Johannesburg, South Africa; tel. (011) 803-8421, fax (011) 807-2365

Accommodation *Cabins and campgrounds in Kruger, lodges and campgrounds in private reserves*

Notes *Reservations required for hikes*

ST **201**

Madagascar

Madagascar

The world's fourth largest island, Madagascar lies 250 miles (400 km) off the East African coast. The Great Red Island—so-called because of its brilliant red soil—separated from the African continent about 100 million years ago, enabling its plants and animals to flourish and diversify in isolation. Its 226,000 square miles (590,000 km²) are a paradise for naturalists, particularly as three-quarters of the flora and fauna here are found nowhere else.

Madagascar is particularly famous for its lemurs—large-eyed primitive primates—and its orchids, of which there are about 1,000 species,

Antserañana
Ankarana Plateau

MILES
0   100   200
0   200
KM

PÉRINET SPECIAL
RESERVE
Antananarivo

RANOMAFANA NP

Pangalanes Canal

BERENTY
Tolagnaro
(Fort Dauphin)

most of them endemic. Half the world's chameleon species are only found here, and almost all the island's butterflies (3,000 species) and nearly half its birds are also endemic.

There are thirteen national parks and reserves in Madagascar, but only seven are protected and administered and many of the island's plants and animals are on the edge of extinction. Poverty and overpopulation have been the spur to aggressive farming practices that have led to about 75 percent of the island's forests being felled. The main threat to the remaining rain forest is from small-scale farmers using slash-and-burn agriculture. Erosion is a devastating problem: the rivers often run blood-red with soil. Fortunately, a stable government and growing awareness of environmental issues is resulting in the establishment of further protected areas on the island.

For the ecotourist, the "must-sees" are in the far north, the far south, and the east of the 1,000 mile (1,600 km) long island, which entails a fair amount of getting about.

The eerie call of the indri (top) is one of Périnet's most distinctive sounds. Red clay from surrounding hills colors the waters of many rivers (left). Erosion, resulting from deforestation, is widespread.

THE EAST COAST

The most accessible park is Périnet–Analamazoatra Special Reserve, which is three hours' drive east from the capital, Antananarivo (known locally as Tana). The reserve is situated in lush tropical rain forest amid rolling hills. Nowhere in Périnet is more than an hour or two's walk along trails that wind through the vegetation and around a series of small lakes covered in massive waterlilies. Guides can be hired in the nearby town of

Andasibe. The reserve also has a delightful orchid garden and the birdlife is impressive.

Périnet's star attraction is the teddy-like indri, the largest of the lemur species. These noisy, black-and-white creatures can be found in the farthest reaches of the forest, leaping from treetop to treetop. The best time to see them is within 30 minutes of daylight.

Other lemurs, such as the gray bamboo and red-fronted, also live in Périnet, as does the tenrec, a small insect-eating mammal. There are several species of tenrec: some resemble water rats while others have rows of spines. Another resident is the Parson's chameleon. Sadly, its future is threatened by the success of the tourist trade, which has encouraged local children to catch chameleons for visitors to photograph.

The Parson's chameleon (above) can grow to 2 feet (60 cm) in length. The pitcher plant (right) feeds on insects.

TRAVELER'S NOTES

Access *International flights to Antananarivo. Air Madagascar serves most major towns. Bush taxis (taxis-brousses) offer cheap local and (if your constitution allows) long-distance transport. Rental cars are available in Antananarivo*

When to visit *May–Sept. Oct–Apr is hot*

Information *Direction du Tourisme, BP 610, Lalana Fernand Kasanga, Tsimbazaza, Antananarivo, Madagascar, tel. 26298*

Accommodation *Hotels only in major towns; otherwise ask around for rooms to rent. Camp only in reserves and parks. Cabins at Berenty. Accommodation in old research camp at Ankarana; take supplies as there are no stores*

Notes *Purchase permits for parks and reserves from ANGAP, opposite American Cultural Center in Antananarivo*

Madagascar's east coast consists largely of long stretches of uninhabited sandy beaches, swept by moist trade winds from the Indian Ocean. An eye-opening experience is to take a day trip from Périnet in a rented *pirogue* (dugout canoe) and follow a stretch of the Pangalanes Canal, which links a series of lagoons running down the east coast of the island. On the landward side of the canal there is thick jungle and to the east savanna stretches down to the sea. There is the occasional fishing village, and baobab trees with their bulbous trunks stand among long grass where rosy periwinkles grow. (Chemical compounds from this periwinkle—grown in plantations near Antsirabe—are used to treat leukemia.)

A place well worth a two-day stopover, if you are driving, is Ranomafana National Park, on the road from Tana to the south. Much of its 160 square miles (416 km²) of rain forest has been logged but a program is now in place that encourages locals to assist with conservation measures. It is situated among rolling hills where white-water rivers tumble. Twenty-nine species of animal can be seen here, including twelve types of lemur.

Eight species of baobab or "bottle tree" (top) occur in Madagascar. A ring-tailed lemur (right).

SUBTROPICAL COUNTRY

At the southeastern corner of the island lies the old French colonial port of Tolagnaro (Fort Dauphin). You can reach the town by road (allow two days) or by air from Tana. The southern part of Madagascar sits below the Tropic of Capricorn and the vegetation here resembles that of the same latitude in neighboring Africa. This is arid country, and spiny desert—a mix of thorn scrub and aloe plants—dominates the region.

At Berenty, a private reserve 50 miles (80 km) west of Tolagnaro on the Mandrare River, 80 acres (32 ha) of dry tamarind forest sprouts from a surrounding sisal plantation like an oasis. (Sisal is a Mexican agave plant that yields strong fibers used to make rope.) In the reserve, over 110 species of animal, insect, and plant thrive. Ring-tailed lemurs are Berenty's "signature species", but you can also see sifakas (another lemur species), flying foxes, fossas (a cat-like animal related to mongooses), and 83 bird species, including the Madagascar buzzard and the paradise fly-catcher. Night walks are mesmerizing. From the bush, the eyes of omnipresent lemurs peer out at you. Move quietly, as the slightest noise will scare the more timid animals away.

The owner of the reserve is Jean de Heaulme. His father cleared scrub and baobab forest to farm sisal but left the Berenty forest intact, later becoming aware of its economic potential as a conservation area. In 1985, Jean de Heaulme was awarded the Getty Prize for nature conservation. In limited numbers, visitors can stay in cabins on the reserve and wander at their leisure, day or night. Guides are available and good ones can add greatly to the pleasure of your stay.

ROCK SPIRES AND UNDERGROUND RIVERS

The best way to reach the spectacular world of limestone rock spires on the Ankarana Plateau, in the island's far north, is to take an organized tour from Antsiranana. Independent travel is not recommended, as the spires form maze-like canyons and water is scarce.

Razor sharp from millenia of rock-dissolving heavy rain, the jagged pinnacles of limestone are known locally as *tsingy*, referring to the metallic ring made by the rain as it falls on them. In caves lying far below the pinnacles,

crocodiles and aggressive 4 foot (1.3 m) eels roam the cold waters of underground rivers. Above ground, lemurs and ring-tailed mongooses live in the forests of baobabs, figs, and palms that grow in the canyons between the limestone peaks. JH

LEMURS

Madagascar's best-known endemic species are the lemurs, named after the *lemures*, the Roman spirits of the dead. The island is home to 28 species of these dainty, agile primates that vary in size from the mouse lemur, weighing only a couple of ounces, to the indri, which is the size of a small child. More than a dozen other species are extinct.

The ancestors of today's lemurs appeared in Madagascar 40 million years ago, traveling on logs that floated across from Africa. The quicker-witted true monkeys never made the trip, nor did lions or wild dogs, leaving the lemurs to evolve with little mammalian competition.

From the orange-spotted crowned lemur in the caves of the north to the playful ring-tailed lemur tamely approaching tourists at Berenty, these graceful animals can be found in most parts of the island, but they're gravely threatened by habitat destruction.

Limestone pinnacles on the Ankarana Plateau (top). A phelsuma gecko (above). Thought evil by many Malagasy, the aye-aye lemur (right) was traditionally killed on sight. It is now a protected species.

The Seychelles

Seychelles

In the nineteenth century, many Europeans considered the Seychelles so idyllic that they thought they must have come across the original Garden of Eden. Here, forests of palm, teak, and mahogany blaze with morning glories and white begonias, and reef-filled waters of surreal clarity wash onto blinding white beaches. Like paradise, the Seychelles—an archipelago in the Indian Ocean just south of the equator—isn't easy to reach. Its 115 islands are scattered widely across an expanse of ocean.

The central islands of the archipelago are the only mid-ocean granite isles in the world. They are the mountaintops of a microcontinent that was stranded mid-ocean when India split from Africa about 650 million years ago. There are 41 of them, Mahé being the largest and most densely populated. The remainder of the Seychelles consists of 74 coral islands, to the southeast of Mahé. Rarely visited, most barely poke above the ocean.

To protect its fragile ecosystems, the Seychelles' government has pursued enlightened ecotourism policies. Charter flights are prohibited and the number of hotel rooms restricted. Forty percent of the land, including almost the entire coastline and whole islands, is protected by reserves or bird sanctuaries. Most of these reserves can be visited during a one-week stay on the islands.

PARADISE FOUND

The Botanical Gardens on Mahé, a short distance from Victoria, the capital city, is a good place to become acquainted with the local flora. If you are feeling energetic, you can then follow the Trois Frères Trail into Morne Seychellois National Park. As the trail rises, so do the heat and humidity. Passing through stands of bamboo, cotton-

The seed and flower spike of the coco-de-mer.

206

Baie Lazare on Mahé Island (above).
A fairy tern on Cousin Island (left).

wood, and antediluvian tree ferns, you'll arrive, two hours later, atop the granite summit for a fabulous 360 degree view.

A short distance from Victoria by boat lies Sainte Anne Marine National Park. Here, visibility in the water reaches an astounding 165 feet (50 m). The strictly protected corals—over 150 types—grow in great Gothic walls, providing a dramatic backdrop for 800 species of fish.

A two-hour ferry journey lands you on Praslin, famed for its fantastically eroded pink and red boulders. Here, a three-hour trail leads into the island's beautiful Vallée de Mai Nature Reserve, a small but remarkable forest where the coco-de-mer grows. This towering palm, unique to the valley, bears huge, heart-shaped seeds that weigh up to 40 pounds (18 kg). Some have said that the coco-de-mer is the tree of knowledge, the seeds of the female tree resembling Eve's genitalia, and the long, pendulous flower-spikes on the male tree resembling Adam's. The extraordinary nuts became known as coconuts of the sea, because when they were washed up on distant shores their origins were a mystery.

The flora includes five other palms, pandans (also known as screw pines), epiphytes, lichens, and mosses. Keep an eye out for flying foxes and the secretive, endangered black parrots, which only exist on Praslin. Other native birds you may see include the Seychelles bulbul and the Seychelles blue pigeon.

Six hundred miles (1,000 km) south of Mahé lies the virtually uninhabited Aldabra Atoll. It consists of a series of beautiful, fragile coral islands surrounding a huge tidal lagoon, where millions of sandpipers, plovers, frigatebirds, sooty terns, and noddies nest. The fearless, flightless white-throated rail (a cousin of the extinct dodo) also lives here, along with 14 other species of landbird. Aldabra is best known, however, for its large population of giant tortoises, which grow up to 5 feet (1.5 m) long and can weigh 880 pounds (400 kg). CB

TRAVELER'S NOTES

Access International flights to Victoria, on Mahé. Domestic flights and ferries to adjacent islands, charter boat or plane to distant islands

When to visit Temperatures around 80°+F (27+°C) year-round. May–Oct relatively cool and dry; Dec–Mar hot and humid. Jan wettest month

Information Seychelles Tourist Board,

Independence House, Box 92, Victoria, Mahé, Seychelles; tel. 225-313

Accommodation Hotels and guest-houses on Mahé. Limited accommodation elsewhere. Reservations essential

Notes Take plenty of water when hiking

Asia

ECOTRAVEL *in* ASIA

The diversity of Asia's cultures is matched by the diversity of its habitats and wildlife. From the peaks of the Himalayas to the jungles of Borneo, an extraordinary range of experiences awaits the ecotraveler.

Asia has held special allure for travelers ever since Marco Polo returned to Italy from his journey to China, Mongolia, Tibet, Burma, Vietnam, and Java, bearing tales of fascinating cultures and riches beyond belief. Today, it's the region's unparalleled natural treasures that beckon visitors. Ecotravelers come to trek among the highest mountains on Earth, look for tigers while riding atop elephants, hike through forests where more than a thousand flower species bloom, and snorkel and scuba-dive around coral reefs.

THE INDIAN SUBCONTINENT

The Indian subcontinent is a biological world unto itself, washed by monsoon rains for half of the year and desiccated by blazing sun for the remainder. Though much of it lies within the tropics, the subcontinent has a range of habitats: alpine, evergreen forest, scrubby plain, riparian woodland, and coastal mangrove.

Most of the subcontinent falls within India's borders, and though the country is one of the most densely populated in the world—one-sixth of the Earth's people lives here—it boasts 55 national parks and 247 nature sanctuaries, constituting some 4 percent of the country's total landmass.

Given the mounting demands from a rapidly expanding population needing land for agriculture, housing, and industrial development, these nature preserves are all the more precious.

PAKISTAN

Tibet

NEPAL

INDIA

SRI LANKA

MIGHTY CREATURES *One of the tigers in Ranthambore National Park (above left). An Indian rhinoceros, wading (left). A painted stork coming in to land (top).*

Many of the country's national parks face the twin problems of poaching and incursion from illegal settlers.

The wealth of flora and wildlife combined with an ancient, rich culture makes India a popular destination for ecotravelers. Many tour companies offer trips that combine visits to several national parks.

They typically divide the continent into north and south. On a loop through northern India, you can expect to visit Bharatpur, home to some of the rarest birds in Asia; view the Taj Mahal, an architectural ode to love; and go looking for tigers in Ranthambore National Park. A loop in the south of the country would generally take in the Periyar Wildlife Sanctuary in Kerala, home to elephants, sloth bears, and lion-tailed macaques; the bird-rich, semi-arid woodlands of Mudumalai National Park in Tamil Nadu; and the deer and tigers at adjacent Bandipur National Park and Tiger Reserve in Karnataka. You will need to allow about two weeks for each loop.

RUSSIAN FEDERATION

MONGOLIA

JAPAN

NORTH KOREA

SOUTH KOREA

CHINA

❺

❹

Taiwan

VIETNAM

❼

LAOS

RMA

THAILAND

CAMBODIA

PHILIPPINES

❻

BRUNEI Sabah

❾

Sarawak

MALAYSIA

❽

Sumatra

SINGAPORE BORNEO

INDONESIA

AT HIGH ALTITUDES *A caravan of yaks making its way across the Tibetan Plateau (left). The snow leopard is at home in the cold of the Himalayas (below). Giant pandas are only found in a few pockets of bamboo forest in mountainous western China (bottom).*

THE HIMALAYAS

The precipitous Himalayas were created by the collision of two tectonic plates 40 million years ago. This rugged region contains 30 peaks exceeding 24,000 feet (7,000 m). Within the range lie Nepal, Tibet, and Bhutan, and parts of India, including Sikkim.

The Himalayas are a biological treasure trove. Nearly a third of the world's mammal species live here, including such species as the snow leopard, sloth bear, barking deer, and red panda. Many bird species nest here between May and October, and broadbills, parrotbills, finfoots, and honeyguides are found here year-round. Flora is also well represented, with conifers and rhododendrons covering the slopes at lower altitudes. More than 250 species of orchid bloom in Sikkim.

There are several national parks and preserves in Nepal and tour operators often include visits to more than one. At Royal Chitwan, you can see numerous species of wildlife, including tigers and crocodiles. To the west lies Royal Bardia, home to a range of bird species and large mammals, plus otters and the Gangetic dolphin. Sagarmatha National Park, on the Tibetan border, offers high-altitude trekking and the chance to view the Himalayas' crown, Mount Everest.

CHINA, MONGOLIA, AND SIBERIA

China sprawls to the north and east of the Himalayas. It has nearly a quarter of the world's population and is experiencing extreme environmental pressures, exacerbated by massive development projects such as the current construction of a dam on the Yangtze River that will drown the spectacular Three Gorges. Despite this, China still has areas of striking beauty and great biological diversity. About 1 percent of the country is set aside in parks and reserves. The best-known reserves are in the mountainous west of the country, protecting the giant panda and other endangered species.

In Tibet, which has been annexed by China, efforts are underway to protect the country's fragile ecosystems from Beijing's development programs. Many of Asia's great rivers rise in Tibet and it is thought that logging by the Chinese in this region has contributed to flooding in parts of China and the Indian subcontinent. Tibet's exiled leader, the Dalai Lama, has called for the creation of a nationwide zone of peace in which plants and wildlife would be protected and a policy of sustainable development would be adopted in populated areas.

Visitors can now cross into Mongolia to go birding, tour the Gobi Desert, or go horseback-riding across the Mongolian steppes. Russia has also opened its borders to ecotourists. Key nature destinations include Lake Baikal, the world's deepest freshwater

VARIED TOPOGRAPHY *The steaming volcanic landscape of the Kamchatka Peninsula, in Russia (left). Alpine scenery in Japan (below). An orang-utan mother and her baby in Borneo (bottom).*

lake; the Kamchatka Peninsula, a spectacular land of glaciers and more than 100 volcanoes; and the taiga forest of Siberia.

JAPAN

Japan's 125 million people live in an area no bigger than California, yet 14 percent of the country is parkland, which is testament to its people's tradition of valuing nature. Because of the mountainous terrain and a policy of buying timber abroad for wood and paper products, 60 percent of the country remains forested.

Among the more popular nature trips are treks through the Kita Alps, a chain of snow-capped peaks dotted with Shinto shrines, and birding trips to see cranes, sea eagles, pelagic birds, cuckoos, and owls. The best-loved trek is up Mount Fuji to view the sunrise.

SOUTHEAST ASIA

Extending from the Tropic of Cancer to south of the equator, Southeast Asia encompasses numerous biomes. Tropical forests cover much of the region, supporting many rare and unusual plants and animals. However, much has been destroyed, and much that remains is at risk from the pressures of a burgeoning population and rampant development. Parks and preserves throughout the region serve as last strongholds for threatened natural treasures.

In Thailand, 16,000 square miles (41,000 km²) of land is set aside in 58 national parks. Nearly 90 percent of Thailand's forest has been destroyed, which has resulted in the disappearance of many species, including the Javan rhino and the kouprey, a type of buffalo. Even the elephant, which once roamed in its tens of thousands, has dwindled to a mere 2,000 or so in the wild.

Southeast Asia is popular for extended touring. Over a few weeks you can visit several key destinations. For instance, you could start your tour by viewing the rich birdlife in northern Thailand, in Doi Suthep-Pui National Park, then head south to the coral reefs at Hat Nopparat Thara National Park. As a contrast, in peninsular Malaysia you could take a boat trip through the rain forest of Taman Negara National Park, followed by a visit to the mon-tane and elfin forests of the Cameron Highlands—a haven for botanists. You could then travel across the Strait of Malacca to Sumatra and the other islands of Indonesia, or across the Java Sea to Borneo.

In Borneo, you can visit the Sepilok Forest Reserve where previously captured young orang-utans are helped, at a rehabilitation center, to return to the wild. At Gunung Leuser National Park, in Sumatra, two similar projects have been established. This park has a wide array of habitats, from swamp to alpine, and you have a good chance of seeing wildlife here, including Sumatran rhinos, elephants, and leopard cats. There are excellent parks elsewere in Indonesia, too, including Mount Gede–Pangrango National Park, near Jakarta, and the Bromo–Tengger National Park in East Java, with its dramatic volcanic landscape. DH

The Himalayas

Nepal

The peaks of the Himalayas are superlative—the highest, grandest, and most admired on Earth. Soaring into the heavens of southwestern Asia, the mountains march more than 1,600 miles (2,600 km) from northern Pakistan in the west, through Kashmir and northern India, across Tibet, Nepal, and Sikkim, and into Bhutan in the east.

Although these mountains are collectively known as the Himalayas, they actually form three separate ranges. The Siwalk Range rises in the south along the Ganges Plain to a height of 4,000 feet (1,200 m), setting the stage for the loftier peaks beyond. Next in line, the Lesser Himalayas reach heights of up to 15,000 feet (4,600 m) and are sprinkled with Indian hill stations such as Darjeeling and Simla. The Great Himalaya chain of Nepal and Tibet boasts the highest peaks on the planet, including 29,028 foot (8,854 m) Mount Everest and 29 others rising to more than 25,000 feet (7,600 m).

THE MOUNTAINS OF NEPAL

Travelers can experience the majesty of the Himalayas in various places in several countries, but nowhere is more popular than Nepal, and for good reason. Breathtaking scenery, well-developed trekking routes, fascinating cultures, and a good range of accommodation have turned the country from an inaccessible mountain kingdom into a renowned adventure travel destination.

Throughout Nepal and Tibet, prayer flags flutter from rooftops and high mountain passes (left). Prayers printed on the cloth are carried heavenward by the wind. Tibetan nomad boy (far left).

Today, about 200,000 tourists visit Nepal each year, bringing foreign exchange and a higher standard of living for some, but at a price. Hillsides are eroding because so many trees have been felled for firewood to keep trekkers and porters, as well as villagers, warm. Trash along the trails piles up higher each season—the world's highest garbage dump is on Everest. The local people's health suffers when they sell food to travelers at high prices instead of eating it themselves. Many visitors are aware of the problems and have taken action to solve them. Tour operators now carry in kerosene for fuel; participants in cleanup treks clear trash from trails; and groups distribute veg-etable seeds so that villagers can grow more food.

Trekkers pass through forests of rhododendron (left) on their way to higher slopes that afford splendid views, such as this of Mount Ama Dablam, Nepal (above). The yak (below) is native to the Himalayas.

Visitors are likely to meet many local people along the trails because trekking areas are quite densely populated. This also means, however, that animal encounters may be limited to domestic creatures such as goats, yaks, and chickens. Most of the forests that once blanketed the slopes of the lower Himalayas have been cleared, but those that remain combine evergreen oak, bamboo, and rhododendron. The red, pink, and white blossoms of rhododendron (the country's national flower) flourish from February to May. Along the mountain trails, sacred pipal trees—the tree under which the Buddha attained enlightenment—shade the stone platforms that provide welcome relief for tired trekkers.

TRAVELER'S NOTES

Access International flights to Kath-mandu, then 1-hour flight or 8-hour bus trip to Pokhara for Annapurna, or 1-hour flight to Namche Bazaar for Everest region.

When to visit Oct–May (dry season). Oct–Nov best weather, but trails most crowded. Feb–April also good.

Information Nepal Department of Tourism, Patan Dhoka, Lalitpur, Nepal; tel. (01) 52-3692, fax (01) 52-7852

Accommodation Throughout Nepal, trekkers overnight in village lodges run by local families. Comfortable Sherpa Guide Lodges in the Everest region are a day's walk apart.

Notes Hire an experienced guide: these mountains are high and remote, the weather can change very suddenly, and avalanches sometimes occur. Also pay attention to signs of altitude sickness (see p. 48)

Langur monkeys are occasionally spotted in the forests, along with various birds, most notably the colorful Himalayan monal pheasant—Nepal's national bird.

At higher elevations, scrubby vegetation marks the transition to bare rock and snow. Argali (wild sheep) and ibex (wild goats) gracefully pick their way over the rocky slopes, while impressive birds of prey, such as golden eagles and Himalayan griffons, glide overhead. The elusive snow leopard haunts the highlands of western Nepal.

In the Pokhara region, tourists can rent boats on Lake Phewa Tal and admire magnificent Mount Machhapuchhare (above). The Himalayan monal pheasant (left) may be seen among the banyan and pipal trees that surround the lake.

TREKKING ROUTES

Trekking is the reason most travelers visit Nepal: about 77,000 trekking permits are issued each year. Since much of the country is connected by footpaths rather than

The endangered snow leopard lives above the treeline. A solitary creature, it preys on bharal (blue sheep) and ibex.

roads, it is possible to trek nearly everywhere in the mountains, but most people choose to follow the Annapurna and Everest circuits.

The Annapurna Conservation Area lies north of Pokhara, a town dominated by the sight of Mount Machhapuchhare (Fishtail Mountain). There are three main ways to explore this awesome region. The first is by following the eastern Kali Gandaki River valley to Jomoson and Muktinath, a sacred pilgrimage site for more than 2,000 years. The other main trail parallels the Marsyangdi River to Manang. Each of these routes takes about one week each way, and they can be joined in what is known as the Annapurna Circuit by crossing the 17,650 foot (5,383 m) Thorung La Pass. This results in a two-week trip of nearly 200 miles (320 km).

Another trek, taking at least 10 days from Pokhara, leads to the Annapurna Sanctuary at the heart of the region. Spectacular, almost perpendicular peaks surround this peaceful meadow, which the local Gurung people believe to be the home of their gods.

THE EVEREST REGION

Although it is second to Annapurna in popularity, the Everest region draws the most serious trekkers. Rugged terrain and lofty altitudes make it suitable only for those who are fit and hardy.

Solu, with altitudes from 8,500 to 11,000 feet (2,600 to 3,350 m), can be explored by walking from Jiri to Namche Bazaar. Steep trails make for some very strenuous hiking, and the trip takes at least a week, passing through the traditional homeland of the Sherpa people and one of the most fascinating areas of Nepal.

The Khumbu area covers the upper reaches of the Everest region and forms Sagarmatha National Park. (Sagarmatha is the Sherpa name for Everest and means "mother of the universe".) Treks begin in Namche Bazaar, where trails lead out into four valleys. Although the trails are not particularly tough, altitudes of over 16,000 feet (4,900 m) make trekking in Khumbu difficult, if not impossible, for some people (see p. 48). Those who can handle it, however, are rewarded with walks among the world's finest mountains: Lhotse, Everest, and Ama Dablam, to name a few. JJ

From Namche Bazaar (top), the main Sherpa town in the Everest region, a trail leads toward the summit ridge of Lobuje East (above).

SHERPAS

Although there are 17 official ethnic groups in Nepal, none is better known than the Sherpas, who have become legendary as guides and porters. Edmund Hillary may get the credit for being the first to climb Mount Everest, but it was his Sherpa guide, Tenzing Norgay (below), who led the way and reached the summit with him in 1953.

The word *Shar-pa* means "people from the East" and, according to Sherpa oral history, they arrived in Nepal from eastern Tibet sometime in the 1500s. The Sherpas speak a dialect of Tibetan and practice Tibetan Buddhism, worshipping at magnificent *gompas* (monasteries) built on the mountainsides.

Traditionally, Sherpas are yak herders, potato farmers, and traders. The Everest ascent, however, fostered the new industry of mountaineering, and today most of Nepal's trekking agencies are Sherpa owned and operated.

The Chitwan Valley

Nepal

A visit to Royal Chitwan National Park offers you the chance to ride an elephant in search of tigers and Indian rhinos against the magnificent backdrop of the Himalayas. Much of the park's 370 square miles (960 km²) is hilly and forested and about one-third lies on a floodplain. The floodplain vegetation is a sea of elephant grass, growing to 25 feet (8 m), combined with riverside forest. Chitwan is Nepal's finest wildlife preserve and 450 bird species and 50 varieties of mammal can be seen here.

Chitwan's ecology is largely determined by the rain and flooding of the monsoons (from June to September) but another major factor is fire. Early in the year, up to 100,000 people from nearby villages cut grass to thatch their homes, and then set fire to the grassland to encourage new growth. The shoots provide rich pasture for animals, such as rhino and chital (spotted deer). This centuries-old practice maintains the grasslands, which otherwise would be succeeded by forests. It also means that until April, when the grasses start to grow back, it is easier to see wildlife.

A memorable way to visit Chitwan is to stay at one of the lodges, where you can arrange elephant rides, river-rafting, and hikes. Allow at least four days to see the park.

SEEING THE WILDLIFE

A highlight of a visit to Chitwan is seeing the Indian rhinoceros. Hunting and poaching almost brought this once-common species to extinction. In Chitwan, where they are well protected by game wardens (combined with the death penalty for killing a rhino), there are now about 400 and you'll almost certainly

There are about 80 tigers in the park.

218

At Chitwan, you can tour the park on the back of an elephant (above). Most of the Indian rhinoceros's habitat is now farmland and the park is one of the few places in which it survives (right).

encounter one feeding in the elephant grass or wallowing in a lake. You'll also see wild boar and hog deer on the floodplain, and possibly a sloth bear or a tiger. The leopard is the park's other large predator, but few visitors see them.

Guides can take you on walks in the sal forest, on higher ground, where vines twine, orchids bloom, and gray langur monkeys swing. At dawn and dusk, you may see giant hornbills fly by. The stork-billed kingfisher, the coucal, and flocks of scarlet minivets are found near water. In winter, numerous waterbirds fly in, such as brahminy duck and black-necked stork. These can be seen when river-rafting, along with osprey and the crested serpent-eagle. You may also spot a gharial, a crocodile that feeds mainly on fish.

Now that poaching is controlled, many park species are increasing in number. Animals such as rhino and deer sometimes feast on crops in nearby villages, and tigers and leopards prey on livestock, occasionally even attacking a villager. This is a major problem, as it is impossible to resettle the thousands of people living around the park. SM

The red junglefowl, domesticated worldwide, still lives in the wild throughout much of Asia.

TRAVELER'S NOTES

Access *International flights to Kathmandu; 30-minute domestic flight to Meghauli (near park) or 6- to 8-hour drive. Also 2- to 3-day rafting trips to Chitwan on the Rapti River from Mugling, at junction of Kathmandu–Pokhara and Narayanghat highways*

When to visit *Dry season Oct–Mar. Peak season Christmas/New Year. Mar best time to see tigers; Oct–Apr best for birding; May–Sept humid, rainy and difficult to get around*

Information *Dept of Tourism, Tripureshwar, Kathmandu, Nepal; tel. (01) 211-203*

Accommodation *Jungle lodges within park; budget hotels in nearby Sauraha*

Notes *Book 6–12 months ahead. Most lodges close mid-May through Aug. Walk in groups of at least three, with a guide, because of dangerous mammals*

Rajasthan

India

R ajasthan combines a wealth of wildlife and a rich 4,000-year-old culture. Situated in northwestern India, the state is divided diagonally by the Aravalli Hills into two regions: arid lands dotted with desert oases in the north and west, and agricultural lands, rivers, marshes, grasslands, and deciduous and bamboo forests in the east and south. The Aravallis are characterized by dramatic canyons and vegetation ranging from arid thorn forest to palm-fringed marshes. Everywhere you will see signs of the

Women collecting water from a well at Jaroli near Bharatpur.

splendors of the past, most notably the lavish palaces and huge forts of the former Rajput princes.

With 4 national parks and 19 wildlife sanctuaries, Rajasthan offers a wide variety of eco-travel experiences. Two national parks should not be missed: Bharatpur, India's premier bird reserve, and Ranthambore, one of Asia's most important tiger reserves. A 10-day circuit from Delhi will enable you to explore both parks and spend some time at cultural sites such as the Taj Mahal, the deserted palaces of Fatehpur Sikri, and the pink city of Jaipur.

AMONG THE MARSHES

Visitors to India usually arrive in Delhi, the nation's capital, and if you're traveling to Rajasthan you will probably go via the Taj Mahal, in Agra. On the road from Delhi to Agra, 127 miles (204 km) south, you'll quickly become familiar with India's roadside birds: peacocks strolling through the fields, and flocks of rose-ringed parakeets, noisy mynahs, and black kites overhead. At the Taj Mahal—a monument of supreme beauty and grace—you'll see white-breasted kingfishers diving

Sunrise over the wetlands of Keoladeo
Ghana National Park (above). A red-crested
pochard (right). An Indian roller (below).

western Gangetic plains, with
lakes and canals fed by the nearby
Gambhir and Bangaga rivers.

Following the monsoons (July
through September), the shallow marshes that
appear throughout the park provide ideal wintering sites for migratory waterfowl from Siberia
and Central Asia. The surrounding forest is a
combination of deciduous, scrub, and thorn trees.

in the pools, purple sunbirds in the gardens, and
Indian river terns along the Yamuna River.

Just 33 miles (50 km) west of Agra, across the
Rajasthan border, Bharatpur provides a natural
spectacle of huge concentrations
of birds. Formerly the duck-
hunting preserve of the maharajas
of Bharatpur, this 11 square mile
(29 km²) area was declared Keoladeo
Ghana National Park in 1983 to
protect an amazing 350 species of
bird and a world-famous heronry
where some 30,000 chicks are born
each year. Bharatpur is a natural,
year-round wetland on the fertile

You can explore 41 miles (66 km) of trails
in a rickshaw, on a bike, or on foot. A boat ride
on the marshes at dawn among the cacophony
of the heronry is a memorable experience.
Waterbirds are everywhere, supported by the
myriad fish, crustaceans,
water plants, and insects.

The painted
stork nests in
large colonies
near water.

TRAVELER'S NOTES

Access International flights to New
Delhi; car, bus, or train to Agra, Bharatpur,
and Sawai Madhopur (for Ranthambore)

When to visit Oct–Mar (dry season);
Apr–Sept hot with heavy rains July–Sept;
Aug–Oct breeding season for birds; Oct–
Mar for wintering Eurasian birds; Mar for
tigers. Christmas and New Year busy

Information Indian Tourist Development Corporation, 88 Janpath, New
Delhi, India; tel. (11) 332-0005

Accommodation Bharatpur:
simple hotels in and near park.
Ranthambore: lodges and camp
near park, and four rooms
available in Jogi Mahal

Notes Ranthambore
closed 1 June to 1 Oct.
Reservations for Jogi
Mahal must be made a
year in advance. Make
safari arrangements at
lodge, as hiking and
private vehicles not
allowed in park

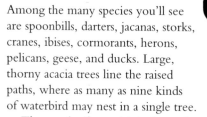

Among the many species you'll see are spoonbills, darters, jacanas, storks, cranes, ibises, cormorants, herons, pelicans, geese, and ducks. Large, thorny acacia trees line the raised paths, where as many as nine kinds of waterbird may nest in a single tree.

Thousands of waterbirds descend upon the park between November and March, among them the endangered Siberian crane—a tall, majestic wader that migrates nearly 4,000 miles (6,400 km) from northeastern Russia to its wintering grounds. A wide variety of landbirds can be seen here too, including babblers, coucals, tree pies, bee-eaters, rollers, warblers, and eagles. At night you may hear the haunting calls of jackals, stone curlews, and seven species of owl. Mammals are also abundant, and include the common mongoose, blackbuck, rhesus macaque, striped hyena, and smooth Indian otter.

Sambar feeding on water plants in Ranthambore (above). A flying fox (left). The rare fishing cat (below) is sometimes seen hunting in the marshes at Bharatpur.

TIGER TRACKING

Lying 109 miles (176 km) southwest of Bharatpur, near the town of Sawai Madhopur and at the junction of the Aravalli and Vindhya ranges, Ranthambore National Park is one of the best places in the world to see tigers in the wild. This 198 square mile (513 km²) park, once the private hunting grounds of the maharajas of Jaipur, became a national park in 1973 as part of Project Tiger. The road into the park winds through a steep desert canyon opening onto a region of marshes, streams, lakes, grasslands, and craggy hills. Much of the area is covered by virgin deciduous forests studded with palms. Mango groves and huge banyans grow around the lakes.

On drives in open-sided jeeps, you'll see abundant wildlife, including sambars (a large deer), Indian gazelles, langur monkeys, blue bucks, sloth bears, marsh crocodiles, and Indian flying foxes. The tigers are elusive, and sightings can never be guaranteed, but, with luck, you may experience the thrill of seeing a tigress with her young as you wind through the forest in the early morning or late afternoon. You'll certainly see a wide range of birds, including paradise flycatchers, green pigeons, pheasant-tailed jacanas, white wagtails, and even crested serpent eagles.

Jogi Mahal, the former hunting lodge of the maharajas, overlooks the main marsh, Padam Talao, where painted storks and spotted deer feed. At night here, you may hear the scream of a leopard or the hoot of an eagle owl. The massive Ranthambore Fort, built in the tenth century and located on a ridge-top in the park's southwestern corner, affords a spectacular panoramic view. Throughout the park you'll see remnants of the past: pavilions, tombs, and hunting blinds. Allow at least three days here in order to make the most of your visit.

India's national parks are islands of native habitat in a country where the pressures of population are making ever-growing demands for farming land. Remarkably, over 300 parks covering 35,000 square miles (90,000 km²) have been set aside to protect endangered species and habitats. There have, however, been significant disputes and unless India's population growth is curbed, the demand for food may become too great to save these preserves. SM

PROJECT TIGER

In 1973, Project Tiger was launched in India to protect and rehabilitate tiger populations in nine sanctuaries and national parks with a variety of habitats. Hunting these magnificent cats has been banned since that time and, as a result, tiger numbers have increased from 1,800 to about 4,000. There are now 18 tiger preserves throughout the country. Much has been learned about tigers by biologists, particularly in Ranthambore, where the tigers are thriving under protection. Tigers here are no longer afraid of humans and are often seen padding about in broad daylight. Previously it was thought that they were strictly nocturnal.

Project Tiger has saved tigers from extinction, but corruption in local management, poaching, and pressures for timber and grazing land pose major threats to their habitat, particularly in times of drought.

Tigers are largely solitary animals.

Ranthambore Fort (top) offers panoramic views over the park's marshes and grasslands. Langur monkeys in a banyan tree (above).

223

The Hengduan Mountains

China

The steep, forested Hengduan Mountains in western China are a refuge for many animals known nowhere else. These include the golden snub-nosed monkey, the takin, the Tibetan blood pheasant, the red panda, and the giant panda.

The giant panda was once widespread in China, but, as a result of several factors, mainly the dramatic increase in human population, it now faces extinction. Only about 1,000 survive in pockets of bamboo high in these mountains. With its round face and cuddly body, the giant panda has become a much-loved symbol of wildlife conservation.

THE WILDLIFE RESERVES
Thirteen reserves, covering 2,340 square miles (6,000 km²), have been set up in western China since 1963. Among the best known are Wolong, Huanglongsi, and Jiuzhaigou. The vegetation in all three areas ranges from subtropical forest at lower altitudes through broadleaf forest, to coniferous forest and

alpine meadows at about 13,000 feet (3,900 m) above sea level.

Covering 780 square miles (2,000 km²), Wolong has about 100 peaks that are over 16,000 feet (4,800 m) above sea level. A popular trip is to visit Mount Balangshan, a drive of 40 miles (64 km) from the administrative office at Shawan, beside the Pitiaohe River. The drive takes you through a landscape of snowy peaks and untouched forests, and you pass the Yingxionggou Valley, with its beautiful limestone peaks. There is a number of trails, some of which lead up to the alpine meadows on Mount Balangshan's higher slopes, where rhododendron and polygonum grow in profusion.

Near the administrative center there is a panda conservation research base where visitors are able to see pandas in captivity.

Huanglongsi, a region of spectacular mountain scenery, is famous for its 2 mile (3.5 km) long Yellow Dragon Gully.

A golden snub-nosed monkey.

224

The giant panda, which feeds almost entirely on bamboo (above), and the Tibetan golden pheasant (right) live in high-altitude forests.

or because they have marked medicinal or aesthetic qualities. Among them are 15 species of high-altitude rhododendron.

Over eons, snowmelt and rainfall have deposited calcium carbonate on plant roots and dead trees, forming strange limestone formations throughout the valley. These are interspersed with shallow pools in an extraordinary range of colors—red, green, yellow, purple, and black—around which grow forests of birch, cypress, azalea, and rattan.

Exquisite Jiuzhaigou Reserve consists of three valleys studded with crystalline lakes, rimmed by mountains and splashed by waterfalls. You can explore the reserve by following numerous trails of varying lengths. If you are lucky, you may see a troup of golden snub-nosed monkeys or even a giant panda.

Over 90 species of plant grow in Jiuzhaigou that are valuable either because they are threatened

Despite great conservation efforts, giant panda numbers and habitat continue to decline as a result of population fragmentation, logging, and poaching. A plan has recently been introduced, which includes the establishment of corridors to maintain contact between panda populations in separate reserves, in order to maintain a viable gene pool for the continuation of the species. WS

TRAVELER'S NOTES

Access International flights from Bangkok, Hong Kong, and Singapore to Chengdu. By bus or car to Wolong Reserve (3–4 hours). From Wolong to Huanglongsi is a 7-hour drive; from there to Jiuzhaigou is another 2 hours

When to visit May–Oct

Information China Science International Travel Service, 55 Kexueyuan Naniu, Zhongguancun, Haidian District, Beijing 100086, China; tel. (010) 257-1104, fax (010) 257-1044. Sichuan

Nature Travel Service, 15 Renmin North Rd, Section 1, Chengdu, Sichuan Province 610081, China; tel./fax (028) 334-2174

Accommodation Guesthouses in reserves and nearby towns and villages. Lodging available in local people's houses. Permits required for camping

Red pandas have a mixed diet of bamboo, other vegetation, and insects.

The Japan Alps

Japan

Although many foreigners imagine Japan to be one giant metropolis, in fact more than 75 percent of the country is mountainous and 60 percent is covered in forest.

A chain of peaks punctuates each of Japan's four major islands—Honshu, Kyushu, Shikoku, and Hokkaido—following the arc of the archipelago as it stretches more than 2,000 miles (3,200 km) from northeast to southwest. The greatest of these mountain groups, the Japan Alps in central Honshu, boasts nine of the country's ten highest peaks. (Mount Fuji, the highest, lies south of the main range, not far from Tokyo.) The alps are formed from three mountain ranges, known by the Japanese as Hida (North Alps), Kiso (Central Alps), and Akaishi (South Alps).

CHUBU SANGAKU

The beautiful North Alps are protected within Chubu Sangaku National Park, which encompasses 673 square miles (1,743 km²) and more than 100 peaks. Forests of spruce, pine, fir, cedar, and maple blanket the lower slopes, providing shelter for macaques, deer, serows (goat antelopes), and black bears. Small mammals such as weasels, raccoon dogs, and hares hide in the thick undergrowth of bamboo grass.

Stunted, creeping pines mark the transition between the regions of forest and the alpine zone. During summer, the rocky slopes are splashed with the varied colors of wildflowers. In a crevice, you may see the ptarmigan, a bird that sports white feathers in winter and brown in summer to blend into its surroundings. Other birds that you

The raccoon dog, which is neither raccoon nor dog but related to the fox, gets its name from its eye patches.

The upper alps are snow-covered for half the year and plants grow close to the ground (above). Macaques warm up in thermal pools (left). A ptarmigan in between-season plumage (below).

might come across include the Siberian meadow bunting, the Chinese bamboo partridge, and the copper pheasant, which is also known as the yamadori or mountain bird.

The Tateyama Mountains, in the north of the range, are the best place to find alpine wildflowers and fauna. From Murodo, a town above the treeline, a day's walk affords splendid views from the peaks of Oyama and Onanji-san, where you are surrounded by perpetual snow. The trail leads through Raicho-sawa (Ptarmigan Vale) to Jigokudani (Hell's Valley), a volcanic crater full of bubbling, steaming vents. Just before the track returns to Murodo, you come to the splendid crater lake of Mikuri-ga-ike.

Farther south is Kamikochi, a small village on the Azusa River that is surrounded by the highest peaks in the range. From here, there are a number of easy walks, including one to Hotaka Shrine and Taisho Pond. The pond was formed in 1915 by the eruption of Mount Yake, the North Alps' only active volcano.

Kamikochi is also the starting point of the ultimate Japanese alpine hike—a 24 mile (38 km) circuit that takes three days. The trail meanders through the Azusa Valley, becoming much more challenging as it ascends the slopes of Mount Yari. To reach the summit, you must climb chains and ladders up vertical rock faces, but the view, especially at sunrise, is spectacular, and on a clear day you can see Mount Fuji in the distance. The trail then leads you to the peak of Mount Hotaka. From there, you continue along a series of smaller peaks, before a steep descent back to Kamikochi.

TRAVELER'S NOTES

Access International flights to Osaka. Murodo: 1-day journey by train and bus from Osaka via Toyama and Tateyama. Kamikochi: 1-day journey by train and bus from Tateyama via Matsumoto and Shin Shimashima

When to visit June–Sept. Murodo and Kamikochi closed Nov–Apr

Information Japan National Tourist Organization, 6-6 Yurakucho 1-chome, Chiyoda-ku, Tokyo 100, Japan; tel. (03) 3502-1461

Accommodation Hotels and lodges in Murodo and Kamikochi, and mountain huts and campgrounds throughout region. Make reservations 6 months ahead

Notes Cold-weather gear essential. 24 mile Kamikochi circuit is for experienced hikers only

The Thai Peninsula

Thailand

Thailand's great natural beauty encompasses mountains, forests, waterfalls, caverns, rugged coastlines, and coral reefs. It has 58 national parks, covering more than 16,000 square miles (41,440 km²), or about 5 percent of the country. A rewarding way to encounter a range of Thailand's flora and fauna is to visit the peninsula in the south. Within this relatively small area, you can explore tropical forest on the mainland and spectacular limestone islands and coral reefs in the coastal waters.

LIMESTONE ISLANDS

Particularly fascinating are the 40 islands scattered across Phang Nga Bay on the west coast, which can be

The sun bear, the smallest of the bears, is known as the dog bear in Thailand.

visited on tours from nearby Phuket Island. They are part of an arc of karst formations—eroded limestone features—that extends from Burma across Thailand, Laos, and Vietnam to China.

Some of the islands harbor cavern–like passages leading to *hongs* (rooms in Thai)—caves dripping with stalactites. The *hongs* are inhabited by bats and visited by kingfishers and herons. The only way to see these caves is to paddle into them by sea kayak, an increasingly popular sport in southern Thailand, and this can be done only when the tide is exactly right. Many caves remain unexplored.

Outside, on the surface of the islands, a quite different world exists. Lush tropical vegetation covers rugged limestone outcroppings, and macaques and langurs scamper about on the cliffs. Here and there, a precarious bamboo ladder to a cave high above indicates the presence of human visitors—daring villagers who gather the nests of swiftlets to be made into the local delicacy, bird's-nest soup.

Farther south, six islands in the Phi Phi group are protected in Hat Nopparat Thara National Park, which also includes Nopparat Thara Beach on the mainland. The Phi Phi Islands are among

Limestone islands in Phang Nga Bay
(top). Colorful fish inhabit these tropical
waters (above). Remarkable stalactites adorn the caves (left).

ON THE BORDER

Although much of the peninsula has been
cleared, pockets of semi-evergreen tropical forest
remain on the slopes. Thaleban National Park,
near the Malaysian border, can be reached by
a half-hour bus ride from the city of Satun.

The wildlife in this beautiful nature preserve
includes sun bears, gibbons, and tapirs, as well as
bat hawks and great argus pheasants. Tigers and
elephants also live here but are seldom seen.
Large areas of the park are inaccessible and many
of the trails are overgrown, so it's a good idea
to hire a guide. A stay here, in one of the
bungalows beside the lake, will give you an
opportunity to see much of the rich bird
community and enjoy a swim in the pools
of Yaroy Waterfall. JJ

the most beautiful in Asia. They rise dramatically
from the sea, edged by sheer cliffs where vines
hang and rare pirate birds roost.

The clear waters off Nopparat Thara Beach
and surrounding the islands provide excellent
visibility for diving and snorkeling. Angel,
butterfly, parrot, and tiger fish glide through
the corals, and the occasional stingray, white-
tipped shark, or moray eel can be seen.

TRAVELER'S NOTES

Access International airport at Bangkok.
Hat Nopparat Thara: by plane from
Bangkok to Phuket, then by bus to Hat
Nopparat or by boat to Phi Phi Islands.
Thaleban: by plane from Bangkok to
Hat Yai, then bus to Satun; or by bus
from Phuket to Satun via Hat Yai

When to visit Thailand has three
seasons: hot (Mar–May), rainy
(June–Oct), and cool (Nov–Feb). The
best time to visit southern Thailand
is Nov–May

Information Tourism Authority of
Thailand, 73–75 Phuket Rd, Amphoe
Muang, Phuket 83000, Thailand;
tel. (076) 212-213, fax (076)
213-582

Accommodation Hotels and resorts
in Phuket, hotels in Phang Nga, hotels
and guesthouses on Phi Phi Islands, and
bungalows at Thaleban

The male great
argus pheasant
performs his
elaborate court-
ship display
within the
forest.

229

Northern Vietnam

Vietnam

Like the regeneration of a forest after a fire, Vietnam has risen from the ashes of a devastating war. The country's luxuriant landscapes, rugged peaks, and glittering beaches stand in sharp contrast to images that many people hold of bombs and battles.

Vietnam stretches southward from its border with China for more than 950 miles (1,500 km). The country is mountainous and nearly one-fifth is forested—less than half the figure of 40 years ago. Deforestation has resulted from the spread of human settlement, slash-and-burn agriculture, logging, and the use of defoliants during the war.

The lay of the land fosters a wide variety of ecosystems, ranging from tropical rain forests and mangroves to deciduous forest and scrub savanna. These habitats host a diverse fauna, which includes sun bears, serows (a type of antelope), elephants, and one-horned rhinos, along with some 773 species of bird and 180 kinds of reptile.

The Vietnamese government has only recently established a national park system, but, already, 10 national parks and 49 nature reserves have been created. These areas are especially important because many of the country's estimated 12,000 plant species have yet to be identified, while the forest may well contain animals that are still unknown. Two of the seven new species of mammal identified this century have been found in Vietnam. The Vu Quang ox and the giant muntjac (a species of barking deer) were both discovered during the past decade in the Vu Quang Nature Reserve in the country's far northwest. Two of Vietnam's most important and accessible national parks—Cuc Phuong and Cat Ba—are situated in the north of the country.

230

Paris peacock butterflies are found throughout the region.

Cuc Phuong National Park features dramatic limestone caves (above). A male douc langur (right). A clouded leopard (below).

THE FIRST PARK

Cuc Phuong, south of Hanoi, was established in 1962 as Vietnam's first national park. Several trails lead through its forests of ancient trees festooned with creeping vines. An explosion of color occurs in January, when many of these trees bloom. In remote parts of the park, leopard sightings are not uncommon, but you are more likely to see red-bellied squirrels, monkeys, gibbons, and spotted deer. The birds here are a delight, including red-headed trogons, pied hornbills, and black-backed kingfishers.

In April and May, the air becomes thick with butterflies, including the orange-banded, leaf-shaped kalima, which is the size of a human hand. There are a number of limestone caves in Cuc Phuong, which can be explored with a guide. The cave entrances are often garlanded with delicate orchids and, inside, you will find stalactites dripping from the ceilings.

Tropical evergreen forests cover the limestone terrain, and after the spring and summer rains, waterfalls cascade down the craggy hills. Woodpeckers and doves flit through the trees, while François monkeys leap from branch to branch, and you may come across the hoof prints of wild boar. Along the shore, waterfowl nest in the mangrove swamps, and if you go snorkeling you'll see some of the park's 200 fish species swimming around the coral reef. On a short boat trip, turtles, dolphins, and seals may also be spotted. JJ

ISLAND LIFE

Cat Ba National Park covers nearly half of Cat Ba Island, about 18 miles (30 km) offshore from Haiphong. The park comprises about 60 square miles (150 km²) of land and 35 square miles (90 km²) of sea.

TRAVELER'S NOTES

Access International flights to Hanoi. Cuc Phuong: hire car or jeep for the 3-hour trip from Hanoi. Cat Ba: domestic flight to Haiphong, then a 3½-hour boat trip (one daily) to Cat Ba Island

When to visit Nov–Apr cool and humid in the north with drizzle Feb–Mar; Mar is sunniest month; rains Apr–Oct

Information Vietnamese National Administration of Tourism, 80 Quan St, Hanoi, Vietnam; tel. (4) 253-314, fax (4) 261-115

Accommodation Lodges in Cuc Phuong, hotels on Cat Ba Island

231

Sumatra

Indonesia

Sparkling crater lakes, rushing rivers, untouched rain forest, and an incredible assortment of wildlife beckon nature travelers to Sumatra. This large island is part of Indonesia, a nation with such extensive flora that scientists estimate only half has been recorded, but also with more endangered plants and animals than most other countries.

Sumatra is home to such exotic mammals as rhinos, tigers, and elephants, and spectacular birdlife including hornbills and the great argus pheasant. The plants can be bizarre: the giant ketapang tree can grow to 200 feet (60 m), while the rafflesia is the largest flower in the world.

The bud of the rafflesia takes 18 months to develop, flowers for less than a week, and smells like rotten meat to attract carrion flies that act as pollinators.

Indonesia's largest wildlife reserve is found in Sumatra. Gunung Leuser National Park extends from the Bukit Barisan mountains to the west coast, with habitats ranging from lowland swamp forest to alpine scrub. A wonderful way to see the park is to take a three-day raft trip down the Alas River, floating through gorges, running rapids, and

The Sumatran rhino (left) was once found throughout Asia. Now only 1,000 are left, 200 of which live in Gunung Leuser National Park. The park is also home to 5,000 orang-utans (above).

drifting in forests where macaques scamper between the branches and the whooping calls of gibbons fill the air.

In the park's north, Gurah Conservation Lodge makes an excellent base for jungle walks. You will have a good chance of seeing orang-utans, barking deer, sun bears, and elephants. At Bukit Lawang, on the eastern border, you can visit the famous Orang-utan Rehabilitation Station. Other park activities include hiking up Mount Leuser, a round trip of about ten days, and up Mount Kamiri, a round trip of three days. Such hikes will take you into mossy montane forest and offer the best opportunities for spotting rhinos and tigers.

VOLCANOES

Sumatra has more than 90 volcanoes, of which 12 remain active. Exquisite lakes lie deep within some of the dormant volcanoes, surrounded by steep crater walls. A 10-hour bus trip south from

From a raft on the Alas River, you can explore the forest of Gunung Leuser National Park (above), where huge rafflesia flowers (below) grow on jungle vines. Lake Toba (left) was created by the explosion of a massive volcano.

Gunung Leuser will take you to Lake Toba, Sumatra's most famous crater lake, which at 480 square miles (1,240 km^2) is the largest lake in Southeast Asia. Prapat, on the shore, and Samosir, a 25 mile (40 km) long island in the center, provide bases from which you can explore. Verdant rice fields surround the lake, while the island is scattered with pine forests, bamboo thickets, and marshes.

Lake Toba is the spiritual home of the Batak people, one of Indonesia's major ethnic groups, whose members live throughout northern Sumatra. The landscape is dotted with their picturesque villages, which contain houses with saddle-shaped roofs and graveyards of elaborately carved tombs.

JJ

TRAVELER'S NOTES

Access International flights to Medan. 5-hour bus trip to Gunung Leuser; 4-hour bus trip to Lake Toba

When to go May–Oct (dry season)

Information Dinas Pariwisata (Tourist Office), Jalan Ahmad Yani 107, Medan, Sumatra, Indonesia; tel. (62) 511-101

Accommodation Losmen (inns) and lodges in Gunung Leuser; losmen and hotels on Samosir Island

Notes Walkers in Gunung Leuser must be accompanied by a park ranger

233

Sarawak and Sabah

Malaysia

The island of Borneo is divided among Indonesia, Malaysia, and Brunei. Here you will find the highest mountain peak in Southeast Asia and the most extensive cave system on Earth. Scientists believe Borneo's forests are the oldest on the planet, and they certainly rank among the most diverse and prodigious. More than 20,000 species of flowering plant, 2,500 species of butterfly, and 100 species of mammal share the island with the Penan, Iban, Kadazan, Kenyah, Ngaju, and other indigenous peoples. These tribal people live in villages in the interior, in longhouses beside the rivers (which serve as roads through the rain forest), or as nomadic hunters and gatherers.

Borneo is the only place, apart from northern Sumatra, where orang-utans are found. These huge, intelligent apes sleep in treetop nests where they are safe from predators such as clouded leopards and crocodiles. Other fascinating creatures in the forests include sun bears, rhinos, elephants, mouse deer, and proboscis monkeys. More easily seen, however, is the island's rich birdlife. The impressive range of bird species you can expect to see includes hornbills, trogons, and bulbuls.

The Malaysian states of Sarawak and Sabah are the most accessible regions of Borneo. Between them, they have 10 national parks ranging from marine preserves teeming with tropical fish to inland regions characterized by rugged peaks and dense rain forest. For those

Dramatic flowers such as the beaked heliconia (left) thrive among the lush growth of the jungle floor, while orang-utans (far left) and harlequin flying tree frogs (opposite) live in the branches above.

234

The Pinnacles on Mount Api (above).
Thousands of wrinkle-lipped bats
emerging from Deer Cave at dusk (right).

interested in getting to know
Borneo, two national parks in
particular—one in Sarawak and one in Sabah—
provide a rich variety of experiences.

GUNUNG MULU

In a jagged ridge of limestone hills near Mount
(Gunung) Mulu in Sarawak, erosion has created
a vast system of caves. The massive Deer Cave
dwarfs all who enter, and is the roosting place
of millions of bats. A remarkable experience is
to watch the bats emerge at dusk, as they wheel
in the air, searching for insects. The bats themselves may fall prey to hawks,
which can often be seen waiting near the mouth of the cave.
The Sarawak Chamber is so
large that 40 Boeing 747s could
fit within it. Extraordinary,
moss-covered stalactites and
stalagmites adorn Eagle, Lang,
and Wind caves.

Other park activities include
hiking up Mount Mulu, which
is Sarawak's second highest
peak. The trail winds through
rain forests up to the stunted
vegetation near the summit.
Equally fascinating is the hike

up adjacent Mount Api to a
group of razor-edged limestone
pillars known as the Pinnacles.
These pillars stand up to 150 feet
(45 m) tall, rising above the
rain forest canopy and often
emerging eerily from a shroud of mist. The trip
requires two or three days. The first day, hikers
take a two-hour boat ride, then walk for 3 miles
(5 km) through the forest to a campsite. From
there, three hours' strenuous walking along
forest paths lined with wild orchids and pitcher
plants takes you to the Pinnacles. As well as bats,
the animals that you might see in Mulu include
gibbons, squirrels, shrews, and deer, and there
are many wonderful frogs, butterflies, and
beetles. The park even has 458 species of ant.

TRAVELER'S NOTES

Access *Mulu: international flights to
Kuala Lumpur, then 2-hour flight to Miri
then 35-minute flight or 7-hour boat
trip to park. Kinabalu: international
flights to Kota Kinabalu, then 2-hour
bus ride to park. Travel between
Kinabalu and Mulu is by plane*

When to visit *Year-round. Rainy
season is Oct–Feb, but it usually rains
only for a short period each day*

Information *Malaysian Tourism
Promotion Board, Wisma Wing Onn
Life, 1 Jalan Sagunting, 88000 Kota
Kinabalu, Malaysia; tel. (088) 248-698,
fax (088) 241-764*

Accommodation *Mulu: ranging from
guesthouses to the first-class Royal
Mulu Resort. Kinabalu: ranging from
cabins and hostels at the base of the
mountain to basic huts near the summit*

Notes *No one can enter Mulu without
an authorized guide. Hikers climbing
Mount Kinabalu must hire a registered
guide at the park*

The landscape of Sabah is dominated by Mount Kinabalu (above), the highest mountain in Southeast Asia. Hiking to the peak is a memorable experience, taking you through cloud forest. The beautiful necklace orchid (left) grows on the forest floor.

MOUNT KINABALU

Sabah's Mount Kinabalu, at 13,455 feet (4,103 m), is the highest mountain between the Himalayas and New Guinea. This spectacular peak towers above Kinabalu National Park, the oldest and most visited in Borneo.

The park's main attraction is the mountain itself. Hiking up it is not particularly difficult but it takes two days to reach the summit. On the way, you pass through three ecological zones. Rain forest covers the first level of the mountain, up to about 4,000 feet (1,200 m), and is home to a variety of animals. Look for orang-utans high in the trees and sun bears and barking deer in

among the thick understory. The smallest and least known of the world's bears, the sun bear gets its name from the crescent-shaped yellowish mark across its chest. The barking deer, also known as the muntjac, has a call that sounds like a loud bark.

Moving up the ecoladder to the next level, the cloud forest, hikers will find some of the park's 1,000 species of orchid, along with a vast array of figs, magnolias, mosses, and pitcher plants. Higher still, 25 species of rhododendron grace the slopes.

Although the summit is barren, cold, and windy, the view of Sabah is superb at sunrise. Most climbers arrive at the top just before dawn and start descending well before 9.00 am, when the clouds begin to close in.

The tree-dwelling reptiles of Sabah include the forest dragon (right) and the oriental whip snake (far right).

236

Even for those who don't climb Mount Kinabalu, a visit to the park is worthwhile. At Poring, a number of hot springs have been channeled into open-air baths, and there is a tree-canopy walkway nearby.

On the trail to Langanan Waterfall, which takes about 2½ hours to walk, you may come across the huge, red rafflesia flower, which can grow to 3 feet (1 m) wide. A keen eye might also spot red leaf monkeys and barking deer.

The Sepilok Forest Reserve, near the town of Sandakan on the east coast, is also well worth a visit. Here you can see orang-utans, both in the forest and at the rehabilitation center where young ones rescued from the illegal pet trade are taught how to live in the wild.

We can only hope that Kinabalu, Gunung Mulu, and the other national parks of Malaysia, Indonesia, and Brunei will continue to preserve remnants of Borneo's natural heritage. Malaysia exports more tropical timber than any other country, and environmentalists estimate that, at present logging rates, Sabah's natural forests will be gone by the end of the decade and Sarawak's by early next century. The tribal people of Sarawak, particularly the Penan, have been at the forefront of the anti-logging efforts, leading blockades and standing before bulldozers. Many have been arrested over and over again, but refuse to give up the struggle to save their forest home for generations to come. JJ

HORNBILLS

With their long, down-curved beaks, often with a prominent casque on top, hornbills are easy to recognize. However, you are likely to hear them first: they make great honks and laughter-like whoops, and the air passing through their wings as they fly sounds like a locomotive.

There are some 45 species of hornbill spread across Africa and Southeast Asia. At least 10 inhabit Borneo, and almost all of them can be found in Gunung Mulu National Park. Few animals mean more to the people of the Borneo rain forest than these great birds, which often appear in the legends, dances, and art of the Iban, Kenyah, Ngaju, and other tribes.

Hornbills have a unique way of nesting. The female builds a nest in a tree cavity, plasters the hole shut, and stays there for the entire incubation period and beyond. A narrow, vertical opening is left, through which she and the brood are fed by the male.

The proboscis monkey (top) is found only in Borneo, where it lives in forests that are close to rivers or the sea. In the nutrient-poor soil of the island's mountain forests, carnivorous pitcher plants (above) supplement their diet by trapping insect prey.

Oceania and Antarctica

ECOTRAVEL *in* OCEANIA *and* ANTARCTICA

Oceania and Antarctica offer the ecotraveler some of the largest remaining wilderness areas in the world.

PACIFIC ISLANDS *such as Palau in Micronesia (below) offer superb diving (left). The koala (far left) is unique to Australia.*

The oceans and land-masses of the southwestern Pacific offer extraordinary biodiversity. Coral reefs and brilliantly colored fish thrive in the warm, clear waters of the Pacific and Indian oceans. Crocodiles bask by Australia's northern rivers, and in the country's dry interior kangaroos hop through the scrub as clouds of chattering budgerigars descend to water holes to drink. Volcanoes and glaciers continue to shape the dramatic landscapes of New Zealand. In the rough waters of the Southern Ocean, whales surface among the icebergs and thousands of seabirds dip and soar. Yet farther south, huge colonies of penguins live on the great, icy continent of Antarctica.

MICRONESIA

Micronesia means "small islands", and refers to the more than 2,000 islands that lie in the western Pacific, approximately midway between Australia and Japan.

Micronesia has a humid, tropical climate with little seasonal variation. The international gateway is Guam. You can easily combine an ecojourney to Australia with a visit to Micronesia by flying from Sydney and taking the "hopper" service from Guam to Honolulu, with up to six island stops in between.

Fewer than 100 of the Micronesian islands are in-habited and in 1994 there was an uproar when it was proposed that a number of the uninhabited ones be used as dumps for nuclear waste.

Some of the islands are volcanic, their lush, green mountains swathed in mist. Others are coral atolls. Their waters are clear and warm, with coral reefs teeming with fish. The diving at Palau is world famous, and is also outstanding at Chuuk in the Caroline Islands, where there are spectacular coral lagoons. The island of Pohnpei, with its profusion of palm and banana trees and brightly flowering plants, is among the many tropical paradises in the region. You can take a guided tour of its mountainous interior and visit the impres-sive ruins of Nan Madol (1285–1485)—the remains of stone towers and bridges—built on a reef. Kosrae is less developed and offers tranquility, secluded beaches, and cool mountain forests.

ANTARCTICA

NEW GUINEA

Mining and forestry have taken their environmental toll in New Guinea, but much of the island remains undisturbed and travel here is still an adventure. Nearly three-quarters of the land is swathed in tropical rain forest vibrant with orchids, butterflies, and dazzling birds. A massive mountain range forms a backbone for the mainland, down which flow great rivers that you can follow deep into the interior. The western half of the mainland is the Indonesian province of Irian Jaya and the eastern half is the country of Papua New Guinea.

Although the cities are growing, the vast majority of the people of New Guinea still live in the traditional way, in tribal groups within villages, practicing subsistence farming, hunting in the forests, and fishing in the rivers and along the coast.

Much of Irian Jaya is impenetrable jungle and its mountains are so high that there are alpine meadows and glaciers on the upper slopes. Most travel is by light aircraft or four-wheel-

THE CASSOWARY (right) *inhabits the dense rain forests of Irian Jaya (far right), Papua New Guinea, and northeastern Australia.*

drive. A 45-minute flight east from Jayapura, the capital, will take you to the Baliem Valley from where you can visit remote villages. Trekking up to the glaciers is possible but you will need a guide. Before setting out, check with the authorities that conditions are peaceful, as confrontations between locals and the government over mining have led to fighting in the past.

THE SOUTHERN PACIFIC

Many island groups in the southwestern Pacific have lost much of their natural environment to logging, mining, and hunting. Once-beautiful Nauru has been devastated by phosphate mining. Large tracts of the Solomon Islands are being stripped of timber. However, increased environmental

awareness and the generosity of the tropical climate are, in places, helping to restore nature's balance. National parks are being established to protect rain forests, beaches, and reefs, although their management is not always effective.

PALAU
❶
MICRONESIA

IRIAN
JAYA
❷
PAPUA
NEW
GUINEA
SOLOMON IS.

❸
❹
AUSTRALIA
❼
❺
VANUATU

❻

❽

NEW
ZEALAND
❾

⓫

A popular ecodestination is Taveuni, in Fiji. On walks through the lush mountain forests of Lavena National Park, you may see the rare collared lory, or kula parrot, which is endemic to the island. Another popular spot in Fiji is Savusavu Province, where there are hot springs, forests, tiny villages, and superb diving. You can kayak to isolated villages, inlets, and reefs.

Almost half of the volcanic islands of Western Samoa is covered in rain forest and the growth of ecotourism is encouraging the local people to protect their environment. All sorts of tours are available. You can travel to the rim of a volcano, down a lava flow, into lava-tube caves and freshwater crater lakes, or through dense rain forest to white sandy beaches.

There are international airports at Nadi in Fiji, Faleolo in Western Samoa, and Port Vila in Vanuatu. Ecotourists traveling between Asia and Australia or the United States can easily include a stopover in the region. The wet season, from November to April, is best avoided.

SOUTHERN SCENES *Magpie geese in Kakadu, Australia (above). A whale shark feeding on plankton (left). Cradle Mountain National Park in Tasmania (below). Red kangaroos (below right).*

AUSTRALIA

Australia was one of the first countries to ratify the World Heritage Convention, nominating three sites soon after it came into force. Eleven Australian sites are now listed. In addition, over 3,000 national parks and reserves have been established.

Australia is an extraordinarily diverse country. Its habitats range from the tropics in the north to the cool, temperate forests of the south. It has more than 22,000 miles (35,000 km) of coastline encompassing cliffs, sandy bays, and pristine beaches. The tropical zone, across the far north, is rich in rain forests and wetlands providing habitats for crocodiles and thousands of birds. Coral reefs teeming with fish lie off the east and west coasts. The heavily forested Great Dividing Range, which extends down the east coast, is popular for walking and camping. Most of the population lives east of this range, along the fertile coast. To the west, the country is flat and dry and this is where you find red kangaroos and emus roaming freely. In the extreme south lies the island of Tasmania, with some of the last great wilderness on Earth.

Australia has a population of only 18 million people in a country about the same size as the continental United States. Distances are considerable but roads and public transport are excellent. It is easy to escape human settlements and even

NEW ZEALAND *offers magnificent wilderness areas such as the South Island's Fiordland (left) and Mount Cook (below) national parks.*

remote areas are safe. On a short stay, you can still visit the backcountry. Sydney, for example, is bordered by three national parks, and walks in the bush-clad valleys of the Blue Mountains are just an hour away. You will find good campgrounds and excellent trails in most national parks.

NEW ZEALAND

New Zealand, deep in the South Pacific, has a sparkling, clean environment, a small population, excellent roads, and magnificent scenery. Thirty percent of the country is designated national park or reserve, and it's the perfect place for driving and cycling. The country's two main islands are linked by a car-ferry service.

At the top of the North Island is the Bay of Islands, with its beaches, tidal inlets, and mangroves, and the Northland Forest Park, a subtropical rain forest where you can see the kauri, New Zealand's biggest tree. In the center lies Rotorua, famous for its geysers and mud pools; Lake Taupo; and Tongariro National Park, which has three active volcanoes.

From the drowned river valleys of the Marlborough Sounds Maritime Park, at the

top of the South Island, you can head south down the west coast to see rain forests, glaciers, and magnificent mountains, or to Kaikoura, on the east coast, for whale watching. New Zealand is renowned for its walking trails in unspoiled country. It has eight "great walks" of from two to four days and numerous shorter ones. It also offers a host of opportunities to go rafting, canoeing, and horse riding.

ANTARCTICA

The coldest and windiest place on Earth, Antarctica is not for the timid and can only be visited on an organized tour. Cruise ships and airliners (day fly-overs from Australia) enable people to experience this world of icebergs, sheer ice

cliffs, and white mountains. The continent and its nutrient-rich waters are a haven for hundreds of thousands of birds, seals, penguins, and whales.

Although many nations have established research stations on Antarctica, no country owns it. It is governed by the Antarctic Treaty which is intended to ensure that it remains free of war, nuclear materials, and sovereign boundaries. A plan has been put forward by the United Nations for Antarctica to become a World Park (see p. 21). SL

ANTARCTICA *supports enormous colonies of Emperor penguins.*

Palau

Palau

Midway between Australia and Japan, in the expanse of the Pacific Ocean, lie the 2,000 dots of land that make up Micronesia. Among these islands, Palau, home to more than 700 species of fish and 1,500 invertebrates, offers some of the best diving in the world.

The Palau archipelago is the westernmost part of Micronesia and consists of over 300 islands. Seventy percent of the total population of 15,000 live on Koror, at the southern end of Babelthuap, the largest island.

MILES
0   5   10
0   10   20
KM

Babelthuap

Koror

Seventy
Islands

Eil Malk Island

Ngemelis
Wall

Jellyfish Lake

Blue Corner

A sightseeing flight over the archipelago is a good way to get your bearings. First, you'll fly along Babelthuap which is volcanic in origin and covered in rich rain forest. Then you'll pass over the myriad islands of the vast 1,675 square mile (4355 km²) lagoon. Seen from above, these islands form a dazzling green mosaic on the azure blue waters. The larger ones to the south of Babelthuap are the Rock Islands. To the west lie the Seventy Islands—an intricately laced pattern of land and water that is one of nature's great wonders.

About 85 species of bird breed in Micronesia, including the cardinal honeyeater, Pacific reef heron, and the endangered ground-dwelling Micronesian megapode. Offshore, you may see dolphins, the occasional sperm whale, or even a timid dugong. However, Palau is primarily a destination for divers. The islands offer a wealth of dive spots, but the three "must-sees" are Blue Corner, Ngemelis Wall, and Jellyfish Lake. You can elect to stay on a live-aboard dive boat or remain ashore and commute to sites by boat.

Sea fans are found throughout the Palau archipelago.

The mosaic of the Seventy Islands from the air (above). Circling barracudas (right) near one of Palau's coral reefs.

THE ULTIMATE DIVE

When dive spots worldwide are rated, Blue Corner invariably appears in every short list. On a typical dive here, you drop through a curtain of silvery fish that shimmer en masse as you pass. Then you come to the wall itself, a rock face covered in live and dead coral. The current, which is strong enough to preclude inexperienced divers, can lift you up and over the wall, so you must find a handhold in the rocks (without touching the coral). Then you can simply watch the passing parade. Sharks, barracudas, parrotfish, sea turtles, and moray eels feed on an array of smaller creatures. Indeed, this restaurant at the end of the universe is patronized by almost the entire aquatic food chain.

Jacques Cousteau, the great French oceanographer, declared Ngemelis Wall to be the world's best wall dive. Descending from 3 to 900 feet (1 to 275 m), the wall is a perpendicular surface covered with marine life. Near the top, there are crowds of sea anemones and small reef fish. Below, you'll find sea stars, feather stars, and a rainbow variety of sponges and corals.

On Eil Malk Island in the Rock Islands there is a unique attraction for both snorkelers and divers—a landlocked lake thick with jellyfish that have no predators and so have lost the ability to sting. You must leave your boat in the coastal mangroves and climb a small, steep, wooded hill, lugging your gear, to reach it. If you swim toward the sunlit part of the lake you'll soon find that every sweep of your hand is brushing scores of jellyfish aside. Finally, there are so many that it becomes impossible to see other swimmers. DM

A diver in Jellyfish Lake (above) in the Rock Islands. The jellyfish have no predators and have lost the ability to sting.

TRAVELER'S NOTES

Access International flights to Guam, then flights to Koror

When to visit Feb–April driest and best time to visit. July–Oct rainy. Palau is not located in a hurricane region

Information Palau Visitors Authority, PO Box 256 Koror, Palau 96940; tel. (680) 488-2793,

fax (680) 488-1453

Accommodation Motels and hotels in Koror. Live-aboard dive boats

Notes Open-water diving certificate and local diving permit required

The Highlands and the Sepik

Papua New Guinea

New Guinea is a wild, mountainous land covered almost entirely in dense jungle. This island of over 300,000 square miles (800,000 km²)—the second largest in the world—lies just south of the equator and about 90 miles (145 km) north of Australia, to which it was linked until 60,000 years ago by a now-submerged land bridge.

Cloud-covered mountain ranges dominate the interior. From above, the plunging gorges and razorback ridges look like a frozen sea of billowing waves. Torrential rivers descend to the coastal plains and meander through some of the world's largest swamp systems; most notably the Sepik region, whose people are renowned for their primitive art. Extremely rugged terrain has isolated as many as 1,000 tribes speaking over 700 languages. Throughout New Guinea, elements of the prehistoric survive.

Another attraction is the mesmerizing wildlife—an astounding 20,000 species of flowering plant (including two-thirds of the world's orchid species), over 6,000 species of butterfly and moth, 650 species of bird, and mammals composed mainly of marsupials and primitive egg-laying monotremes. Most are unique to the island, and their habitats are relatively secure.

While subsistence agriculture is spreading gradually outward from the main population centers and chainsaws tear at the more accessible forests, large areas of New Guinea remain free from commercial logging and the island retains around 70 percent of its tree cover.

The spotted cuscus (far left) is a tree-climbing marsupial native to the lowland rain forests of New Guinea. An extraordinary communal spiders' web in the Southern Highlands (left).

Map labels:
Wewak
Sepik River • Karawari Lodge
BAYER RIVER SANCTUARY
Wabag • ▲ Mount Wilhelm
Mendi • Mount Goroka
Hagen Highlands Hwy
• Lae
IRIAN JAYA
PAPUA NEW GUINEA
MILES 0 80 160
0 200 KM
Port Moresby

THE HIGHLANDS

The Highlands Highway is the only road leading into the mountains of the interior. It snakes uphill from Lae, on the eastern seaboard, to the town of Goroka and on through the Eastern and Western Highlands. To reach Goroka—the logical base for exploring the Highlands—from Port Moresby, the capital on the southwest coast, you must fly.

The Highlands Highway (above) cuts through the heart of the high country. Young green tree pythons (left) are bright yellow. A mudman from Asaro (below).

From Goroka, follow the highway west past coffee plantations to the Asaro Valley where, at the local cultural center, you can watch "mudmen" daubed in clay and wearing fearsome helmet-masks of mud and fiber re-enacting a traditional legend. Next, a spectacular drive takes you over the Daulo Pass (8,151 feet [2,486 m]), gateway to Chimbu Province, the most densely populated area in New Guinea. The region was unknown to outsiders until 1933 when European explorers came over the mountains and looked down in amazement on valley after valley quilted with thatched huts and gardens of *kaukau* (sweet potato), the staple crop. Looming to the north is Mount Wilhelm (14,759 feet [4,501 m]), the island's highest mountain. The trip to its summit, a grueling overnight hike from Kundiawa, should not be attempted without a guide.

Listen for the raucous calls of birds of paradise as you continue westward along the highway through moss-shrouded forest to the wide, fertile Wahgi Valley and the boom town of Mount Hagen.

TRAVELER'S NOTES

Access *International airport at Port Moresby. Flights to Mount Hagen from Cairns, Australia. Extensive domestic air network. Car rental in Goroka, Mount Hagen, Port Moresby. Boats ply the Sepik from Karawari and other lodges*

When to visit *Hot and humid year-round. Higher elevations cooler. Wet season Dec–Apr in Highlands, Oct–Nov in the Sepik, but rains occur year-round*

Information *Papua New Guinea National Tourist Board, PO Box 7144, Boroko, Papua New Guinea; tel./fax (25) 9447*

Accommodation *Lodges along Highlands Highway and the Sepik*

Notes *Insect repellent essential along the Sepik*

IN QUEST OF THE BIRD OF PARADISE

Of the world's 43 species of bird of paradise, 38 inhabit New Guinea. Their plumage is unrivaled and in the nineteenth century was esteemed in Europe's fashionable milliners' shops. Five species are almost extinct, and exporting feathers is now banned. Still, every year thousands of birds are killed to garland the ceremonial human-hair wigs that are the cultural hallmark of Chimbu Province and the Western Highlands. Hunting with firearms is outlawed— only traditional bows and arrows may be used.

For a tantalizing glimpse of these beautiful birds, drive north from Mount Hagen 35 miles (56 km) to the Baiyer River Bird of Paradise Sanctuary. Here, among the dense mid-mountain rain forest of oak, southern beech, araucaria, and pandanus, and in the tall pitpit grass along the river flats, about two dozen species can be seen flaunting their plumes like denizens of an exotic harem. The flamboyant plumage, however, is exclusive to males, who put it to good use in elaborate courtship displays.

ALONG THE SEPIK

A brief flight from Mount Hagen will whisk you to the Sepik River. At the best-known lodge, Karawari, tourists are often greeted in traditional manner by war canoes loaded with painted warriors. Don't be alarmed: the government banned head-hunting years ago.

The Sepik—a realm of exotic plants and animals—is one of four principal rivers that rise in the mountains of central New Guinea. A major portion of its 745 miles (1,200 km) is navigable year-round, meandering in great loops through a scarcely explored swampy plain. It was discovered by Europeans in 1886 but only in recent decades has the Sepik been made safe for visitors.

Limestone pinnacles near Tari in the Southern Highlands (above). During the elaborate courtship display of the male Raggiana's bird of paradise (left), the bird quivers its long flank plumes and calls raucously to its prospective mate.

The dugout canoe (above) is the most common means of transport along the Sepik. A ceremonial mask from the Middle Sepik (left).

Independent travelers can hire canoes to investigate the jungle-fringed waterways. Others can explore in comfort aboard cruise ships and houseboats that travel to isolated villages on the upper reaches. These settlements are repositories of spectacular artworks—ceremonial shields, face masks, intricately carved figurines— evolved from an elaborate spirit-based culture. Each village has its own distinctive art.

A CROCODILE'S TEARS

The Iatmul people of the Middle Sepik are the region's most prolific carvers. They worship ancestor spirits in *haus tambarans*, sacred houses with soaring gables. A haunting insistence of bamboo flutes and log drums may lure you inside to witness the traditional way of life of these fearsome yet hospitable people.

According to Iatmul legend, the Sepik was born of the tears of a *pukpuk*, the local crocodile, which grows to over 20 feet (6 m) and is much revered. Keep your eyes peeled for *pukpuks* as you follow the maze of channels, where snapper turtles scuttle about and brilliant butterflies flutter. Birding is excellent. Squadrons of eclectus parrots streak by; egrets and brolgas pick among the reeds; white-bellied sea eagles soar on the thermals; and hornbills, herons, cockatoos, and kingfishers are all around. CB

LAND OF THE WIGMEN

Until 25 years ago, the lives of the Wopkaimin people of the Star Mountains had changed little in thousands of years. Now, almost overnight, they are having to cope with twentieth-century western ways, and mass tourism is changing their lives. Yet at the same time it is helping to preserve customs that might otherwise die out.

A vital example is *bilas*, startling body and face decoration that is the principal artistic impulse of these warrior-farmers. Adornments include magnificent toupees of human hair garnished with flowers and feathers. Thousands of gaudily painted natives—the wigmen—gather each July for the Highland Show, the most elaborate sing-sing (a festival of singing, dancing, and feasting), held alternately in Goroka and Mount Hagen. Excitement rises as the wigmen chant in unison and dance to the throbbing of drums. In creating the ritual for visitors, the local people demonstrate pride in their traditional culture.

Kakadu and Arnhem Land

Australia

Kakadu National Park encom-passes an entire tropical river system and some of the oldest rock art in the world. From a 311 mile (500 km) long rocky escarpment in the east, through forests and luxuriant wetlands to tidal flats and mangroves in the north, it contains all the major habitats of this part of Australia.

The seasons in Australia's north differ spectacularly from one another. From May to September, no rain falls, then, as the year ends, the skies release torrents of rain, flooding vast areas and bringing new life. The region nurtures well over a thousand plant species, 75 reptile species, numerous mammals, amphibians, and freshwater fish, and billions of insects. But it's the birds most people come to see.

There are about 2.5 million birds in Kakadu, of which half are mag-pie geese. In the wetlands, birds are everywhere. Look for several species of heron; the pelican; the jabiru (Australia's only stork); the brolga, a large, stately bird that dances; and the comb-crested jacana, whose long toes enable it to walk over aquatic vegetation. The best time to see the birds is during the dry season when diminished wetlands restrict their range. Cruises operate at Yellow River, a 45-minute drive south of Jabiru, and on the East Alligator River near Ubirr. On these trips you may also see the two species of crocodile found in Kakadu: the smaller freshwater variety and the larger, and more dangerous, saltwater crocodile.

Drier areas are home to eight species of kangaroo and numerous lizards, although

The comb-crested jacana nests on water plants (left).
Aboriginal rock art at Nourlangie Rock (above).

generally only the wallabies, frill-neck lizards, and goannas show themselves. Sometimes a northern quoll (a small carnivorous marsupial), a dingo, or an echidna makes a brief appearance.

WATERFALLS AND LOOKOUTS

The park is large (7,722 square miles [20,000 km²]) and the main features are far apart, so allow two to five days to explore. All main roads are paved, but you will need a four-wheel-drive on some side roads. The best camping is near waterfalls such as Jim Jim and Gunlom, which have permanent pools. However, be aware that although the falls thunder over the escarpment in the wet season, they become mere trickles in the dry.

There are extensive views of the wetlands, plains, and the escarpment from Ubirr and Nourlangie lookouts, both of which also feature excellent examples of Aboriginal rock art. In the nearby valleys, pockets of monsoon rain forest provide welcome shade in the heat of the day.

The park is managed by local Aboriginal people and the National Parks and Wildlife Service. No animal species has been lost and many creatures that have lost their habitats elsewhere have found refuge here. Efforts are being made to control introduced plants and animals including feral pigs and water buffalo.

Adjoining Kakadu is Arnhem Land, a vast, wild area owned and managed by the Aboriginal people. Access is restricted but a few small camps give adventurous travelers a unique experience, and the rock art and bird life are prolific. SL

TRAVELER'S NOTES

Access International flights to Darwin. Flights from Darwin and Katherine to Jabiru. Numerous tours from Darwin. If not on a tour, a car is essential

When to visit Dry season (May–Sept) is most comfortable and best time to see birds. The wet (Dec–Mar) is lush and hot and floods often close roads. The build-up to the wet (Oct–Nov) is oppressive

Information The Park Manager, Kakadu National Park, Kakadu Hwy,

(PO Box 71) Jabiru, NT 0886, Australia; tel. (089) 799-101, fax (089) 381-115

Accommodation Hotel, holiday complex with motel and camping facilities and a youth hostel (dry season only) within park. Four official campgrounds plus bush campsites. Backcountry camping allowed but permit required

Notes Permit needed for Arnhem Land

Wetlands at Sandy Billabong (top). A saltwater crocodile (above). The sandstone escarpment of Arnhem Land (above right). **251**

The Kimberley

Australia

Bounded by desert and a precipitous coastline, the Kimberley, in northwestern Australia, is an almost square region of semi-arid plains, patches of rain forest, fat-bellied boab trees, waterfalls, and gorges that have seen relatively few humans. Archeological evidence shows that Aboriginal people have been here for at least 18,000 years, but their numbers, and those of the cattlemen that arrived 100 years ago, have always been small.

Much of this untouched, ever-changing landscape can be visited on a drive or tour from Kununurra or Broome.

THE BUNGLE BUNGLE

The most acclaimed feature of the region is the bell-shaped domes of the magnificent Bungle Bungle Range in Purnululu National Park. This mysterious part of the country was unknown to most Australians until the 1980s.

These "honeypot mountains", some 820 feet (250 m) high, are of soft sandstone held together by bands of black lichen and orange silica. Because of the mountains' fragility, visitors must walk only on the trails and on creek beds. A maze of canyons invites you to explore and you will find remnant rain forest and Livistona palms flourishing around water holes and seeps. There are thousands of frogs and 130 species of bird, including the Gouldian finch and flocks of noisy budgerigars. Three wallaby species also live here.

Walks range from a trail from the Ranger Station to Walanginjdji Lookout (1½ miles [2.5 km]), to the two-day Piccaninny Gorge hike, past deep water holes and richly varied rock formations. One of the best ways to take in the size and strangeness of the Bungle Bungle

The frill-neck lizard erects its ruff-like collar to deter predators.

Part of the Bungle Bungle Range (above). A magnificent tree frog (left). Large flocks of budgerigars (below) live throughout the Kimberley.

is to take a scenic flight. These are available from most of the towns in the vicinity.

Some 350 million years ago, the Kimberley was partly covered by a sea which, when it receded, exposed a giant limestone reef. The ancient reef extends for 600 miles (1,000 km) and is studded with fossilized marine creatures from the Devonian period, before the evolution of reptiles and mammals. Over the eons, seasonal rivers have cut gorges, exposing the fossils and creating caves where Aborigines sheltered. The best places to see such features are in the national parks of Geikie Gorge, Tunnel Creek, and Windjana Gorge in the southwest. These gorges are treasure troves of fossils, Aboriginal art, fish, freshwater crocodiles, bats, and birds. The water holes are fringed with paperbarks, river gums, native figs, and freshwater mangroves.

Most spectacular is Geikie Gorge, with its cream and reddish brown walls. You need a flashlight and a strong constitution to visit the caves of Tunnel Creek where colonies of bats live. You have to wade through icy pools and past freshwater crocodiles. Windjana Gorge has a lovely walking trail between high cliffs.

The coast can be explored from Broome and Derby on charter boats. Waterfalls spill into the ocean and birds and crocodiles live among the mangroves. Broome Bird Observatory is an important site for shorebirds. Of its 240 bird species, 33 are migratory. SL

TRAVELER'S NOTES

Access International flights to Darwin, Perth, and Broome. Domestic flights and coaches to Kununurra and Broome. Many tours available. 4WDs, campervans, and camping gear can be rented locally

When to visit May–Sept. Other months, particularly Jan–March, hot and wet; some roads and parks may close.

Information Western Australia Tourist Centre, Forrest Place, Perth, WA 6000, Australia; tel. (09) 483-1111. Kununurra Tourist Bureau, Lot 75, Coolibah Dr.,

Kununurra, WA 6743, Australia; tel. (091) 681-177. Broome Tourist Bureau, Cnr Bagot Rd and Great Northern Hwy, Broome, WA 6725, Australia; tel. (091) 922-222

Accommodation Hotels, motels and campsites in towns. Campsites in parks

Notes Always carry water on walks. Saltwater crocodiles along the coast and in estuaries are dangerous

The spectacular rock walls of Geikie Gorge were formed by the Fitzroy River.

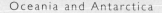

Coastal Queensland

Australia

Along Australia's far north-eastern coast, ancient rain forests grow from the mountaintops to the tropical sea. Beneath the sea lies the greatest coral reef in the world, the Great Barrier Reef, which stretches for 1,430 miles (2,300 km). Both the rain forest and the reef are World Heritage listed. The patches of rain forest listed as the Wet Tropics of Queensland run along the coast for nearly 360 miles (600 km). An Aboriginal culture developed here, and on Cape York Peninsula there is an extensive body of prehistoric art.

In this wonderful part of Australia, you can swim in clear forest streams in the morning and in a world of coral and tropical fish in the afternoon. The best place to base yourself is either Cairns or Port Douglas, but you might also like to spend a few days on one of the many islands.

THE RAIN FOREST

In the rain forest, many plants retain characteristics from millions of years ago. Here, among 1,160 species of flora, you will find the world's largest concentration of ancient flowering plants and the greatest diversity of wildlife in the country. Some of the finest areas of rain forest lie a couple of hours north of Cairns, in Daintree and Cape Tribulation national parks. Once you cross the Daintree River, by ferry, the drive is spectacular, through tunnels of trees and

To attract a mate, the male satin bower bird decorates its bower with any blue objects it can find (right). A Cairns birdwing butterfly (above).

254

Cape Tribulation Beach and Mount Sorrow (above). The aerial roots of this strangler fig have formed a dense curtain (right).

over hillcrests with magnificent views of the forest and long, golden beaches. From the river, it's a 24 mile (40 km) drive to Cape Tribulation, named by Captain Cook when he damaged his ship here in 1770.

Along the road, walking trails lead through the trees and board-walks cross mangrove swamps to isolated beaches. In the forest, the buttress roots of tall trees and mighty strangler figs compete for space. Ferns, mosses, orchids, lichens, and colorful fungi thrive in the moist mulch of fallen leaves and branches.

Reptiles and possums scuttle away when disturbed. The brilliant colors of the birds are rivalled by the magnificence of the butterflies.

Walkers may come across a cassowary, a glossy black, flight-less bird up to 6 feet (2 m) tall with a casque on its head. These birds are quite aggressive but their sight is poor, so you can safely watch them from behind a tree. If approached, they raise their feathers and hiss loudly.

At the town of Daintree, you can take a cruise along the river to see the crocodiles and birds that inhabit the mangrove-lined creeks and tributaries. Forty-nine species of bird live here, including herons, egrets, cuckoos, honeyeaters, sea-eagles, kookaburras, and bright blue kingfishers.

Mossman Gorge, to the west of Port Douglas, is a lush valley of towering rain forest and sparkling streams and waterfalls.

Tree frogs abound in the moist rain forest environment.

TRAVELER'S NOTES

Access *International flights to Cairns and Brisbane. Domestic flights to mainland towns and some islands. Train from Brisbane to Cairns (32 hours). Reef cruises from Port Douglas, Cairns, Townsville, Airlie Beach, Bundaberg*

When to visit *Year-round. Dec–Mar hot, wet and steamy*

Information *Far North Queensland Promotions Bureau, PO Box 865, Cairns, QLD 4870, Australia; tel. (070) 513-588, fax (070) 510-127. Queensland Tourist and Travel Corp., GPO Box 328, Brisbane, QLD 4001,*

Australia; tel. (07) 3406-5400, fax (07) 3406-5496

Accommodation *Range of accommodation along coast. Lodges and camping at Mossman and on Cape Tribulation road. Resorts and camping on many islands including Heron and Lady Elliot*

Notes *Deadly box jellyfish along mainland coast (but not on reef) Oct–May. Swim only in enclosures*

An easy 2½-hour hiking trail follows a stretch of the Mossman River which is strewn with huge boulders. It crosses a bridge, then meanders back through the forest where you can see Boyd's forest dragons (a type of lizard) in the trees.

Heron Island and Wistari Reef (above). A silvertip reef shark (left).

THE GREAT BARRIER REEF

The Great Barrier Reef is a maze of thousands of small reefs and hundreds of islands and coral cays. Covering an area of 134,600 square miles (348,600 km²), it's the world's largest system of corals and associated plants and animals. In 1975, the Great Barrier Reef Marine Park was established to protect the area. It is managed by the Great Barrier Reef Marine Park Authority, which monitors commercial and leisure activities, undertakes a range of research activities and conducts education programs.

Black noddy terns nest on many reef islands.

To reach the reef from the mainland, you take a charter cruise or fly to one of the cays or islands. Most trips are day trips but some outfitters offer accommodation on cruise boats. Cruises also depart from many of the resort islands, few of which are on the reef. (There are resorts on about 20 islands but choose carefully because some are crowded, party places and some are overrun by daytrippers.)

Boat charter operators generally offer beginners a scuba lesson and then a shallow dive with an instructor. Some visitors prefer to snorkel in the shallows or view the reef from a glass-bottomed boat. In all, the reef supports 1,500 species of fish, 400 species of coral, 500 species of seaweed, and 4,000 species of mollusk. You will see corals in blues, pinks, and greens; giant clams; crabs; harmless reef sharks; moray eels; butterfly fish; parrotfish; and schools of little fish in shades of silver, gold, orange, red, and green.

Experienced divers are taken to renowned dive spots where they may also come across dugong, sea turtles, rays, sharks, sea snakes, and enormous whale sharks.

The seagrass beds around the reef feed some 12,000 dugong—large, herbivorous marine mammals. These gentle creatures resemble fat dolphins. The reef is also the wintering ground

for humpback whales which arrive from the Antarctic in June to breed in warmer waters.

The islands are the breeding grounds of vast numbers of turtles and seabirds. Over a million wedge-tailed shearwaters and about half a million black noddy terns nest here, as do gulls, gannets, and frigatebirds.

Two of the most appealing places to stay, both of which are on the reef, are Heron and Lady Elliot islands, in the south of the park. These "islands" are in fact coral cays. They support numerous seabirds, turtles nest on their beaches, and their reefs are superb for snorkeling and diving. The research center on Heron is open to the public and an ecocenter on Lady Elliot provides information on the reef.

As in all ecosystems, there is a fine balance between animals and plants. In the 1960s and '70s,

vast numbers of crown-of-thorns starfish (sea stars) consumed whole reefs. When their numbers fell, the reefs recovered. Researchers are trying to find out whether population explosions such as these are natural or result from human activities. SL

NESTING SEA TURTLES

Tens of thousands of sea turtles live and breed around the Great Barrier Reef. It has one of the largest remaining green turtle rookeries in the world, is a nesting ground for loggerheads and hawkbills, and a refuge for the giant leatherback, the flatback, and, occasionally, the olive Ridgley.

From October to February, the females lumber ashore. Each digs a depression with her front flippers to accommodate her, then, with her back flippers, scoops out a hole into which she lays soft, white eggs. From January to April, the hatchlings dig their way out and run to the sea. Large numbers are eaten by crabs, birds, and fish before they reach deep water.

Females live for about 50 years and start laying when they are about 30 years old. They produce several clutches of eggs a season, but only lay every three to six years. They nest on many beaches so there is a good chance of visitors seeing them.

A giant Maori wrasse (above). Purple anthias, angelfish, and golden damselfish among the coral (top). One of the many thousands of green turtles that nest on the reef islands (right).

257

Southwestern Australia

Australia

Few places in the world are as acclaimed for the diversity of their flora as southwestern Australia. Isolated by sea and desert, the flora here has developed over eons, unaffected by invaders. Primitive forms sway beside those that are more evolved. There are plants that use tricks to catch insects; orchids that grow underground; and stunning orange-flowering Christmas trees, the largest root parasite in the world. Current estimates put the number of species at 8,000, but new plants are found every year.

A good way to start a wildflower tour is with a visit to King's Park and Botanic Garden in Perth. This beautiful park has a huge section devoted to native plants. Where you go next depends upon your interests and the time of year, as the mixture of species and the timing of flowering vary from region to region. Around Kalbarri, 350 miles (560 km) north of Perth, the flowers burst into life in July, starting to open farther and farther south as the weather warms up. In the south, they are blooming from September through February.

The coast road north from Perth, leading to Kalbarri National Park, is rich with heath and woodlands. A deep river gorge slashes through Kalbarri's dry sandplains and some 300 species of flowering plant bloom in the park in July and August. If you return to Geraldton and follow the inland road toward Mullewa, you will find everlastings covering the ground like spilled paint, especially after rain. The 80 miles (130 km) from Mullewa to Perenjori are exceptional, with foxgloves, everlastings, and yellow wattles in flower.

The flowers attract a variety of birds that pollinate the plants as they flit from one to another. Among the most common species are honeyeaters, western spinebills, and red wattlebirds.

Many feather flowers are pollinated by the jewel beetle (left).

In spring, everlastings carpet the fields (above). Karri trees near Albany (left). The western pygmy possum is one of a number of small marsupials that pollinate flowers such as the grevillea (below).

TALL TREES AND ORCHIDS

South of Perth, the country is richer and wetter. Following the coast road through the vineyards of Margaret River, you come to Albany where mighty forests of karri, tuart, and jarrah grow. Eastward, toward Esperance, the countryside is famous for its feather flowers and orchids.

Botanists from all over the world flock to Stirling Range National Park, which lies 40 miles (65 km) north of Albany. The range was declared a national reserve early this century and so escaped being cleared for farming, unlike the surrounding country. The park has over 1,000 species of flowering plant, of which 60 are found nowhere else. From towering peaks shrouded in mist to sprawling heathlands grow leschenaultias, grass trees, scarlet banksia, pea flowers, blue smoke bush, rare and delicate mountain bells, and orchids.

Among the estimated 300 species of ground orchid in the region are such beauties as the blue lady, the charming dwarf blue China, spindly spider varieties, and the remarkable *Rhizanthella gardneri*. This plant grows and flowers entirely below the soil surface and is pollinated by termites.

Some of the insect-eating plants have sticky pads that trap insects, while others use subterranean bladders to catch soil microbes. The Albany pitcher plant is a lethal pit into which insects drop and cannot get out.

Western Australia's floral emblem is the lovely, velvety kangaroo paw from the Haemodoraceae family. Species range in size from a ground-hugging 4 inches (10 cm) to the giant *Anigozanthos flavidus* at 8 feet (2.5 m). SL

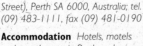

TRAVELER'S NOTES

Access International flights to Perth. Many driving and walking tours from Perth, or rent a car

When to visit Starting in the north at Kalbarri in July and moving south till Dec. Stirling Range blooms Sept–Nov

Information Western Australia Tourist Centre, Forrest Place (Cnr Wellington Street), Perth SA 6000, Australia; tel. (09) 483-1111, fax (09) 481-0190

Accommodation Hotels, motels and guesthouses in Perth and other towns throughout region. Camping in most national parks.

The Red Center

Australia

From above, the center of Australia spreads in a panorama of red soil speckled with dusty vegetation, rows of brown mountain ranges and pencil-thin roads. Much of the history of this ancient landscape is in its rocks, some of them nearly two billion years old.

Compared with most arid areas, Central Australia is rich in vegetation and wildlife. All sorts of marsupials, from rock wallabies to the mouse-like hairy footed dunnart, leave their footprints in the sand, as do dingos, and many birds, rodents, frogs, and lizards. This country is home to the world's second-largest lizard, the perentie, which grows to 8 feet (2.5 m), and the bizarre thorny devil, a small, slow-moving lizard that is covered with spines.

The richest natural areas lie deep within gorges that were formed by ancient rivers, where cool water holes give life to a profusion of plants and creatures.

There are any number of secluded gorges in the MacDonnell Ranges, which are only a day trip from the town of Alice Springs. The closest is Simpsons Gap, which can be reached along a 10 mile (16 km) bicycle path from the Alice. Energetic walkers can do the completed sections of the Larapinta Trail, which will eventually run for 132 miles (213 km) from Alice Springs west along the backbone of the West MacDonnell Ranges.

Palm Valley in the Finke Gorge National Park, 90 miles (145 km) from Alice Springs, is an oasis where hundreds of red cabbage palms grow. It's a jolting four-wheel-drive trip to the valley, but you are rewarded

Uluru (Ayers Rock) rises 1,050 feet (340 m) from the desert floor (left). A red kangaroo (right).

Glen Helen Gorge (above). A spiny devil near Kata Tjuta (right). This slow-moving lizard eats thousands of ants each day.

with an abundance of plants, including palms, ferns, and mosses, their greenery contrasting with sheer rock walls of burning red.

Australia's most famous rock, Uluru (Ayers Rock), is a sandstone monolith that rises from the broad plains of red sand and golden spinifex. Uluru and the rock humps of Kata Tjuta (the Olgas) lie within the World Heritage listed Uluru–Kata Tjuta National Park, which is owned by the Aboriginal people who have lived here for at least 23,000 years. Their tours describe how their ancestors lived in this harsh environment and introduce visitors to the Aboriginal view of the natural world, which sees the landscape and all living things as having deep spiritual significance. You can walk the 6 mile (9.5 km) trail around Uluru, to see its changing rock forms, the water holes, and various caves containing Aboriginal art. Visitors are drawn to climb the rock but the local people regard this as disrespectful.

BACK ROADS

For a drive that encompasses the Center's unique features, take the Mereenie Loop Road from Alice Springs to Yulara, the resort near Uluru. The road links Glen Helen, Kings Canyon, and Yulara, returning to Alice Springs via the Lasseter and Stuart highways. Side roads lead to the chasms and waterholes of Simpsons Gap, Standley Chasm, Ellery Creek Big Hole, Serpentine Gorge, and Ormiston Gorge. You should allow five days for the trip, to have plenty of time for swimming and walking. SL

TRAVELER'S NOTES

Access Domestic flights from capital cities to Alice Springs. Coach and 4WD tours from Alice Springs, where 4WD vehicles and campervans can be rented. Uluru is 288 miles (480 km) from Alice Springs, 45 minutes by air

When to visit Year-round. Hot during the day; coolest Apr–Sept. Cold at night

Information Central Australian Regional Tourism Industry Association,

Cnr Gregory Tce and Hartley St, Alice Springs NT 0871, Australia; tel. (089) 525-199, fax (089) 530-295

Accommodation Hotels, motels, hostels, campsites in Alice Springs and Yulara; hotel, hostel, campsites at Kings Canyon; motel, campsites at Glen Helen; campsites in national parks

Notes Carry water on all walks: 8 pints (4 l) per person per day. Register with rangers before going on long hikes

The Tasmanian Wilderness

Australia

The island of Tasmania, lying off Australia's southeastern corner, is a place of spectacular scenery where more than 30 percent of the land is secure in World Heritage areas, national parks, and reserves. The Tasmanian Wilderness World Heritage Area, in the west, encompasses a mountainous, magical wilderness. Occasionally, a scenic flight buzzes over the crags of Cradle Mountain, a cruise boat shatters the reflections on the Gordon River, or a white-water raft bounces down the untamed Franklin. Otherwise, the whole 5,400 square miles (14,000 km²) is pretty much free of people. Yet archeological evidence, including some of the world's oldest cave paintings, shows that humans lived here during the last ice age.

The scenery changes markedly as one moves from north to south. The north is

mainly wet, alpine country with a large plateau in the east that receives heavy snowfalls. The mountains are mostly rounded, with some sharp ridges to challenge climbers. Glaciers once covered the land, gouging valleys and hollows where clear lakes now glitter. The central region is lower, with rivers that tumble through forested gorges. In the south, there are two huge artificial lakes, Gordon and Pedder, and the coast is characterized by mountains and dunes.

The dense rain forests throughout lowland areas contain sassafras, celery top pine, King Billy pine, myrtle beech, and stands of Huon pine.

The Tasmanian devil (left) lives throughout the island. Grass trees (right) grow in heath country.

Higher up, the trees are stunted, leaving the plateaus to fields of buttongrass, flowering herbs, dwarf shrubs, and bright green cushion plants.

Wildflowers are at their best in December but many people come in April to see the native beech when it turns brilliant orange. On walks, look for quolls (cat-like marsupials), wallabies, pademelons (small wallabies), wombats, platypuses, and Tasmanian devils.

WONDERFUL WALKING

The Overland Track, the island's best-known walk, runs north–south through Cradle Mountain–Lake St Clair National Park. It can be done in five days if you're reasonably fit. As you walk, mountains, forests, and moors become your home and cockatoos, honeyeaters, and rosellas your companions. Huts are a day apart, but hikers should carry a tent in case they are full.

The less energetic can walk along the shores of Lake Dove to a forest of myrtle, sassafras, King Billy pine, and grass trees or wander through moorland and past waterfalls.

A delightful way to visit the wilderness is to take a cruise from the town of Strahan, on the west coast, up the Gordon River. Trips go as far as Heritage Landing, where a boardwalk loops through the dense rain forest.

The South Coast Track, in Southwest National Park, is not for the faint-hearted. Walkers usually fly in to Melaleuca, near Bathurst Harbour, and exit at Cockle Creek in the east. The track goes along beaches and through swampland, and includes two mountain crossings. There are no huts and it's an exhausting eight to ten days, but experienced walkers rave about it. If you'd prefer a day walk, you can walk from Cockle Creek to South Cape Bay and back in a day. SL

Cradle Mountain, viewed from the shore of Lake Dove (above). The platypus (left) is found in subalpine lakes.

TRAVELER'S NOTES

Access International flights to Melbourne. Ferry or domestic flights to Launceston or Hobart, then by rental car. Comprehensive coach network: if no regular service, company will arrange connection at start and end of walks

When to visit Year-round. Dec–Apr best for walking. Feb driest month. Snow on mountains June–Sept

Information Dept of Tourism, Sport and Recreation, Tasmania Government Travel Information Service, GPO Box

399, Hobart, Tasmania 7001, Australia; tel. (002) 30-8250, fax (002) 30-8232

Accommodation Lodges, huts, and camping in World Heritage Area. Motels, cabins, and camping in nearby towns

Notes When camping, carry fuel stove as fires are banned in many areas. Weather is wet and changeable so be prepared

263

The South Island

New Zealand

Jewels in the temperate South Pacific, the islands of New Zealand broke from the ancient southern landmass, Gondwana, about 80 million years ago, and their plants, fish, birds, insects, one reptile (the tuatara), and only two mammals (both bats) evolved in isolation. Without predators, many plants did not evolve defence mechanisms, and some birds became flightless. This proved the birds' downfall when humans arrived. The Maori came about 900 years ago, Europeans 200 years ago. The flightless kiwi, takahe, kakapo, and weka are only surviving because of programs to protect them; the mighty moa and others have gone.

Wildlife conservation is now a high priority in New Zealand. Fortunately, because the human population is small, it has been possible to set aside large areas as parks and preserves. Programs are in place to eradicate introduced animals and plants and much captive breeding work is being done.

The South Island is a geological wonderland, with the Southern Alps running its entire length, dividing the plains of the east from a slip of land on the west. The rainfall on the west coast is high, resulting in dripping rain forest where the air smells of mosses and ferns. From November to April, the rata trees shroud the forest in a red haze.

The southwest of the South Island is a wilderness of knife-like, snow-capped mountains, lakes, glaciers, rain forests, wetlands, and deep, brooding fiords. The air is pure and people are few. Here you will find the national parks of Mount Cook, Westland, Mount Aspiring, and Fiordland which, together with neighboring protected areas, were listed in 1990 as the South-West New Zealand World Heritage Area.

The takahe is among a number of flightless birds species in the country that survive only because of programs to protect them.

MOUNT COOK NATIONAL PARK

Driving from Christchurch (about three hours), the first of these parks you come to is Mount Cook. In 1991, the top of Mount Cook collapsed and millions of tons of rock and ice blitzed down the Tasman Glacier. Avalanches are common in the Southern Alps, sometimes as a result of weather conditions, but also because the mountains are constantly being uplifted by movements in the Pacific and Indian plates.

Most walks start from Mount Cook Village and helicopters take skiers and sightseers from here onto

Mount Cook lilies (left) bloom in December. The kea (right) is the world's only alpine parrot.

Magnificent Mount Cook rises to 12,316 feet (3,754 m), crowning the alpine national park that carries its name.

the Tasman Glacier. From November to March, the park is bright with alpine wildflowers, birds, and butterflies. This is the time to do the many easy walks. The one-hour Governor's Bush Walk takes you through silver-beech forest, and the Hooker Valley Trail, which is a round trip of about three hours, leads to the terminal lake of the Hooker Glacier. Watch out for the roguish kea, a parrot found throughout the mountains. It will steal anything left lying around.

Experienced hikers might like to take the Copland Track that leads over the alps to the West Coast Road near Fox Glacier. The crossing takes three to four days but is often closed by bad weather. You must check with the ranger station at Mount Cook before setting out. Guides are available to take groups over the pass. To reach Fox Glacier by car, you have to either cross the alps farther south at Haast Pass (284 miles/457 km) or to the north at Arthurs Pass (402 miles/ 647 km).

TRAVELER'S NOTES

Access International flights to Christchurch. Domestic flights to Hokitika, Mt Cook, Queenstown. Best to rent a car

When to visit Mount Cook year-round, walking best Nov–Apr. Westland, Fiordland wet all year, walking best Nov–Apr, other times cold and bad weather can close tracks. Milford Track open late Oct to mid-Apr

Information Mt Cook: DOC, Mt Cook Village, Mt Cook, NZ; tel. (03) 435-1819. Westland: DOC, PO Box 14, Franz Josef, NZ; tel. (03) 752-0727.

Fiordland: DOC, PO Box 29, Te Anau, NZ; tel. (03) 249-8514. Kaikoura: Whale Watch Kaikoura Ltd, PO Box 89, Kaikoura, NZ; tel. (03) 319-5045

Accommodation Hotels, motels and camping in towns. Huts or camping on most tracks. No camping on Milford Track

Notes Passes required for Milford Track: book several months ahead with Te Anau DOC office

265

RAIN FOREST AND GLACIERS

Fed by snowfall in the Southern Alps, the Franz Joseph and Fox glaciers, in Westland National Park, terminate 2,300 feet (700 m) above sea level, almost in the rain forest. These mighty rivers of ice are fascinating to visit, with or without a guide. Isolated chunks of ice and masses of boulders mark the points at which they end.

Westland's relatively mild climate and diversity of wetlands provide habitats for birds such as the New Zealand scaup, pukeko, royal spoonbill, black swan, paradise shelduck, kingfisher, and the rare and graceful white heron. You can visit the herons' breeding ground on a tour from Wateroa or Franz Joseph from November to February and walk along

Stella Falls (above) at Doubtful Sound, in Fiordland. Walkers at the terminal of Fox Glacier (left) in Westland. The kiwi (below left) is the best known of New Zealand's flightless birds.

beaches where fur seals and the quaint Fiordland crested penguins live. Lake Matheson, near Fox Glacier, is a place to slow down and listen to the whispers of nature. In the park there are also traces of early mining endeavors: the Maori came for greenstone, Europeans for gold.

FIORDLAND NATIONAL PARK

Writers and artists have tried to capture the grandeur of Fiordland National Park but nothing prepares you for its wildness, its sheer rock walls, its lakes and waterfalls, and the mists wafting around towering peaks. Long-gone glaciers have cut U-shaped valleys where sea water now penetrates deep inland, forming fiords. Forests of podocarp (ancient conifers with fleshy fruit) line the shores.

The main center for Fiordland is the lakeside village of Te Anau. To the south lies Manapouri from where day-trips depart for the remote fiords of Doubtful Sound. To the north, a spectacular drive, the 75 mile (120 km) Milford Road, leads to Milford Sound. It runs along the shores of Lake Te Anau and through beech forests before making a dramatic descent through a magnificent, glacier-

gouged valley to the water's edge, where occasional cruise boats and kayaks, dwarfed by towering cliffs, carve through the still water. A number of walks depart from points along the road.

The high rainfall (200 days a year) and milder temperatures in the valleys nurture forests of podocarp, silver beech, and kamahi, which form a protective canopy for tree ferns and mosses. More than 700 plant species are endemic. At every turn you come across waterfalls, and when the rains are heavy many of the creeks flood, carrying debris downstream. Parts of the park have never been explored and the trails have a pioneer feel to them.

Three hundred miles (500 km) of walking tracks crisscross the park. Some are easy, others, such as the Milford, the Routeburn, and the Kepler, are more challenging. The Milford Track links Lake Te Anau to Milford Sound. It's 33 miles (53 km) long and you need to be moderately fit as the route is quite strenuous. The track climbs from lush valleys around canyon walls and over the Mackinnon Pass, where alpine herbs color the ground. As you walk, you will notice the changing bird life: bellbirds, tomtits, grey warblers, and tiny riflemen in the lower areas; rock wrens

and cheeky keas higher up. At dusk, you may hear the whistle of the kiwi. When you reach the fiords you'll see seals, dolphins, and the Fiordland crested penguin which live along the coast. SL

WHALE WATCHING

For generations, the Māori people of Kaikoura, a fishing village north of Christchurch, have marveled at whales, dolphins, and New Zealand fur seals playing in the nutrient-rich, deep water close to shore. In the 1980s, the Ngai Tahu tribe, seeing the growing interest worldwide in whale watching, decided to set up whale-watching boat trips to provide jobs for their people. They raised money and trained staff and Whale Watch Kaikoura trips are now a great international drawcard. (In 1994 they won the British Airways Ecotourism Award.) Few other places in the Southern Hemisphere offer better opportunities for seeing marine mammals.

The boats go out every day, weather permitting. Sometimes it's just too rough. Immature male sperm whales and the endangered Hector dolphin live here permanently and are joined throughout the year by orcas, humpbacks, and dusky dolphins. Even on shore there is plenty to see, with more than 2,000 seals sunning themselves on the rocks and albatrosses and petrels soaring above.

Milford Sound is surrounded by peaks up to 5,000 feet (1,500 m) high (top). Sometimes the whales at Kaikoura (above right) come so close to the boats that they cover their audience with sea spray.

The Antarctic Peninsula

Antarctica

The 1,000 mile (1,600 km) long mountainous spine that juts from the Antarctic continent toward South America is known as the Antarctic Peninsula. Here you will find dramatic mountains, glaciers, and fiords, vast penguin rookeries, seal colonies, and seabird nesting sites, all of which ensure the peninsula's reputation as one of the world's great, undisturbed wildlife paradises.

Since the founding father of tourist travel to Antarctica, Lars Eric Lindblad, took the first groups of ship-based ecotravelers to the area in the early 1960s, the peninsula has become the most frequently visited part of the continent. Compared with the rest of Antarctica, it is relatively accessible and the summers (December to February) here are mild, with the temperature averaging −3°C to +3°C (27°F to 37°F). As a result, the peninsula is the only place in Antarctica where flowering plants occur.

Falkland Islands
Port Stanley
ARGENTINA
CHILE
Punta Arenas
Ushuaia
MILES
0   160   320
0   300   600
KM
Drake Passage
South Shetland Islands
Deception Island
Antarctic Circle

HEADING SOUTH

Each summer, ice-strengthened tour ships head south into the stormy waters of the Drake Passage, making for the western flanks of the peninsula. After a day or so at sea, you enter the magical world of castle-like icebergs, then the ship makes its way into the sheltered waters between the South Shetland Islands and the northern tip of the Antarctic continent. Mountains rise steeply from the sea—an icebound continuation of the Andes.

Beyond the South Shetlands, the volcano of Deception Island (which last erupted in 1967) sits in brooding contrast to its snow-covered neighbors. Small ships can pass through a gap in the crater wall into the seawater-filled caldera

Inflatable boats are used to take travelers from ship to shore.

Adélie penguins on one of the islands of the peninsula (above). A minke whale (right). Chinstrap penguins (below).

where, at the water's edge, steam rises among scattered groups of chinstrap penguins.

As you cruise farther south, there are opportunities to visit ice-filled bays along the deeply indented coast. The ice comes from the winter freeze, nearby ice shelves, and calving glaciers. (Sometimes, when a glacier calves, millions of tons of ice collapse into the sea like a 10-story building exploding in a city demolition.)

In many of the bays just north of the Antarctic Circle there are Adélie, gentoo, and chinstrap penguin rookeries with between 5,000 and 300,000 birds busily laying eggs, hatching chicks, and weaning their young. The Adélie penguin has an endearing habit of dropping a pebble at the feet of its mate as he or she sits on the nest. This seems to be a token of affection.

Whale sightings are common. These waters are the summer feeding grounds for minke, orca, and migrating humpback whales. Humpback whales sometimes become curious about passing inflatables and come to take a look. Often they pass so close that you can smell krill on the whale's blow-hole breath.

You will also see crabeater seals lolling about on passing ice-floes, huge elephant seals lying in groups on the shore, and leopard seals cruising in menacing patrols near penguin rookeries.

In order to protect the peninsula, quotas may soon be placed on the most commonly visited sites, particularly in fragile, mossy areas where a single footprint can last for years. GM

TRAVELER'S NOTES

Access Ships depart from Punta Arenas in Chile, Ushuaia in Argentina, and Port Stanley in the Falklands

When to visit Early Dec to late Feb

Information International Antarctic Tour Operators Association,

111 East 14 St, Suite 110, New York, NY 10003, USA; tel. (212) 460-8715, fax (212) 529-8684

Notes Book ahead. Cruises range from 8 to 14 days. Ensure ship is ice-strengthened and the crew experienced in traveling in antarctic waters. Ships take between 35 and 400 passengers

The Ross Sea

Antarctica

The Ross Sea, off the shores of Antarctica, lies about six days' sailing southward across the Southern Ocean from Tasmania or New Zealand. For most of the year, the Ross Sea is covered by pack ice (frozen sea), which can stretch hundreds of miles out from the coast. Visits must therefore be made in summer, when the ice has melted enough to allow ships to approach the shore.

The journey south is frequently rough but always rewarding. After about four days sailing you'll see icebergs. They come in an infinite variety of shapes and range from the size of a table to that of a city. Where the cold waters of Antarctica meet the warmer, northern seas, nutrient-rich water upwells, forming the Antarctic Convergence—an immensely rich feeding ground for seabirds and marine mammals. These waters are home to the millions of Adélie and emperor penguins that you will see resting on icebergs, along with crabeater and Ross seals. Large numbers of orca, minke, humpback, fin, and sei whales live here, too.

Tens of millions of seabirds live on the Southern Ocean, from majestic albatrosses that feed on squid, to tiny, darting petrels that pluck plankton from the surface of the ocean with their clawed feet.

THE ROSS ICE SHELF

As the ship enters the Ross Sea, the Transantarctic Mountains dominate the view to the west, rising straight from the water to an average height of over 9,000 feet (2,750 m). At the northern tip of the mountains, the volcanic peninsula of Cape Adare pokes into the Southern Ocean. To the south, the flat expanse of the Ross Ice

Weddell seals are usually seen on the dense pack ice.

(map labels) MILES · 0 · 150 · 300 · 0 · 250 · 500 · KM · ROSS SEA · McMurdo Sound · Ross Island · Transantarctic Mountains · Ross Ice Shelf

The Ross Ice Shelf (above) is more than 650 feet (200 m) thick and is about the size of France. Adélie penguins around Shackleton's hut on Ross Island (left), which was built in 1908.

Shelf meets the sea in 100 foot (30 m) ice cliffs. Its seaward margin is 500 miles (800 km) across, from Ross Island in the west to Marie Byrd Land in the east. This is the phenomenal wall of ice that early explorers named the Barrier.

West of Ross Island, McMurdo Sound gives access to the Barrier. In late summer, it is some-times possible to cruise right up to the largest Antarctic research station, the US McMurdo Base. New Zealand's Scott Base is nearby.

It was from Ross Island that Amundsen, Scott, and Shackleton made their epic journeys toward the South Pole early in the century. The huts of Scott and Shackleton are still standing, lovingly preserved by the New Zealand Antarctic

Heritage Trust. Mount Erebus (12,450 feet [3,797 m]), an active volcano, looms behind them, vapor rising from its summit.

Visiting tourists live on board ship and are taken in inflatable boats to visit various sites along the coast, such as penguin nesting colonies. Visitors must take great care as the Antarctic environment is extremely fragile. In summer, the temperature averages −10°C to +1°C (14°F to 34°F). The sun barely sets in summer and the days are prefaced by glorious apricot, orange, and pink skies as the sun dances close to the horizon for hours on end. GM

Emperor penguins breed in large colonies on the ant-arctic ice.

TRAVELER'S NOTES

Access Ships depart from Hobart, Tasmania; Invercargill, New Zealand; and Christchurch, New Zealand

When to visit Late Dec to late Feb

Information International Antarctic Tour Operators Association, 111 East 14 St, Suite 110, New York, NY 10003, USA; tel. (212) 460-8715, fax (212) 529-8684

Notes Book ahead. Cruises range from 21 to 25 days. Ensure ship is ice-strengthened and the crew experienced in traveling in Antarctic waters. Each ship takes between 35 and 180 passengers

We need wilderness whether or not we ever set foot in it.
We need a refuge even though we may never need to
go there … We need the possibility of escape as surely
as we need hope.

Desert Solitaire: A Season in the Wilderness, EDWARD ABBEY (1927–1989),
American writer

RESOURCES
DIRECTORY

FURTHER READING

Books
GENERAL

The Backpacker's Handbook,
by Hugh McManners
(Houghton Mifflin, 1995).
Sound advice on wilderness
hiking and camping.

Discovering the Wonders of Our
World (Reader's Digest, 1993).
A colorful guide to 138 of the
world's natural wonders.

Earthtrips: A Guide to Nature
Travel on a Fragile Planet, by
Dwight Holing (Living Planet
Press, 1991). An overview
of international ecotravel
destinations.

Ecotourism. A Sustainable Option?,
by Lowman Gwen (Wiley,
1994). A study of ecotourism
as a sustainable economic
source as well as a conservation management tool.

Ecotourism: The Uneasy Alliance,
by Karen Ziffer (Conservation
International/Ernst Young,
1989). An analysis of the
growth of ecotourism.

Ecotours and Nature Getaways:
A Guide to Environmental
Vacations Around the World, by
Alice M. Geffen and Carole
Berglie (Clarkson Potter,
1993). A guide to tours,
operators, and activities.

Ecotravel, edited by Buzzworm
Magazine (Buzzworm, 1992).
A round-up of ecotravel
destinations and operators.

Eco Vacations: Enjoy Yourself and
Save the Earth, by Evelyn Kaye
(Blue Penguin Publications,
1991). A sampler of volunteer
vacations.

The Green Travel Sourcebook,
by Daniel Grotta and Sally
Wiener Grotta (Wiley, 1992).
Hints and tips on planning
an ecoadventure.

Holidays That Don't Cost the
Earth, by John Elkington and
Julia Haines (Victor Gollancz,
1992). Good, practical advice
on planning an ecotour.

Nature's Last Strongholds, (Time-
Life, 1993). A survey of
conservation issues and protected areas around the world.

Nature Tourism: Managing for the
Environment, by Tensie Whelan
(Island Press, 1991). A study of
ecotourism as a conservation
management tool.

Paradise on Earth, by the IUCN–
The World Conservation
Union (JIDD Publishers,
1995). A lavishly illustrated
guide to UNESCO's natural
World Heritage sites.

Staying Healthy in Asia, Africa,
and Latin America (Volunteers
in Asia Publications, 1988).
Advice on health matters.

The Traveller's Health Guide, by
Dr Anthony C. Turner
(Roger Lascelles, 1985).
Recommendations on how to
stay healthy while traveling.

TRAVEL GUIDES

The following series of travel
guides are recommended:

Insight Wildlife Guides (APA
Publications). Cover the wildlife and preserves of the most
popular ecotravel destinations,
including Amazonia, East
Africa, and Southeast Asia.

Lonely Planet Guides (Lonely
Planet Publications). Re-
nowned and reliable guides
for independent travelers.
Over 180 titles covering most
corners of the globe.

Moon Guides (Moon Publications,
Inc.). Practical handbooks for
international travel.

The Outdoor Traveler's Guides
(Stewart, Tabori & Chang).
Detailed, illustrated guides
to the flora and fauna of a
number of regions, including
the Caribbean and Australia.

FIELD GUIDES

Collins Guides (HarperCollins).
International series of field
guides to birds, mammals,
and plants.

Finding Birds Around the World,
by Peter Alden and John
Gooders (Houghton Mifflin,
1981). A useful international
birdfinder.

Peterson Field Guides (Houghton
Mifflin). Field guide series
covering North America and
some international destinations.

Sierra Club Handbook of Whales
and Dolphins (Sierra Club
Books, 1983). An excellent
international guide.

NORTH AMERICA

ABA Birdfinding Guides,
(American Birding Association,
Inc.). Guides to the best
birding locations in the USA.

Birding, by Joseph Forshaw et al.
(The Nature Company, 1994).
A fascinating introduction
to birding and the most
common American species.

Desert Solitaire: A Season in the
Wilderness, by Edward Abbey
(Simon & Schuster, 1968).
A classic work about the
Desert Southwest from one
of America's most contro-
versial nature writers.

The Exploration of the Colorado
River and its Canyons, by John
Wesley Powell (Penguin
Books, 1987). One of the
earliest accounts of this region.

Fodor's National Parks and
Seashores of the East
(Fodor's, 1994).

Fodor's National Parks of the
West (Fodor's, 1994).

Golden Guides (Western
Publishing Co.). Series of
field guides for identification
of birds, plants, mammals, and
reptiles in North America.

Guide to the National Wildlife
Refuges, by Laura and William
Riley (Collier Books, 1992).

John Muir: Eight Wilderness
Discovery Books (Diadem
Books and The Mountaineers,
1992). John Muir's inspira-
tional nature writings
collected in one volume.

National Audubon Society Field Guides (Alfred A. Knopf). Excellent photographic field guides to a range of topics.

The National Parks of Canada, by Kevin McNamee (Key Porter Books, 1994).

Nature Travel, by Dwight Holing et al. (The Nature Company, 1995). A lavishly illustrated guide to North America's top ecotravel destinations.

Roadside Geology, (Mountain Press Publishing Co.). A series of geological identification guides to western North America.

A Sand Country Almanac, by Aldo Leopold (Oxford University Press, 1949). Outlines the great conservationist's philosophy.

A Sense of Wonder, by Rachel Carson (The Nature Company, 1990). Observations on developing an appreciation of nature.

The Sierra Club Guides to Natural Areas of the United States: including *California; Colorado and Utah; Idaho, Montana, and Wyoming; Florida; New England; New Mexico, Arizona, and Nevada; Oregon and Washington.* (Sierra Club Books).

The Sierra Club Guides to the National Parks: including *Desert Southwest; East and Middle West; Pacific Northwest and Alaska; Pacific Southwest and Hawaii; Rocky Mountains and the Great Plains.* (Stewart, Tabori & Chang).

Silent Spring, by Rachel Carson (Houghton Mifflin, 1962). A classic conservation book.

The Smithsonian Guide to Natural America (Random House, 1996). A series of 16 guides to natural areas in the USA.

Walden, by Henry David Thoreau (Viking, 1993). A lyrical conservation classic.

Wildlife in America, by Peter Matthiessen (Penguin Nature Library, 1994). An outstanding overview of the natural history of North America.

CENTRAL AND SOUTH AMERICA

Baja California, by Lisa and Sven-Olof Lindblad (Rizzoli, 1987). An excellent introduction to Baja, with natural-history essays and photographs.

Belize: A Natural Destination, by Richard Mahler and Steele Wotkyns (John Muir Press, 1991). An invaluable guide.

The Birds of Colombia, by Steven L. Hilty and William L. Brown (Princeton University Press, 1986). Also useful for Ecuador, Peru, and the Amazon.

A Bird Watcher's Adventures in Tropical America, by Alexander Skutch (Texas University Press, 1977). A naturalist's experiences in Central America in the 1930s and '40s.

Costa Rica: A Natural Destination, by Ree Strange Scheck (John Muir Publications, 1990). An introduction to the country's ecosystems, parks, and reserves.

Costa Rica Handbook, by Christopher P. Baker (Moon Publications, 1996). Includes concise, informative profiles on ecosystems, plus details of prime places to visit.

Costa Rican Natural History, by Daniel H. Janzen (University of Chicago Press, 1987). A comprehensive guide.

Ecotourism: The Potentials and Pitfalls, by Elizabeth Boo (World Wildlife Fund, 1990). An in-depth analysis of the impact of ecotourism on the Caribbean and South America.

Galápagos: A Natural History Guide, by M.H. Jackson (University of Calgary Press, 1985). An introduction to the natural history of the Galápagos Islands.

Life Above the Jungle Floor, by Donald Perry (Simon & Schuster, 1986). A fascinating account of life in the forest canopy and of Perry's studies at Rara Avis in Costa Rica.

The Log of the Sea of Cortez, by John Steinbeck (Viking Press, 1941). A highly personal account of Baja California.

Naturalist on the River Amazon, by Henry Walter Bates (Penguin Books, 1989). First published in Great Britain in 1863, a classic account by the first biologist to explore the Amazon.

A Neotropical Companion, by John Kricher (Princeton University Press, 1989). An introduction to the ecosystems and natural history of the New World tropics.

The Quetzal and the Macaw: The Story of Costa Rica's National Parks, by David Rains Wallace (Sierra Club Books, 1992). A compelling tale of how diminutive Costa Rica established a heralded national park system.

Rainforests: A Guide to Research and Tourist Facilities, by James L. Castner (Feline Press, 1990). A comprehensive guide to research facilities and accommodation in Central and South America.

Running the Amazon, by Joe Kane (Alfred A. Knopf, 1989). The story of the first expedition to travel the entire length of the world's longest river.

Savages, by Joe Kane (Alfred A. Knopf, 1995). An account of the current conflict in the Amazon between the petroleum industry and native people and conservationists.

Tales of a Shaman's Apprentice, by Mark Plotkin (Penguin, 1994). A wonderful book about an ecobotanist who lived with Indian tribes in Venezuela.

Tropical Nature, by Adrian Forsyth and Kenneth Miyata (Scribner, 1984). An introduction to tropical ecosystems.

The Voyage of the Beagle, by Charles Darwin (Doubleday, 1962). Includes Darwin's famous account of his visit to the Galápagos Islands.

Where to Watch Birds in South America, by Nigel Wheatley (Princeton University Press, 1995). A guide to birding sites throughout South America.

EUROPE

Birds of Europe, North Africa and the Middle East, by Lars Jonssom (Princeton University Press, 1993). The definitive guide to the birds of Europe.

British National Parks (Webb and Bower/Michael Joseph, 1987). A series of high-quality guides to 10 national parks.

A Guide to the National Parks and other Wild Places of Britain and Europe, by Bob Gibbons (New Holland, 1994).

Last Places: A Journey to the North, by Lawrence Millman (Houghton Mifflin, 1991). An amusing and informative description of a tour to the islands of the North Atlantic.

The Living Isles: A Natural History of Britain and Ireland, by Peter Crawford (BBC Books, 1985). Excellent background material.

Mammals of Britain and Europe, (HarperCollins, 1995). An excellent all-in-one guide.

The Nature Parks of France, by Patrick Delaforce (Windrush, 1996). A fine overview.

Ordnance Survey Leisure Guides (AA/Ordnance Survey). Highly practical guides to regions of the British Isles.

Scotland's Highlands and Islands, by Richenda Miers (Cadogan, 1994). A detailed guide to the wilds of Scotland.

Walking the Alpine Parks of France and Northwest Italy, by Marcia R. Lieberman (The Mountaineers, 1994). Includes information on Vanoise and Gran Paradiso national parks.

Wild Flowers of Britain and Europe, by Bob Press and Bob Gibbons (New Holland, 1993).

Wild Italy, by Tim Jepson (Aurum Press, 1987). Italy's habitats, flora, and fauna.

Wildlife of the British Isles, by Bob Gibbons (Hamlyn, 1987). British habitats, flora, and fauna.

Wildlife Traveling Companion: France, by Bob Gibbons and Paul Davies (Crowood Press, 1992).

Wildlife Traveling Companion: Great Britain and Ireland, by Martin Walters (Crowood Press, 1992).

Wildlife Traveling Companion: Spain, by John Measures (Crowood Press, 1992).

AFRICA

Adventuring in East Africa, by Allen Bechky (Sierra Club Books, 1990). A terrific travel guide to the great safaris of East Africa.

Among the Elephants, by Iain and Oria Douglas-Hamilton (Penguin, 1975). The authors detail their many years living among elephants in Tanzania.

Cry of the Kalahari, by Mark and Delia Owens (Houghton Mifflin, 1984). Describes seven years of work by two biologists in the Kalahari.

Elephant Memories, by Cynthia Moss (Fawcett Columbine, 1988). An excellent account of 20 years spent studying elephants in Amboseli, Kenya.

A Field Guide to the National Parks of East Africa, by J. G. Williams (Collins, 1984). An indispensable guide.

Gorillas in the Mist, by Dian Fossey (Houghton Mifflin, 1983). Studies of gorilla behavior by a heroic naturalist.

Guide to Southern African Game and Nature Reserves, by Chris and Tilde Stuart (New Holland, 1992). A highly practical guide to 400 reserves.

In the Shadow of Man, by Jane Goodall (Collins, 1971). Recounts the author's studies of chimpanzee behavior.

On Safari in East Africa: A Background Guide, by Ernest Neal (HarperCollins, 1991). Advice on travel and wildlife watching.

Out of Africa, by Isak Dinesen (Random House, 1938). A classic account of the author's life in Kenya.

Portraits in the Wild, by Cynthia Moss (University of Chicago Press, 1982). An in-depth natural history of the large mammals of Africa.

Robert's Birds of Southern Africa, by Gordon Lindsay Maclean (Trustees of the John Voelcker Bird Book Fund, 1993). The Southern African ornithologist's bible.

The Safari Companion: A Guide to Watching African Mammals, by Richard D. Estes (Chelsea Green Publishing Co., 1993).

The Tree Where Man Was Born, by Peter Matthiessen (Dutton, 1972). Eliot Porter's stunning photos accompany a riveting account of the author's trek across the continent.

West with the Night, by Beryl Markham (Virago, 1984). A lyrical account of life in Kenya's wilderness.

Wildlife Parks of Africa, by Nicholas Laird (Salem House, 1986). A regional guide to national parks.

ASIA

The Birds of South-East Asia, by Ben King et al. (Collins, 1976). An excellent field guide.

The Malay Archipelago, by Alfred Russel Wallace (Oxford University Press, 1989). An evocative account of an exploration made in 1854–62.

Mountains of the Middle Kingdom, by Galen Rowell (Sierra Club Books, 1983). Exquisite photographs of the Himalayas.

The Narrow Road to the Deep North, by Matsuo Basho (Penguin, 1991). A poet's account of his travels around seventeenth-century Japan.

A Pictorial Guide to the Birds of the Indian Subcontinent, by Salim Ali and S. Dillon Ripley (Oxford University Press, 1983). Excellent photographs and informative text.

The Snow Leopard, by Peter Matthiessen (Viking Press, 1978). A trek through the Himalayas in search of the snow leopard.

Southeast Asia Rainforests: A Resource Guide and Directory, by Dirk G. Schroeder (Rainforest Action Network of San Francisco, 1993).

Stranger in the Forest: On Foot Across Borneo, by Eric Hansen (Houghton Mifflin, 1988). An excellent book about Borneo by a first-rate writer.

Trekking in the Indian Himalaya, by Garry Weare (Lonely Planet, 1996).

Trekking in the Nepal Himalaya, by Stan Armington (Lonely Planet, 1994).

Wild India, by Gerald Cubitt and Guy Mountfort (Collins, 1985). Informative text and excellent photos.

OCEANIA AND ANTARCTICA

Antarctica: A Guide to Wildlife, by Tony Soper (Bradt, 1994).

Australia Down Under, by Christine Deacon (Doubleday, 1986). A guide to diving in Australian waters.

Birds of New Guinea, by Bruce Beehler, Thane Pratt, and Dale Zimmerman (Princeton University Press, 1986).

Bushwalking in Australia, by John and Monica Chapman (Lonely Planet, 1996).

Bushwalking in Papua New Guinea, by Yvon Perusse (Lonely Planet, 1993).

The Crystal Desert: Summers in Antarctica, by David Campbell (Houghton Mifflin, 1992). An account of the author's sojourns on the Antarctic Peninsula.

Ecotourism and Nature-based Holidays, by Janet Richardson (Simon & Schuster, 1993). A guide to ecotourism and tour operators in Australia and New Zealand.

The Fragile South Pacific: An Ecological Odyssey, by Andrew Mitchell (University of Texas Press, 1990). A brilliant study of the ecology of the region, from Palau to Tahiti.

The Slater Field Guide to Australian Birds, by Peter, Pat, and Raoul Slater (Landsdowne Publishing, 1989). A superb, compact field guide.

Stepping Lightly on Australia: A Traveller's Guide to Ecotourism, by Shirley LaPlanche (HarperCollins, 1995). A guided tour of the nation's parks and reserves, with information on tours, activities, and accommodation.

Tramping in New Zealand, by Jim DuFresne and Jeff Williams (Lonely Planet, 1994). A hiker's guide.

Under the Mountain Wall, by Peter Matthiessen (Harvill, 1989). The author's experience of living among the indigenous peoples of New Guinea.

Wild Australia (Reader's Digest, 1984). A comprehensive guide to Australia's wildlife and wilderness areas.

Magazines

Australian Geographic, 321 Mona Vale Rd, Terrey Hills, NSW 2084, Australia. A quarterly journal devoted to the natural history of Australasia.

BBC Wildlife, PO Box 125, Tonbridge, Kent TN9 1YP, UK. Natural history and conservation from a British viewpoint.

EcoTraveler, 7730 SW Mohawk St, Tualatin, OR 97062, USA. A bimonthly survey of international ecotravel.

National Geographic, Box 37448, Washington DC 20013-7448, USA. Superb natural history journal.

Wildlife Conservation, PO Box 56696 Boulder, CO 80323-6696, USA. Reports on conservation issues from around the world.

Computer Information Services

Most online information services offer a variety of travel-related material, including flight information, government advisories, and reference material. On the Internet, the World Wide Web includes a huge number of useful and regularly updated web pages relating to ecotravel. You can begin by searching one of the main Web directories, such as Yahoo (http://akebono.stanford.edu/yahoo/Reference/), or by consulting some of the web sites listed below.

http://greenarrow.com
An interactive magazine offering information on eco-travel in Central America.

http://www.igc.apc.org/econet/
A good website with links to environmental topics.

http://www.natureco.com
The Nature Company website. Contact the Nature Company naturalist and obtain updates on in-store and natural events.

http://www.nps.gov
US National Park Service website. Information on park services and links to home pages for individual parks.

http://www.peg.apc.org/~tasol/gogreen.html
GoGreen Forum features advice on responsible travel.

http://www.planeta.com
Reports on ecotourism projects in Central and South America.

http://www.travelsource.com/ecotours
An interactive, international travel guide for ecotravelers.

ORGANIZATIONS

Ecotravel Organizations

The Center for Responsible
Tourism, PO Box 827,
San Anselmo, CA 94979,
USA; tel. (415) 258-6594,
fax (415) 454-2493
The Ecotourism Association of
Australia, PO Box 130,
Terrey Hills, NSW 2084,
Australia; tel. (02) 486-3316,
fax (02) 486-3353
The Ecotourism Society,
PO Box 755, North
Bennington, VT 95257,
USA; tel. (802) 447-2121
The Ecumenical Coalition on
Third World Travel,
PO Box 9-25, Bangkhen,
Bangkok 0900, Thailand
Tourism Concern, Froebel
College, Roehampton Lane,
London SW15 5PU, UK;
tel. (081) 878-9053

Conservation Organizations

African Wildlife Foundation,
1717 Massachusetts Ave NW,
Washington DC 20036, USA;
tel. (202) 265-8393
Friends of the Earth,
Global Building, Suite 300,
1025 Vermont Avenue NW,
Washington DC 20005, USA;
tel. (202) 783-7400
Greenpeace,
1436 U St NW,
Washington DC 20009, USA;
tel. (202) 462-1177
National Audubon Society,
950 3rd Ave,
New York, NY 10022, USA;
tel. (212) 832-3200

The Nature Conservancy,
1815 North Lynn St,
Arlington, VA 22209, USA;
tel. (703) 841-5300
Rainforest Action Network,
450 Sansome St, Suite 700,
San Francisco, CA 94111,
USA; tel. (415) 398-4404
The Rainforest Alliance,
65 Bleecker St 6th,
New York, NY 10012-1420,
USA; tel. (212) 677-1900
Wilderness Society,
900 17th St NW,
Washington DC 20006, USA;
tel. (202) 833-2300
World Tourism Organization
Calle Capitan Haya, 42,
28020 Madrid, Spain;
tel. (01) 571-0628,
fax (01) 571-0757
e-mail: omt@dial.eunet.es
World Wildlife Fund,
1250 24th St NW, Suite 500,
Washington DC 20037, USA;
tel. (202) 293-4800

Medical and Security Matters

For a list of names of English-speaking physicians
worldwide, send a self-addressed envelope to:
International Association for
Medical Assistance to
Travelers, 736 Center St,
Lewiston, NY 14092, USA;
tel. (716) 754-4883.
You can obtain a similar list
from Intermedic, 777 Third
Ave, New York, NY 10017,
USA; tel. (212) 486-8974.
The US Centers for Disease
Control operate two travel
health hotlines with the latest
information on diseases and
vaccination requirements.
Call (404) 332-4559. For fax-back information, call (404)
332-4565 and follow the
automated prompts.
The US State Department
operates a 24-hour
travel advisory
hotline for US
travelers. Call
(202) 647-5225.
Travel advisories
are also available
on computer information
services such as Compuserve.

Information about vaccination
requirements in the United
Kingdom is available from
the International Relations
Division, Department of
Social Security, Alexander
Fleming House, Elephant and
Castle, London SE1 6BY, UK;
tel. (071) 407-5522, ext. 6749.

Volunteer Vacations

The following nonprofit organizations act as intermediaries
for volunteer vacations:
Australian Trust for
Conservation Volunteers,
PO Box 423, Ballarat,
VIC 3350, Australia;
tel. (053) 327-490,
fax (053) 332-290
Australian and New Zealand
Scientific Exploration Society,
PO Box 174, Albert Park,
VIC 3206, Australia;
tel. (03) 690-5455,
fax (03) 690-0151.
Earthwatch, 680 Mt Auburn St,
Watertown,
MA 02272, USA;
tel. (617) 926-8200
Field Studies Council,
Preston Montford,
Montford Bridge, Shrewsbury,
Shropshire SY4 1HW, UK;
tel. (0743) 850-674
International Research
Expeditions, 140 University
Dr., Menlo Park,
CA 94025, USA;
tel. (415) 323-4228
National Wildlife Federation,
1400 16th St NW,
Washington DC 20036, USA;
tel. (703) 790-4363
Oceanic Society Expeditions,
Fort Mason Center,
Building E, Room 230,
San Francisco,
CA 94123-1394, USA;
tel. (800) 326-7491,
(415) 441-1106
Sierra Club, Service Trips,
730 Polk St, San Francisco,
CA 94109, USA;
tel. (415) 923-5630
University Research Expeditions
Program (UREP),
University of California,
2223 Fulton St,
Berkeley, CA 94720, USA;
tel. (510) 642-6586

INDEX *and* GLOSSARY

CONTRIBUTORS

Christopher P. Baker (CB) is an award-winning writer of travel and natural history based in Oakland, California. British-born, his area of interest is Latin America and his books include *Costa Rica Handbook*, *Cuba Handbook*, and *Passport Illustrated Guide to Jamaica*. He founded British Pride Tours and was its president for seven years.

Ben Davidson (BD) is a San Francisco-based writer and photographer specializing in outdoor recreation and adventure travel. A native Californian, he has been a travel editor at *Sunset Magazine* and currently contributes to numerous magazines and newspapers.

Jeremy Hart (JH) has traveled far and wide, from the Canadian Arctic to the Gobi Desert. A former radio journalist, he is now a London-based adventure writer and foreign correspondent for a range of international newspapers and magazines, including the *Independent* in London, the *Bulletin* in Sydney, and *Le Figaro* in Paris.

Dwight Holing (DH) writes on natural history subjects and environmental issues for leading US and international magazines from his base in the San Francisco Bay Area. His nature-travel guidebooks include *The Smithsonian Guide to Natural America: The Far West* and *EarthTrips: A Guide to Nature Travel on a Fragile Planet*.

Brian Jackman (BJ) is a freelance journalist who writes on travel and wildlife. He is especially interested in Africa and is currently working on a book for BBC Books called *The Big Cat Diary*. His other publications include *Roaring at the Dawn* and *The Countryside in Winter*.

Judy Jacobs (JJ) has traveled widely to remote areas of Asia and the Pacific, including Ladakh, Borneo, Papua New Guinea, the Shan States of Burma, and Cambodia. Her writing has appeared in magazines and newspapers around the world and her books include *Indonesia: A Nation of Islands*.

Shirley LaPlanche (SL) grew up in the wild beauty of New Zealand but has traveled extensively in Australia, writing on ecotourism and the environment. Her book *Stepping Lightly on Australia* is an excellent guide to ecotourism in that country.

Bobbie Leigh (BL), a former teacher and headmistress in a private elementary school, now works as a freelance writer. She is based in New York, but travels widely in Africa, the Middle East, and Pacific Rim countries, working on travel and wildlife magazine articles and film scripts.

David McGonigal (DM) is a prize-winning travel writer and photographer based in Australia. An accomplished scuba diver, he has dived at many of the world's most remarkable sites. Author of several books on nature and travel, his next major project is a journey by motorcycle through all seven continents.

Susanne Methvin (SM) is General Manager of Inca Floats, a nature-travel tour operator specializing in tours to the Galápagos Islands and mainland Ecuador. A former Safari Director at the Nature Company, she has been active in organizing and leading nature tours throughout the world since 1979.

Greg Mortimer (GM) is a geologist who runs a Sydney-based tour company specializing in travel to Antarctica. A leading mountaineer, he made the first Australian ascents of Mount Everest, Annapurna 2, and K2, as well as Mount Minto and the Vinson Massif in Antarctica.

Paolo Perna (PP) is a biologist with a keen interest in the flora and fauna of the Central Appenines. Since 1987, he has worked at the Fiastra Abbey Nature Reserve, near Macerata in Italy. He has been involved in numerous local conservation projects, education programs, and the publication of a number of nature guides.

Everett Potter (EP) has worked as a professional travel writer for more than 10 years, contributing to both the Fodor and Birnbaum series of guides. He has traveled widely in the US, Latin America, Europe, and Asia, and is the author of *The Best of Brazil*.

Dan Strickland (DS) is a writer and commercial fisherman who has made his home in Alaska for the past 24 years. His articles on biological, environmental and fisheries-related issues appear regularly in magazines such as *Natural History*, *Oceans*, and *Islands*.

Steven Threndyle (ST) is a Vancouver-based writer and photographer specializing in outdoor activities. He has published articles in more than 30 North American magazines and newspapers and is currently the editor of *Coast*, British Columbia's outdoor recreation magazine.

Theresa Waldrop (TW) is a graduate of Alabama and Boston universities. Since 1980 she has been based in Bonn, Germany. She has traveled widely in Europe and currently works as a special correspondent for *Newsweek International*.

Eugene J. Walter Jr (EW) is a New Jersey-based freelance writer specializing in natural history and environmental conservation. From 1974 to 1991 he was Director of Publications at the New York Zoological Society and Editor-in-Chief of the society's *Wildlife Conservation* magazine. His books include *Why Animals Behave the Way They Do*.

Wang Sung (WS) is a Research Professor with the Chinese Academy of Sciences, and Executive Vice Chairman of the Endangered Species Commission. His work includes the compilation of a biodiversity database and the setting up of a conservation program in China.

Michael J. Woods (MW) grew up in England's West Country. He spent 15 years managing nature reserves before becoming a freelance wildlife and travel journalist and photographer. He now visits wilderness areas as a consultant assessing endangered animal populations.

CAPTIONS

Page 1: A young mountain gorilla in Rwanda.

Page 2: Chinstrap penguins leaping from an iceberg in Antarctica.

Page 3: Young polar bears shelter behind their mother in Churchill, Canada.

Pages 4–5: A proboscis monkey leaps across the canopy near the Sekunir River in Kalimantan.

Pages 6–7: A majestic boab tree in the Kimberley in northwestern Australia.

Pages 8–9: Hikers on Kanchenjunga in Sikkim, India, in the Himalayas.

Pages 10–11: The Seventy Islands, Palau, Micronesia.

Pages 12–13: Zabriskie Point in Death Valley National Park, California, USA.

Pages 24–5: A traveler at Victoria Falls in Zimbabwe.

Pages 42–3: Backcountry camping in the New Zealand Alps.

Pages 65–6: Ecotourists at an Adélie penguin colony on Paulet Island in the Weddell Sea, Antarctica.

Page 68–9: The Grand Canyon, Arizona, USA.

Page 69 (inset top): A humpback whale breaching in the waters of Alaska, USA.

Page 69 (inset bottom): Lava flowing from Mount Kilauea in Hawaii Volcanoes National Park, Hawaii.

Page 104–5: Lush rain forest in Belize.

Page 105 (inset top): A flame bromeliad.

Page 105 (inset bottom): A red-eyed tree frog.

Page 142–3: Gran Paradiso National Park, Italy.

Page 143 (inset top): White storks in Estremadura, Spain.

Page 143 (inset bottom): Wildflowers in Crete.

Page 172–3: A lion and lioness in the Okavango Delta, Botswana.

Page 173 (inset top): A school of Rathbourne's sweepers in the coral reefs of the Red Sea.

Page 173 (inset bottom): A leaf-tailed gecko in Madagascar.

Page 208–9: A langur monkey in Ranthambore National Park, India.

Page 209 (inset top): A close-up of a tiger's coat.

Page 209 (inset bottom): Mount Everest in the Himalayas.

Page 238–9: Diving on the Great Barrier Reef, Australia.

Page 239 (inset top): Uluru (Ayers Rock), central Australia.

Page 239 (inset bottom): Emperor penguins, Antarctica.

Page 272–3: Lesser flamingos flying over Lake Magadi in Kenya.

ACKNOWLEDGEMENTS

The publishers wish to thank the following people for their assistance in the production of this book: Dan Bickle; Steven Bray; Lynn Cole; Melanie Corfield; Greg Hassall; Rita Joseph; Ionas Kaltenbach; Toomas Kokovkin; James McGahey; Margaret McPhee; Lisa Neuchew, Traveller's Medical and Vaccination Centre, Sydney, Australia; Paddy Pallin Ltd; Oliver Strewe; Tashi Tenzing.

PICTURE AND ILLUSTRATION CREDITS

(t = top, b = bottom, l = left, r = right, c = center, i = inset A = Auscape International; AL = ARDEA London Limited; AM = Australian Museum; BCL = Bruce Coleman Limited, UK; Bridgeman = Bridgeman Art Library, London; HI = Horizon International; HH = Hedgehog House, New Zealand; LT = Lochman Transparencies; NHM = Natural History Museum, London; NHPA = Natural History Photographic Agency; OSF = Oxford Scientific Films; PE = Planet Earth Pictures; PL = The Photo Library, Sydney; REI = Recreational Equipment Incorporated; SNH = Scottish National Heritage Slide Library; TS = Tom Stack and Associates; TSI = Tony Stone Images; VIREO = Visual Resources for Ornithology; WWF = World Wide Fund For Nature)

1 Steve Turner/OSF 2 Jean-Paul Ferrero/A 3 Wayne Lynch/Masterfile/Stock Photos 4-5 Gerald Cubitt 6-7 Oliver Strewe 8-9 Tashi Tenzing 10-11 David McGonigal 12-13 Jeff Foott/BCL 14tl Painting by Edward Lear/Bridgeman; c Chip and Jill Isenhart/TS 14-15 Martyn Colbeck/OSF 15t Tashi Tenzing; tr Mark N Boulton/BCL 16tl Royal Geographical Society, London/Bridgeman; c Jill Lomer/Thomas Cook Travel Archive; bl Hulton-Deutsch/PL 17tl Osterreichische National Bibliothek; c Research Library/Nature Focus/AM; br British Museum, London/Bridgeman 18t Robert Holmes; b Michel Gunther/WWF 19tl Alain Compost/BCL; b Inga Spence/TS; br Jean-Paul Ferrero/A 20tl John Cancalosi/A; c Michael and Patricia Fogden; cr BCL; b Ferrero/Labat/A 21t Kevin Deacon/ Ocean Earth Images; b Colin Monteath/HH 22tl Jiri Lochman/ LT; cr Michael and Patricia Fogden; bl Sorrel E Wilby/Wild Side 23tr Baron Wolman/TSI/PL; c Tashi Tenzing; b Mark N Boulton/BCL 24-25 Leonard Lee Rue/BCL 26tl Robert Holmes; c Mike Langford/A; bl Hans Reinhard/BCL 27tr Oliver Strewe; tl Tashi Tenzing; b David Nicholas Green/PL 28 Thomas Kitchin/TS 28-29 Grant Dixon/HH 29tr John Netherton/OSF; cr Norbert Rosing/OSF 30tl Oliver Strewe; b Tashi Tenzing 31t Jean-Paul Ferrero/A; cr Oliver Strewe; br BCL 32tl and cr Oliver Strewe; b Colin Monteath/HH 33 Oliver Strewe 34t American Express; bl Oliver Strewe 35 Oliver Strewe 36 Oliver Strewe 37t Ionas Kaltenbach; b Oliver Strewe

38 Oliver Strewe 39tl Colin Monteath/A; cr Tashi Tenzing; br Oliver Strewe 40tl and br Colin McRae Photography; tr Oliver Strewe; bl Joe McDonald/TS 41t Colin Monteath/A; bl courtesy REI; br Tashi Tenzing 42-43 Andris Apse/PL 44tl Oliver Strewe; c Jean-Paul Ferrero/A; bl Mark N Boulton/BCL 45t Bruce Herrod/OSF; c Michael W Richards/OSF; b Bert Hilger/TSI/PL 46tl Oliver Strewe; c Peter Ryley/OSF; b HI 47t Sorrel E Wilby/Wild Side; cr C B and D W Frith/BCL; b Michael Freeman/BCL 48tl courtesy REI; tr Nick Green/PL; cr Mike Powell/TSI/PL; bl Tom Bean/TSI/PL 49t Geoff Spearpoint/HH; b Bob Thomason/TSI/PL 50tl Ionas Kaltenbach; cr J Lotter/TS; cl courtesy REI 51tr Tashi Tenzing; cr courtesy Paddy Pallin; b Chip Porter/TSI/PL 52tl Ionas Kaltenbach; b Stewart Cohen/PL 53tr Christer Fredriksson/ BCL; cl Peter Ryley/OSF; br HI 54tl Ionas Kaltenbach; cr Dennis Harding/A; bl Robert Fried/PL 55tl Andris Apse/PL; cr S Wilby and C Ciantar/A; b Karl Weatherly/TSI/PL 56tl Ben Davidson; cr Arnulf Husmo/TSI/PL 56-57 Stuart Westmorland/TSI/PL 57tl Becca Saunders/A; br Joe Bennett/OSF/PL 58tl David Kjaer/PE; c Wes Walker 59tl Andrew J Purcell/BCL; tr Mark N Boulton/BCL; br Jiri Lochman/LT 60tl Maurice Ortega/AM; cr Jean-Paul Ferrero/A; b Robert Rattner 61tl David Austen/BCL; tr Jen and Des Bartlett/BCL; b Ionas Kaltenbach 62tl Ionas Kaltenbach; cr M Melodia/Panda Photo; bl Mark Newman/A 62-63 Kathie Atkinson/A 63t Galen Rowell/PL 64-65 Colin Monteath/A 68-69 Alan Kearney/TSI/PL 69ti Daniel J Cox/OSF; bi Mark Newman/TS 70tl John Shaw/A; tc Atlantide SDF/BCL; tr Jeff Foott Productions/BCL; b Lon E Lauber/OSF/PL 72tl Johnny Johnson/BCL; tr Jean-Paul Ferrero/A; b Jeff Foott/Jeff Foott Productions 73t David Nicholas Green/PL; cl John Shaw/A; bl David Maisel/PL; br Stan Osolinski/OSF 74 Tom Bean/TSI/PL 74-75 Pascal Crapet/TSI/PL 75 Stuart Westmorland/TSI/PL 76t Mary Bee Kaufman/BCL; c Erwin and Peggy Bauer/A; bl Leonard Lee Rue/BCL; br John Warden/TSI/PL 77t Steven C Kaufman/BCL; cr Tim Davis/TSI/PL; b Joel Bennett/Survival Anglia/OSF 78-79 Bob Anderson/Masterfile/Stock Photos 79c Erwin and Peggy Bauer/A; br John Shaw/A 80bl Jeff Foott/BCL; br Jeff Foott/A 80-81 Francois Gohier/A 81

Norbert Rosing/OSF **82** Frans Lanting/BCL **82-83** Francois Gohier/A **83** Jeff Foott/A **84-85** Thomas Kitchin/TS **85**cr John Shaw/A; bl Harry Angels/PL **86** Erwin and Peggy Bauer/A **86-87** Randy Wells/TSI/PL **87** Jim Nilsen/TS **88**bl Jeff Foott/A; br Krafft/A **88-89** Jeff Foott/BCL **90** Tom Tietz/TSI/PL **90-91** Jeff Foott/A **91** Jeff Foott/A **92-93** Doug Sokell/TS **93**c Jeff Foott/BCL; br Wayne Lankinen/BCL **94**t Ben Davidson; cl Bob and Clara Calhoun/BCL; b David Hiser/TSI/PL **95**t Charlie Oass/PL; cr Jeff Foott/TS; b John Shaw/A **96** John and Ann Mahan **96-97** Terry Donnelly/TS **97** Thomas Kitchin/TS **98-99** John Shaw/BCL **99**c Stephen J Krasemann/BCL; b Erwin and Peggy Bauer/A **100-101** Lynn M Stone/A **101**cl and cr Lynn M Stone/A; bl John Netherton/OSF **102-103** Soames Summerhays/PL **103**c Greg Vaughn/TS; b Robert Holmes **104-105** Will and Demi McIntyre/TSI/PL **105**ti Kjell B Sandved/OSF; bi Mike Bacon/TS **106**t Erwin and Peggy Bauer/A; cr Atlantide/BCL; bc Art Holfe/PL; br Mike Bacon/TS **107** Tui de Roy/A **108**t Ivor Edmonds/PE, cr Michael Fogden/OSF; bl Sid Bahrt; br Jaques Jangoux/PL **109**t Andy Price/BCL; bl Hans Reinhard/BCL; br Francois Gohier/A **110-111** Jeff Foott/A **111**c Tammy Peluso/TS; bl Francois Gohier/A; br G C Kelley/TS **112** Stephen Coyne/BCL **112-113** HI **113** James D Watt/PE **114**t Ivor Edmonds/PE; cr Chris Prior/PE; bl Robert Rattner **115**t Murray and Associates/TSI/PL; cl Wayne Lankinen/BCL; br Rod Williams/BCL **116** David Nicholas Green/PL **116-117** Luiz Claudio Marigo/BCL **117** Kevin Schafer/TS **118-119** Atlantide/BCL **119**cl Alan and Sandy Carey/OSF; cr Norbert Wu/TSI/PL; br Erwin and Peggy Bauer/A **120**bl Michael Fogden/OSF; br Mike Bacon/TS **120-121** Chip and Jill Isenhart/TS **121**c Roy Toft/TS; br Schafer and Hill/TSI/PL **122-123** Michael Fogden/OSF **124-125** Juan Silva/IB **125**cr Ken Welsh/PL; bl D Weschler/VIREO **126-127** Tui De Roy/A **127**cr David Fleetham/TS; br Mark Jones/OSF **128**t Barbara Von Hoffmann/TS; c Tui De Roy/OSF; bl Wes Walker **129**t D and M Plage/Survival Anglia/PL; bl Wes Walker; br Tui De Roy/A **130-131** Bill Curtsinger **131**c Michael and Patricia Fogden; br Art Wolfe/TSI/PL **132**t Jacques Jangouk/A; b Jany Sauvanet/A **133**t Max Gibbs/OSF; cr Rod Williams/BCL; b Andrea Florence/AL **134** Hans Reinhard/BCL **134-135** Michael Fogden/OSF **135** Paul Thompson/PL **136**t Dr Morley Read/SPL/PL; b David Simonson/OSF **137**t and br Jerry Alexander/TSI/PL; cl Staffan Widstrand/BCL **138**bl Joe McDonald/TS; br Schafer and Hill/TSI/PL **138-139** Eric A Soder/TS **140** D Parer and E Parer-Cook/A **140-141** D Parer and E Parer-Cook/A **141** Colin Monteath/OSF **142-143** Henry Ausloos/NHPA **143**ti Angelo Gandolfi; bi R L ManuelOSF **144**t Ivor Edmonds/PE; c David Woodfall/NHPA; b Richard Packwood/OSF **146** tl Tui De Roy/A; tr Kuvasuomi Ky Matti Kolho; c Neil Latham/OSF; b Joe Cornish/PL **147** t Hans Reinhard/BCL; bl B and C Alexander/NHPA; br Ferrero/Labat/A **148** June Perry/PE **148-149** Tui De Roy/A **149** Tui De Roy/A **150-151** L Vinco/Panda Photo **151**c S Pirovano/Panda Photo; br Tony Tilford/OSF **152** Daniel J Cox/Silvestris **152-153** t Mikko Tiittanen/Luonnonkuvaaja; **153** Maier/Silvestris **154-155** T Leito **155**c Frithjof Skibbe/OSF; br Patrick Clement/BCL **156-157** L Gill/SNH **157**c L Gill/SNH ; br L Campbell/SNH **158-159** W Lapinski/Panda Photo **159**cr Jan Walencik/PE; bl Konrad Wothe/OSF **160** Brett Baunton **160-161** Brett Baunton **161** Konrad Wothe/OSF **162-163** G Pollini/Panda Photo **163**c Bob Gibbons/OSF; b M Branchi/Panda Photo; br William S Paton/Survival Anglia/OSF **166** Angelo Gandolfi **166-167** Angelo Gandolfi **167** Michael Leach/OSF **168**t Angelo Gandolfi; c Richard and Julia Kemp/Survival Anglia/OSF; bl William S Paton/Survival Anglia/OSF **169**t Stephen Mills/OSF; b Jorge Sierra Antinolo/OSF **171**c David T Horwell; b John Netherton/OSF **170-171** David T Horwell **172-173** Peter Davey/BCL **173**ti Marc Chamberlain/TSI/PL; bi Art Wolfe/TSI/PL **174**t Nigel J Dennis/NHPA; c S Wilby and C Ciantar/A; b Marc Chamberlain/PL **176**t Christer Fredriksson/BCL; c Andrew Plumptre/OSF/PL; b Jen and Des Bartlett/BCL **177**t Johnny Johnson/BCL; cl Michael Howard/BL; cr Kim Taylor/PL; b Peter Davey/BCL **178** S Wilby and C Ciantar/A **178-179** Robert Holmes **179** Tony Deane/BCL **180** Charles and Sandra Hood/BCL **180-181** John Murray/BCL **181** Mike Bacon/TS **182** Margaret Gowan/TSI/PL **182-183** Warren and Genny Garst/TS **183** Gunter Ziesler/BCL **184-185** Ferrero/Labat/A **185** Stan Osolinski/OSF **186-187**

Ferrero/Labat/A **187** David W Breed/OSF **188**t Ian Murphy/TSI/PL; cr Erwin and Peggy Bauer/BCL; b Ferrero/Labat/A **189**t Manoj Shah/TSI/PL; br Robin Smith/PL **190-191** Spencer Swangel/TS **191**c Darrell Gulin/TSI/PL; br Johnny Johnson/BCL **192** Bill Everitt/TS **192-193** Gerald Cubitt/BCL **194-195** Jen and Des Bartlett/BCL **195**c Jen and Des Bartlett/BCL; b Gerald Cubitt/BCL **196-197** Peter Davey/BCL **197**c Raymond Valter/A; b Rod Williams/BCL **198-199** Gerald Cubitt/BCL **200-201** Janos Jurka/BCL **202** Konrad Wothe/BCL **202-203** Gerald Cubitt **203** Jiri Lochman/LT **204**t Konrad Wothe/BCL; b Art Wolfe/TSI/PL **205**t Jiri Lochman/LT; cl Mike Bacon/TS; b Konrad Wothe/BCL **206** Michael W Richards/OSF **206-207** Michael Howard/TS **208-209** Manoj Shah/TSI/PL **209**ti Robert Winslow/TS; bi Sorrel E Wilby/Wild Side **210**tl Brian J Coates/BCL; c Andy Rouse/NHPA; b Galen Rowell/PL **212**tl Tashi Tenzing; tr Rod Williams/BCL; b Jean-Paul Ferrero/A **213**tl Evgeny Neskozomny/Survival Anglia/OSF; tr PL; c Konrad Wothe/OSF/PL **214** Clare Forte **214-215** Tashi Tenzing **215**c Gerald Cubitt; br Tashi Tenzing **216**t Robert Holmes; c Gerald Cubitt **217**t Adrian Masters/TSI/PL; bl Tashi Tenzing; br Royal Geographical Society **218-219** Gerald Cubitt **219**cr Gerald Cubitt; bl Joe B Blossom/Survival Anglia/OSF **220** David Tipling/OSF **220-221** Peter Gasson/PE **221**c Belinda Wright/OSF; bl Anup Shah/PE **222**t Gunter Ziesler/BCL; c Vivek Sinha/Survival Anglia/OSF; bl Rod Williams/BCL **223**t Gerald Cubitt; bl Gunter Ziesler/BCL; br International Photographic Library **224**b Gary Milburn/TS **224-225** Jean-Paul Ferrero/A **225**c Brian Parker/TS **226-227** Cosmo and Action/PL **227**cl Steven C Kaufman/BCL; br Norio Yamagata/Nature Production **228-229** Andris Apse/HI **229**c and cl John Everingham; br Gerald Cubitt **230-231** Jeffrey Alford/Asia Access **231**c Rod Williams/BCL; b Jeanne Drake/PL **232** Jean-Paul Ferrero/A **232-233** Gerald Cubitt/BCL **233**c Paul Nevin/PL; br Alain Compost/BCL **234**bl Jean-Paul Ferrero/A; br Daniel J Cox/TSI/PL **234-235** Robert Holmes **235**c Robert Holmes; br Michael and Patricia Fogden **236**t Harold Taylor Abipp/OSF; bl and br Michael and Patricia Fogden **237**t Jean-Paul Ferrero/A; cl Robin Smith/PL; br Art Wolfe//TSI/PL **238-239** Dave Fleetham/TS **239**ti J M La Roque/A; bi G Robertson/A **240**l Gary Lewis/PL; c Stuart Westmorland/PL; r David McGonigal **241**l Steve Turner/OSF; r Wayne Lawler/A **242**t Wayne Lawler/A; c Kevin Deacon/Ocean Earth Images; bl Dennis Harding/A; br Nick Green/PL **243**tl Andris Apse/PL; tr Oliver Strewe; b Art Wolfe/PL **244-245** David McGonigal **245**c Kevin Deacon/A; Kelvin Aitken **246**bl Hans and Judy Beste/A; br Jean-Paul Ferrero/A **246-247** Catherine Secula/PL **247**c Pavel German; br Christopher Arnesen/TSI/PL **248-249** Jean-Paul Ferrero/A **250** Jean-Paul Ferrero/A **250-251** Jocelyn Burt/PL **251**c Jean-Paul Ferrero/A; cr Oliver Strewe **252-253** Oliver Strewe **253**c Hans and Judy Beste/A; cr Jiri Lochman/LT; br Oliver Strewe **254** Gary Lewis/PL **254-255** Nick Green/PL **255**c Tom Till/A; br Hans and Judy Beste/A **256**t and bl D Parer and E Parer-Cook/A; c Kevin Deacon/Ocean Earth Images **257**t Kevin Deacon/A; bl Kevin Deacon/Ocean Earth Images; br Geoff Taylor/LT **258-259** Richard Woldenorp/Photo Index **259** Jiri Lochman/LT **260** J M La Roque/A **260-261** Jocelyn Burt/PL **261** Mike Langford/A **262**bl J Cancalosi/A; br Ted Mead/PL **262-263** Mark Lang/Wildlight **264** Shaun Barnett/HH **264-265** Oliver Strewe **265**cl Geoff Spearpoint/HH ; br Nick Groves/HH **266**t Warren Jacobs/PL; c Shaun Barnett/HH; **267**t Philip Temple/HH; b Barbara Todd/HH **268** Konrad Wothe/OSF **268-269** Dr Nick Gales/LT **269** Kim Westerskov/HH **270-271** Tui De Roy/A **271**cl Colin Monteath/HH; br Hans Reinhard/BCL **272-273** Steve Turner/A

ILLUSTRATIONS: Rob Mancini Chapter Four; **Genevieve Wallace** Resources Directory; **Mike Lamble** maps pages 71, 106, 144, 174, 210, 240; **Mark Watson, Pictogram** all other maps.

JACKET: Front cover: *Elephants and penguin:* Art Wolfe/PL *Boy and prayer flags:* Clare Forte *Totem:* Frans Lanting/BCL *Orangutan:* Daniel J Cox/PL *Sea kayaker:* Ben Davidson *Scarlet macaw:* Erwin and Peggy Bauer/A *Masai man:* Robin Smith/PL **Front flap:** *The Paine Horns:* Colin Monteath/OSF *Women collecting water:* David Tipling/OSF **Back flap:** *Hippopotamus:* Bill Everitt/TS **Back cover:** *Woman:* Jerry Alexander/PL *Wigman:* Jean-Paul Ferrero/A *Coyote:* John Shaw/A *Northern lights:* Norbert Rosing/OSF *Roseate spoonbill:* Lynn M Stone/A

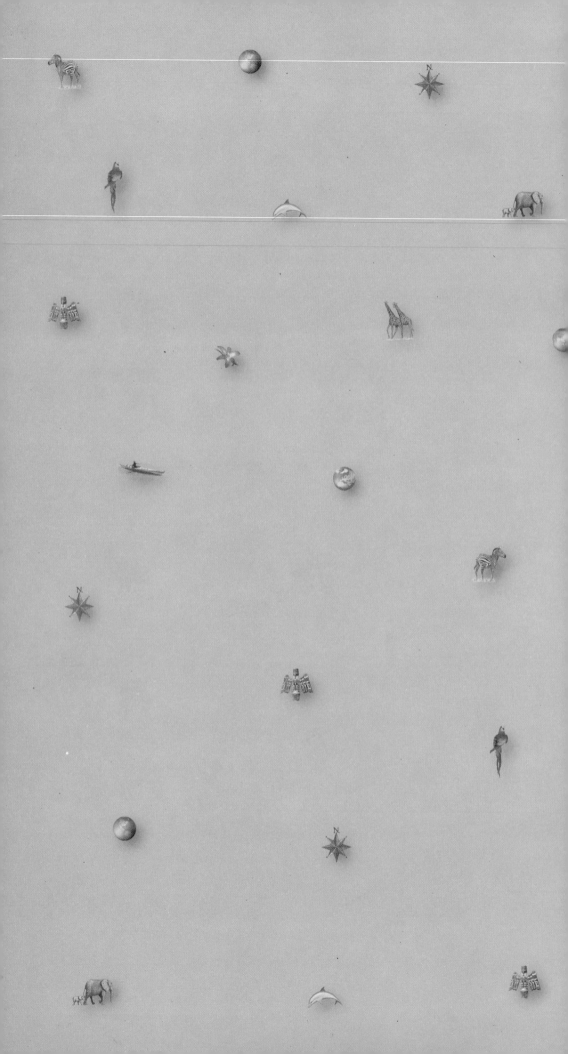